About Island Press

Island Press is the only nonprofit organization in the United States whose principal purpose is the publication of books on environmental issues and natural resource management. We provide solutions-oriented information to professionals, public officials, business and community leaders, and concerned citizens who are shaping responses to environmental problems.

Since 1984, Island Press has been the leading provider of timely and practical books that take a multidisciplinary approach to critical environmental concerns. Our growing list of titles reflects our commitment to bringing the best of an expanding body of literature to the environmental community throughout North America and the world.

Support for Island Press is provided by the Agua Fund, The Geraldine R. Dodge Foundation, Doris Duke Charitable Foundation, The Ford Foundation, The William and Flora Hewlett Foundation, The Joyce Foundation, Kendeda Sustainability Fund of the Tides Foundation, The Forrest & Frances Lattner Foundation, The Henry Luce Foundation, The John D. and Catherine T. MacArthur Foundation, The Marisla Foundation, The Andrew W. Mellon Foundation, Gordon and Betty Moore Foundation, The Curtis and Edith Munson Foundation, Oak Foundation, The Overbrook Foundation, The David and Lucile Packard Foundation, Wallace Global Fund, The Winslow Foundation, and other generous donors.

The opinions expressed in this book are those of the author(s) and do not necessarily reflect the views of these foundations.

About The Wildlife Conservation Society

Founded in 1895, the Wildlife Conservation Society saves wildlife and wild places through science, international conservation, education, and the management of the world's largest system of urban wildlife parks, led by the flagship Bronx Zoo in New York City. Together these activities change attitudes toward nature and help people imagine wildlife and humans living in harmony. WCS is committed to this mission because it is essential to the integrity of life on Earth.

2008–2009

STATE OF THE WILD

A Global Portrait of Wildlife, Wildlands, and Oceans

State of the Wild

Kent H. Redford, series editor

Editorial Board: Debbie Behler, Nancy Clum, Stephen Sautner, Bill Weber, Dan Wharton, Peter Zahler

State of the Wild 2006: A Global Portrait of Wildlife, Wildlands, and Oceans, edited by Sharon Guynup, with a special section, "Hunting and the Wildlife Trade"

State of the Wild 2008–2009: A Global Portrait of Wildlife, Wildlands, and Oceans, edited by Eva Fearn, with a special section, "Emerging Diseases and Conservation: One World—One Health"

2008–2009

STATE OF THE WILD

A Global Portrait of Wildlife, Wildlands, and Oceans

With a special section

Emerging Diseases and Conservation:
One World—One Health

VOLUME EDITOR
Eva Fearn

SERIES EDITOR
Kent H. Redford

Wildlife Conservation Society

FOREWORD BY
Ward Woods

ISLANDPRESS

WASHINGTON · COVELO · LONDON

Catherine Grippo, *Photo Editor*
Sandra Alcosser, *Poetry Editor*

ISLAND PRESS is a trademark of The Center for Resource Economics.

ISSN 1556-0619
ISBN (cloth) 978-1-59726-134-0
ISBN (paper) 978-1-59726-135-7

The opinions expressed in this book are those of the authors and do not
necessarily reflect the view of the Wildlife Conservation Society.

Design by John Costa and Maureen Gately

Printed on recycled, acid-free paper ♻
Manufactured in the United States of America
10 9 8 7 6 5 4 3 2 1

One touch of nature makes the whole
world kin.

Contents

BY THE NUMBERS

Emerging Diseases and Conservation

Of some 1,407 human pathogens, 58 percent (816) are zoonotic, and 177 are categorized as emerging or reemerging. Zoonotic pathogens are twice as likely to be in this category. —*Emerging Infectious Diseases*[1]

As of January 2008, there were 348 cases of avian influenza in humans, with 216 deaths. —World Health Organization[2]

Ghana reported its first case of H5N1 outbreak in May 2007, after 100 chickens died each day for three days. In response, 1,700 chickens were slaughtered to prevent further spread. In September 2007, 32,600 ducks were culled in the Panyu district of China to prevent the spread of H5N1. In October 2007, 50,000 chickens were euthanized in Saskatchewan, Canada, to prevent the spread of H7N3. —CIDRAP News, The Standard News, and News.Medical.Net[3]

The influenza epidemic of 1918–1919 would have an economic impact in today's dollars of $4.4 trillion. In 2005–2006, the world spent almost US$2.5 billion on new flu vaccine development in preparation for avian influenza. —*Foreign Affairs*[4]

US$16.1 billion: The global animal health product market in 2006 for wild animals and livestock. Europe, North America, east Asia, and Latin America held 97 percent, leaving 3 percent to all of Africa and south Asia. —International Federation for Animal Health[5]

Both drought and flood can trigger malaria epidemics: During El Niño years, the death toll from malaria increased by 36 percent in Venezuela, and in northwest India, malaria epidemics increased by 500 percent. —*Orion*[6]

Within endemic countries, malaria consumes 0.25 to 1.3 percent of per capita gross national product. —*Nature*[7]

Thirty of thirty-three provinces in Indonesia are infected with avian influenza. About 60 percent of Indonesian households keep chickens in their backyards or shared yards, and Indonesia has the highest number of H5N1 human fatalities, at 87 as of October 2007. —*Science*[8]

In 2007, human demography hit the point at which now more of the global population lives in urban or semi-urban areas than in rural areas. By 2015 there will be at least 550 cities with populations over 1 million people, and the world population is expected to be 10 billion by 2050. China's population of 1.3 billion people is growing at a rate of 3.7 percent per year in urban areas. —*Planet of Slums*[9]

Over the next 22 years, meat consumption in developing nations is expected to double. If the world's population today were to eat a Western diet of roughly 176 pounds (80 kg) of meat per capita per year, the global agricultural land required for production would be about 2.5 billion hectares—two-thirds more than is presently used. —*Science*[10]

In northern Canada, 40 percent of the former range of the wood bison would be available for wood bison reintroductions if it were not for the presence of brucellosis and bovine tuberculosis in the current herds in Wood Buffalo National Park.[11]

In 2005, 23,305 cases of Lyme disease were reported to the Centers for Disease Control and Prevention (CDC). Lyme disease is transmitted primarily by the deer tick (*Ixodes scapularis*) and is the most common vector-borne disease for people in the United States. —CDC and *Emerging Infectious Diseases*[12]

Scientists estimate that over 170 amphibian species have gone extinct in recent years. Nearly half of all amphibian species are declining, and 30 to 50 percent of amphibian species are threatened with extinction, in large part due to chytrid fungus. —"Amphibian Ark" and *Science*[13]

Lassa fever, occurring in northern and central Liberia, has caused five deaths as of April 2007, and at least thirteen people have been infected. The disease is transmitted by the saliva of rodents and by the excrement and urine of the multimammate mouse (*Mastomys natalensis*). —Panapress[14]

Mexico identified 27,000 cases of dengue fever in 2006, more than four times the number in 2001. Dengue viruses are transmitted between people or between monkeys through mosquitoes of the genus *Aedes*. Dengue fever is the most common vector-borne disease of humans, infecting some 50 million people in tropical and subtropical regions of the world each year. —*Economist* and *Molecular Biological Evolution*[15]

Following the Severe Acute Respiratory Syndrome (SARS) outbreak of 2003, 838,500 wild animals were reportedly confiscated from markets in Guangzhou, China. Three species of horseshoe bat (*Rhinolophus* spp.) were found to be the natural reservoir host for closely related SARS-like coronaviruses. —*Science*[16]

The economic impacts of the Nipah virus outbreak in Malaysia in 1997–1998 was estimated at US$350 to $400 million, and the 2001 foot-and-mouth disease outbreak in England and Europe was estimated to have cost markets almost US$20 billion. —Bio Economic Research Associates[17]

Over 317 species of birds, as well as a small number of domestic and wild mammals, have been affected by West Nile virus. In 2007, there were 3,107 incidences of West Nile virus-related illnesses. —Centers for Disease Control and Prevention[18]

In the northeast part of Tasmania, where facial tumor disease has been observed for several years, there has been a 90 percent decline in populations of Tasmanian devil (*Sarcophilus harrisii*). An estimated 50 percent of the entire devil population has been wiped out. A lack of genetic diversity in the population is allowing the disease to spread at a rate that may lead to extinction within 20 years. —Tasmania Department of Primary Industries and Water and *The Australian*[19]

Ebola virus killed approximately 5,000 western lowland gorillas over the past several years. Ebola causes viral hemorrhagic fever, which can kill up to 90 percent of those infected. Ebola has killed more than 1,000 people since it was first recorded in 1976. Twenty-five human cases of Ebola were confirmed in the Democratic Republic of Congo in 2007. —*Science* and the World Health Organization[20]

Whirling disease affects fish in the trout and salmon families, and has been found in 24 US states, either in wild fish or in hatcheries. The parasitic disease damages cartilage and causes fish to swim in an uncontrollable whirling pattern, rendering them unable to properly function. —Whirling Disease Initiative[21]

About half of southern Africa's 47 million cattle are under threat from transboundary animal diseases, despite improvements in regional surveillance and management. —Botswana Press Agency[22]

FOREWORD

The Value of Conservation

WARD WOODS

Forests, grasslands, freshwater systems, oceans, and their many animals have always supported human societies and economies. Throughout human history, we have known the economic values of wildlife and wild places in terms of what we extract from them. There is now in the conservation community an increased effort to value economically the services wild nature provides by its very existence. One of these studies indicates that services provided by intact nature—carbon sequestration, fresh water, fertile soil, rainfall, protein, and others—may equal twice the $44 trillion product of the global economy. At present, we are paying for few of these services and, if lost, they must be replaced—if they are replaceable—through expensive investments in infrastructure.

It would appear compelling to retain these services. So why are these valuable ecosystems being destroyed, with little consideration of future loss? Basically, it's the difference of time scale. The benefits to us of destroying these ecosystems—agricultural development, logging profits, bushmeat, fishing, land development—are immediate, whereas the loss of ecosystems services will occur over decades. In many cases, a human population just relocates when ecosystem services are lost. Ultimately, of course, there will be no place to go.

There is a further argument that the cost today of protecting ecosystems would be so high it would wreck both developed and developing country economies. In fact, many scholars and practitioners believe the opposite is

WARD WOODS is chairman of the board of trustees of the Wildlife Conservation Society and a director of Bessemer Securities Corporation and Bessemer Trust Company. He is a former trustee of Stanford University; chairman of Stanford Management Company; chairman of the advisory board of the Woods Institute for the Environment, Stanford University; a director of the National Fish and Wildlife Foundation; a member of the Council on Foreign Relations; and a trustee of the Boys' Club of New York.

true—that transforming industrial, agricultural, and other practices to save natural capital and biodiversity will create economic growth and new industries while reducing wasteful consumption. But this would require transformed enterprises to replace existing ones, disrupting the status quo and reducing prospects for a number of entrenched industries.

The economic arguments are compelling but are not the complete solution to preventing loss of biodiversity and the lands and waters species need to survive. In most cases involving a threatened habitat, there are trade-offs that involve human practices, economic opportunity, habitat integrity, and political will. It is both a science and an art to understand the natural systems that allow a particular ecosystem to thrive, what the limits of tolerance are for the critical flora and fauna, and what incentives are required to convince the local human populations and political authorities that it is in their interest to protect certain habitats and to then establish and support a framework for adequate long-term conservation. Successful conservation cannot occur without hard science and local knowledge. Mutual respect and communication are also critical. But none of this will work without sufficient financial support from the public and private sectors.

Having been actively engaged in the financial and business community most of my adult life, I am astounded by how relatively few dollars are required to establish the framework for long-term conservation of ecosystems around the world. As an ardent supporter of conservation and the Wildlife Conservation Society, I have become closely involved in the economics of conservation at WCS, which currently protects about 200 million terrestrial acres globally. We believe that these critical ecosystems contain about 25 percent of terrestrial vertebrate biodiversity of the planet and that this biodiversity can be sustained for an average of about $1 per acre per year, or for approximately $200 million per year. This is a small price to protect a quarter of the vertebrates on Earth. Future pressures on land and resources will undoubtedly increase this price to between $3 and $5 per acre per year. Yet I am sure that most in the financial and business community would find it hard to believe that saving such a large percentage of the world's critters can be such an incredible bargain.

As with a for-profit enterprise, this relatively low-cost operation is the result of an organization's proprietary capabilities. In most of these wild areas, WCS has been active for many years conducting field science and advising governments and local populations, helping to create the framework for conservation success, and providing the financial support to create the incentives to protect these intact ecosystems. WCS's renowned field science capabilities, the quality of its people, and its global reputation combine with its skills in wildlife health and veterinary medicine derived from caring for wildlife at its zoos and aquariums to deliver the formula for success.

For example, in Rwanda, WCS helps protect two of Africa's highest-priority mountain forest areas—home to rare mountain gorillas, the most important population of chimpanzees in eastern Africa, and 12 other kinds of primates. These protected areas also support more than 300 bird species. There is incredibly high biodiversity value here. From an ecosystem service perspective, these forests provide critical water sources for local people, and significant ecotourism revenue. WCS recognized this important conservation opportunity and has worked to strengthen the protection of these parks, train guards, advise government agencies, and monitor species' well-being. The budgeted cost to successfully defend this natural abundance is $320,000 per year.

In Cambodia's northern plains, WCS works to protect regionally rare lowland forest and globally rare bird species, such as giant ibis and sarus cranes. With knowledge of the declines in these magnificent birds, and of the threats to their habitat and nests, WCS worked with the government of Cambodia to incorporate conservation into landscape-level planning processes. To ensure the protection of the birds, WCS established an ingenious incentive program to encourage local villagers to protect nests rather than poach them. This increased the number of nests successfully protected by 150 percent. For bird lovers, that is a conservation solution worth every cent of investment. This successful effort costs $28,000 per year.

These are but two examples of many similar conservation projects managed by WCS. I support the long-term mission of conservation organizations as they strategically invest time and energy to protect wildlife and wild places to benefit future generations, so they can benefit from, appreciate, and admire nature's diversity.

State of the Wild covers emerging issues in wildlife conservation and the conservation of wild places and helps us to assess where to invest in conservation over the next five to ten years. Should it be in more efforts to stem wildlife trade? Or wildlife disease control? Or in the restoration of western US grasslands? All of that and more is in the following pages.

WARD WOODS
NEW YORK CITY
NOVEMBER 2007

2008–2009

STATE OF THE WILD

A Global Portrait of Wildlife, Wildlands, and Oceans

Introduction: Future States of the Wild

Polar bear (*Ursus maritimus*).

KENT H. REDFORD

Wondering and worrying about the future has long been a human preoccupation. We have always wanted to foretell what will happen next and have invented a myriad of ways to try to do so, through reading the veination on the livers of sacrificed oxen, through casting of astragali of deer, or through interpreting patterns in the flight of birds.

A conscientious appreciation of the past—a responsible memory—has become a vital part of conservation. The Wildlife Conservation Society, which celebrates its 113th anniversary in 2008, is the proud owner of a history that now includes parts of three centuries; a history that has spanned much of the history of modern conservation and has included raising captive animal populations, developing wildlife health, establishing protected areas, educating the public, and conducting wildlife research. Our history has also spanned the time of the wide-scale destruction of nature and the rise of modern threats unthought of at the time of our birth. Perhaps most importantly for the future, during the time of our existence, humans have gone from rejoicing in the bounty and thrill of the full richness of nature to forgetting that such richness even existed. Largely extinguished from our collective memory is the feel of the ground shaking under the hooves of tens of millions of bison; the smell of millions of acres of prairie in bloom; the sight of thousands of whales calving in sheltered lagoons; and the sound of the wings of millions of passenger pigeons rising at dawn.

Appreciation of this wasting away of ecological memory has recently been brought to the fore by people referring to this phenomenon as sliding baselines or landscape amnesia. As these observers point out, we must remember the ecological fullness of the past in order to imagine a full future. Recent research has suggested that this is not just the wail of the despondent conservationist but a critical piece in enabling creation of an ecologically replete future. Work on the structure and function of the human brain by neurophysiologists and psychologists[1] shows that memory enables humans to both remember past events as well as imagine future ones: measuring electrical activity in human brains has shown that memory functions to allow the brain to reassemble pieces of the past as a means of imagining possible futures. In fact, people who lose their memory also lose their ability to imagine the future.

Understanding this important link between the past and the future, WCS established a Futures Group to help identify and consider alternate futures that would affect our ability to achieve the mission of conserving wildlife and wild places. The group worked with consultants from Bio Economic Research Associates (bio-era) to develop six scenarios of the future that can help WCS explore the ways in which conservation activities and strategies may need to shift in the decades ahead in response to global changes and the dynamic interplay of geopolitics, technology, economics, and the environment. Connecting the past to the future is a powerful and vital function of conservation. But it must be done in ways that inspire people to act by offering powerful alternate visions of the future from which to choose and powerful ways to reach the desired condition. This volume, *State of the Wild*, is part of our work in this effort.

State of the Wild, a product of the Wildlife Conservation Society Institute, is dedicated to the conservation of the wild. This is the second volume in a series that began in 2006. With this series we hope to inform and inspire others who dream of the wild and care about ensuring its future. Our objective is to fulfill a need for a science-based publication that focuses on achievable conservation of wildlife and wild places.

We have four main goals: (1) to offer to the public insightful, timely analyses of the most pressing global conservation issues confronting wildlife and wild places; (2) to present global conservation news highlights; (3) to promote innovative, science-based solutions to conservation problems; and (4) to influence global public policy. We are committed to exploring both successes and shortcomings of conservation practice from the perspective of over 113 years of work. The first volume of *State of the Wild* featured a focus on wildlife hunting and trade in addition to a broad set of essays addressing other topics.

In this volume, we focus on the integration of wildlife health, human health, and the health of domestic animals—an increasingly critical dimension of conservation that is underappreciated by the mainstream conservation community. This focus is complemented with a range of essays clustered into sections addressing conservation of wildlife; conservation of wild places; people, culture and conservation; and the art and practice of conservation. We have drawn upon a set of authors from WCS as well as other institutions and environmental authors and poets.

State of the Wild brings critical issues into public discussion in an accessible fashion that will both educate a broad range of audiences and inspire many to bring about change.

Within our own lifetimes we have learned the tough lesson that wildlife and wild places cannot take care of themselves in the face of human caused change—no matter how high the fences. Humanity is facing the paradox of having to manage that which we wish to remain unmanaged. Saving the wild is a task that can never falter and never stop. We have become responsible for choosing not only our own future, but the future of Earth as well.

KENT H. REDFORD is director of the Wildlife Conservation Society Institute and vice president for conservation strategy at WCS. He previously worked at The Nature Conservancy and the University of Florida. His areas of interest include biodiversity conservation, sustainable use, the politics of conservation, and the mammals of South America.

Could it be true we live on earth?
On earth forever?

Just one brief instant here.

Even the finest stones begin to split,
even gold is tarnished,
even precious bird-plumes
shrivel like a cough.

Just one brief instant here.

NEZAHUALCOYOTL
MEXICO
(1403–1473)

PART I

STATE OF THE WILD

The state of the wild is at once fascinating, because there is so much to learn about each region and type of wild, and concerning, because all human endeavors impact the wild in some way. The contributions in this section provide an overview of several areas of concern, as well as glimmers of hope for the current state of the wild.

James Hansen's contribution, "Tipping Point: Perspective of a Climatologist," gives us a truly global assessment of what climate change will do to our planet's wildlife. From this overarching view, the focus narrows to "Global Conservation News Highlights," a section containing brief updates on regional conservation victories and losses since the publication of *State of the Wild 2006*.

In "Discoveries," Margaret Kinnaird discusses new species discovered since 2006 and reminds us of the richness that still remains to be explored. In "The Rarest of the Rare," contributors from three conservation organizations—Wildlife Conservation Society, World Wildlife Fund, and The Nature Conservancy—profile some of the world's rarest animals and ecosystems and pinpoint where extinctions are imminent. We hope "The Rarest of the Rare," rather than serving as an epitaph, serves as a poignant time capsule to spur further conservation efforts.

Harkening back to the theme of *State of the Wild 2006*, which featured a special section on hunting and the global wildlife trade, Elizabeth L. Bennett provides a sobering update on the species threatened by trade in "Continuing to Consume Wildlife."

These entries are meant to provide context for and enrich the in-depth essays that follow in parts II and III of this book.

Tipping Point

PERSPECTIVE OF A CLIMATOLOGIST

JAMES HANSEN

"Animals are on the run. Plants are migrating too."[1] I wrote those words in 2006 to draw attention to the fact that climate change was already under way. People do not notice climate change because it is masked by day-to-day weather fluctuations, and we reside in comfortable homes. Animals and plants, on the other hand, can survive only within certain climatic conditions, which are now changing. The National Arbor Day Foundation had to redraw its maps for the zones in which tree species can survive, and animals are shifting to new habitats as well. Are these gradual changes in the wild consistent with dramatic scientific assessments of a crystallizing planetary emergency? Unfortunately, yes. Present examples only hint at the scale of the planetary emergency that climate studies reveal with increasing clarity.

Our home planet is dangerously near a tipping point at which human-made

JAMES HANSEN is director of the National Aeronautics and Space Administration Goddard Institute for Space Studies, but the perspectives here are his own. Hansen is also Adjunct Professor of Earth and Environmental Sciences at Columbia University's Earth Institute, and he appeared in An Inconvenient Truth. *He has also criticized the Intergovernmental Panel on Climate Change for not adequately addressing the danger of large sea level rise.*

greenhouse gases reach a level where major climate changes can proceed mostly under their own momentum. Warming will shift climatic zones by intensifying the hydrologic cycle, affecting freshwater availability and human health. We will see repeated coastal tragedies associated with storms and continuously rising sea levels. The implications are profound, and the only resolution is for humans to move to a fundamentally different energy pathway within a decade. Otherwise, it will be too late for one-third of the world's animal and plant species and millions of the most vulnerable members of our own species.

We may be able to preserve the remarkable planet on which civilization developed, but it will not be easy: special interests are resistant to change and have inordinate power in our governments, especially in the United States. Understanding the nature and causes of climate change is essential to crafting solutions to our current crisis.

Tipping Point

Earth is heated by sunlight and, in balance, reaches a temperature such that an amount of heat equal to the absorbed solar energy radiates back to space. Climate forcings are imposed, temporary changes to Earth's energy balance that alter Earth's mean temperature. Forcings include changes in

> We are at the tipping point because the climate state includes large, ready positive feedbacks provided by the Arctic sea ice, the West Antarctic ice sheet, and much of Greenland's ice.

the sun's brightness, volcanic eruptions that discharge sunlight-reflecting particles into the stratosphere, and long-lived human-made greenhouse gases that trap heat.

Forcings are amplified or diminished by other changes within the climate system, known as feedbacks. Fast feedbacks—changes that occur quickly in response to temperature change—amplify the initial temperature change, begetting additional warming. As the planet warms, fast feedbacks include more water vapor, which traps additional heat, and less snow and sea ice, which exposes dark surfaces that absorb more sunlight.

Slower feedbacks also exist. Due to warming, forests and shrubs are moving poleward into tundra regions. Expanding vegetation, darker than tundra, absorbs sunlight and warms the environment. Another slow feedback is increasing wetness (i.e., darkness) of the Greenland and West Antarctica ice sheets in the warm season. Finally, as tundra melts, methane, a powerful greenhouse gas, is bubbling out. Paleoclimatic records confirm that the long-lived greenhouse gases—

methane, carbon dioxide, and nitrous oxide—all increase with the warming of oceans and land. These positive feedbacks amplify climate change over decades, centuries, and longer.

The predominance of positive feedbacks explains why Earth's climate has historically undergone large swings: feedbacks work in both directions, amplifying cooling, as well as warming, forcings. In the past, feedbacks have caused Earth to be whipsawed between colder and warmer climates, even in response to weak forcings, such as slight changes in the tilt of Earth's axis.[2]

The second fundamental property of Earth's climate system, partnering with feedbacks, is the great inertia of oceans and ice sheets. Given the oceans' capacity to absorb heat, when a climate forcing (such as increased greenhouse gases) impacts global temperature, even after two or three decades, only about half of the eventual surface warming has occurred. Ice sheets also change slowly, although accumulating evidence shows that they can disintegrate within centuries or perhaps even decades.

The upshot of the combination of inertia and feedbacks is that additional climate change is already "in the pipeline": even if we stop increasing greenhouse gases today, more warming will occur. This is sobering when one considers the present status of Earth's climate. Human civilization developed during the Holocene (the past 12,000 years). It has been warm enough to keep ice sheets off North America and Europe, but cool enough for ice sheets to remain on Greenland and Antarctica. With rapid warming of 0.6°C in the past 30 years, global temperature is at its warmest level in the Holocene.[3]

The warming that has already occurred, the positive feedbacks that have been set in motion, and the additional warming in the pipeline together have brought us to the precipice of a planetary tipping point. We are at the tipping point because the climate state includes large, ready positive feedbacks provided by the Arctic sea ice, the West Antarctic ice sheet, and much of Greenland's ice. Little additional forcing is needed to trigger these feedbacks and magnify global warming. If we go over the edge, we will transition to an environment far outside the range that has been experienced by humanity, and there will be no return within any foreseeable future generation. Casualties would include more than the loss of indigenous ways of life in the Arctic and swamping of coastal cities. An intensified hydrologic cycle will produce both greater floods and greater droughts. In the US, the semiarid states from central Texas through Oklahoma and both Dakotas would be-

Brünnich's guillemot (*Uria lomvia*), an Arctic seabird, has advanced its egg-laying date at its southern boundary, a phenological change due to global warming.

Source: Tom Vezo/naturepl.com.

come more drought-prone and ill suited for agriculture, people, and current wildlife. Africa would see a great expansion of dry areas, particularly southern Africa. Large populations in Asia and South America would lose their primary dry season freshwater source as glaciers disappear. A major casualty in all this will be wildlife.

State of the Wild

Climate change is emerging while the wild is stressed by other pressures—habitat loss, overhunting, pollution, and invasive species—and it will magnify these stresses.

Species will respond to warming at differing paces, affecting many others through the web of ecological interac- tions. Phenological events, which are timed events in the life cycle that are usually tied to seasons, may be disrupted. Examples of phenological events include when leaves and flowers emerge and when animals depart for migration, breed, or hibernate. If species depend on each other during those times—for pollination or food— the pace at which they respond to warmer weather or precipitation changes may cause unraveling, cascading effects within ecosystems.

Animals and plants respond to climate changes by expanding, contracting, or shifting their ranges. Isotherms, lines of a specific average temperature, are moving poleward by approximately thirty-five miles (56 km) per decade, meaning many species ranges may in turn shift at that pace.[4] Some already are: the red fox is moving into

The Mount Graham red squirrel (*Tamiasciurus hudsonicus grahamensis*) survives on a single mountain in Arizona. "Green islands" on mountains, and the species that live on them, are pushed higher as temperatures rise, and will be pushed off the planet if global warming continues.

Arctic fox territory, and ecologists have observed that 943 species across all taxa and ecosystems have exhibited measurable changes in their phenologies and/or distribution over the past several decades.[5] However, their potential routes and habitat will be limited by geographic or human-made obstacles, and other species' territories.

Continued business-as-usual greenhouse gas emissions threaten many ecosystems, which together form the fabric of life on Earth and provide a wide range of services to humanity.

Some species face extinction. The following examples represent a handful. Of particular concern are polar species, because they are being pushed off the planet. In Antarctica, Adelie and emperor penguins are in decline, as shrinking sea ice has reduced the abundance of krill, their food source.[6] Arctic polar bears already contend with melting sea ice, from which they hunt seals in colder months. As sea ice recedes earlier each year, populations of polar bears in Canada have declined by about 20 percent, with the weight of females and the number of surviving cubs decreasing a similar amount. As of this writing, the US Fish and

Wildlife Service is still considering protecting polar bears, but only after it was taken to court for failure to act on the mounting evidence that polar bears will suffer greatly due to global warming.[7]

Life in many biologically diverse alpine regions is similarly in danger of being pushed off the planet. When a given temperature range moves up a mountain, the area with those climatic conditions becomes smaller and rockier, and the air thinner, resulting in a struggle for survival for some alpine species.

In the Southwest US, the endemic Mount Graham red squirrel survives on a single Arizona mountain, an "island in the sky," an isolated green spot in the desert. The squirrels, protected as an endangered species, had rebounded to a population of over 500, but their numbers have since declined to between 100 and 200 animals.[8] Loss of the red squirrel will alter the forest because its middens are a source of food and habitat for chipmunks, voles, and mice.

A new stress on Graham red squirrels is climatic: increased heat, drought, and fires. Heat-stressed forests are vulnerable to prolonged beetle infestation and catastrophic fires. Rainfall still occurs, but it is erratic and heavy, and dry periods are more intense. The resulting forest fires burn hotter, and the lower reaches of the forest cannot recover.

> Prior major warmings in Earth's history, the most recent occurring 55 million years ago . . . resulted in the extinction of half or more of the species then on the planet.

In the marine world, loggerhead turtles are also suffering. These great creatures return to beaches every two to three years to bury a clutch of eggs. Hatchlings emerge after two months and head precariously to the sea to face a myriad of predators. Years of conservation efforts to protect loggerhead turtles on their largest nesting area in the US, stretching over 20 miles of Florida coastline, seemed to be stabilizing the South Florida subpopulation.[9] Now climate change places a new stress on these turtles. Florida beaches are increasingly lined with sea walls to protect against rising seas and storms. Sandy beaches seaward of the walls are limited and may be lost if the sea level rises substantially.

Some creatures seem more adaptable to climate change. The armadillo, a prehistoric critter that has been around for over 50 million years, is likely to extend its range northward in the US. But the underlying cause of the climatic threat to the Graham red squirrel and other species—from grizzlies, whose springtime food sources may shift, to the isolated snow vole in the mountains of southern Spain—is "business-as-usual" use of fossil fuels. Predicted warming of several degrees Celsius would surely cause mass extinctions. Prior major warmings in Earth's history, the most recent occurring 55 million years ago with the release of large amounts of Arctic methane hydrates,[10] resulted in the extinction of half or more of the species then on the planet.

Might the Graham red squirrel and snow vole be "saved" if we transplant them to higher mountains? They would have to compete for new niches—and there is a tangled web of interactions that has evolved among species and ecosystems. What is the prospect that we could understand, let alone reproduce, these complex interactions that create ecological stability? "Assisted migration" is thus an uncertain prospect.[11] The best chance for all species is a conscious choice by humans to pursue an alternative energy scenario to stabilize the climate.

State of the Planet

There is a huge gap between what is understood about global warming—by the scientific community—and what is known about global warming—by those who need to know: the public and policymakers.

The crystallizing science points to an imminent planetary emergency. The dangerous level of carbon dioxide, at which we will set in motion unstoppable changes, is at most 450 parts

Loggerhead turtle (*Caretta caretta*) hatchling emerging from egg. Loggerhead decline has been arrested by the protection of nesting areas on Florida beaches and other measures, but these areas will be threatened by rising sea level.

Source: Turtle Time, Inc.

per million (ppm), but it may be less.[12] Carbon dioxide has already increased from a preindustrial level of 280 ppm to 383 ppm in 2007, and it is now increasing by about 2 ppm per year. We

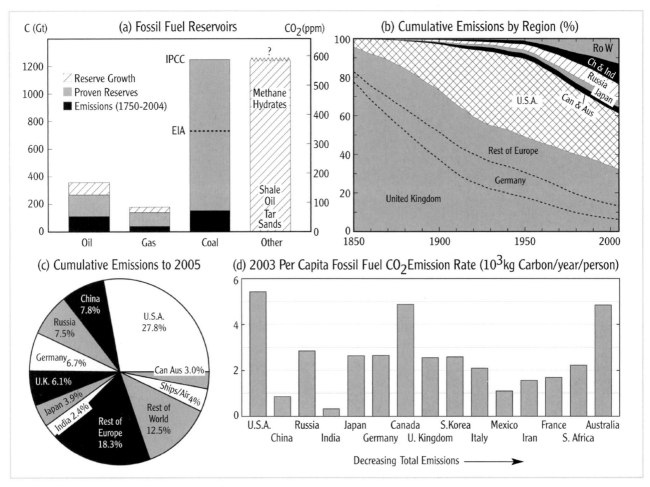

Carbon dioxide contained in fossil fuel reservoirs, (a) the dark areas being the portion already used; (b, c) cumulative fossil fuel carbon dioxide emissions by different countries as a percent of global total; (d) per capita emissions for the 10 largest emitters of fossil fuel carbon dioxide.

must make significant changes within a decade to avoid setting in motion unstoppable climatic change.

We need to address carbon dioxide emissions immediately. Global industrialization, powered first by coal, and later by oil and gas, resulted in fossil fuel pollutants that choked London on smog, set a river on fire in the US, and damaged forests by acid rain. We are solving those pollution problems, but we did not address them until they hit us with full force. That approach, to wait and see and clean up the mess post facto, will not work in the case of carbon dioxide emissions and climate change because of inertial effects, warming already in the pipeline, and tipping points. On the contrary, ignoring emissions would lock in catastrophic climatic change.

Instead, we must resolve to move rapidly to the next phase of the industrial revolution—expanding the benefits of advanced technology to help maintain the atmosphere, and consequently the wonders of the natural world. A review of basic fossil fuel facts reveals why the shift must be made soon. Based on the estimated amount of carbon dioxide locked in each remaining fossil fuel reservoir—including oil, gas, coal, and unconventional fossil fuels (tar sands, tar shale, heavy oil, methane hydrates)[13]—burning readily available oil and gas resources alone will take atmospheric carbon dioxide to levels near 450 ppm. Burning coal and unconventional fossil fuels, which energy companies are now exploring, could take atmospheric carbon dioxide to far greater levels.

To understand the limits on future

> In my view, special interests have undue sway with our governments and have effectively promoted minimalist actions and growth in fossil fuels, rather than making the scale of investments necessary.

use of fossil fuels, an awareness of the carbon cycle is critical. In this cycle, the ocean quickly takes up a fraction of carbon dioxide emissions, but uptake slows as carbon dioxide added to the ocean exerts a "back pressure." Further uptake depends upon carbon dioxide mixing into the deep ocean and precipitating out of ocean water via carbonate sediments. This means that about one-third of carbon dioxide emissions remain in the atmosphere after 100 years and one-quarter still remain after 500 years. Indeed, carbon dioxide from the Industrial Revolution still around today implies heavy responsibilities for Europe and the US.

Carbon reservoirs and the ocean's pace of removing carbon dioxide are important boundary conditions in framing solutions to the climate crisis. We can avert planetary transformation —eventual disintegration of ice sheets

and massive extinctions— only if the planetary energy balance is restored at an acceptable global temperature. Temperature fluctuates from year to year, but it is increasing by about 0.2°C per decade. Although estimates of permissible warming must be refined as knowledge advances, the upshot of crystallizing science is that the "safe" global temperature level is, at most, about 1°C greater than the year 2000 global temperature.

This 1°C limit on additional global warming implies the aforementioned carbon dioxide ceiling of about 450 ppm.[14] Pinpointing this carbon dioxide ceiling is complicated due to other human-made forcings, especially methane, nitrous oxide, and "black soot." For example, an alternative scenario allows carbon dioxide levels to peak at 475 ppm because it assumes a large reduction of methane.[15] However, human-made sulfate aerosols (reflective particles that have a cooling effect) are likely to decrease, neutralizing these potential reductions in methane. Therefore 450 ppm is a good comprehensive estimate of the maximum allowable carbon dioxide. Indeed, if recent ice loss from Antarctica is a sign, it may be that even 450 ppm is excessive.

Since we could reach 450 ppm within two to three decades, we should be inspired now to change our energy systems. Based on the preceding boundary conditions, the following is a four-point strategy to avoid dangerous climate change.

1. Coal and unconventional fossil fuels must be curtailed and used only with capture and sequestration of the carbon dioxide underground. Existing coal-fired power plants should be phased out over the next few decades.

2. Carbon price and efficiency standards must be implemented. Recognizing the unusual energy concentration and mobility of fossil fuels—with which little else can currently compete—the practical way to transition to a postpetroleum era is to impose a moderate but continually rising carbon price. The price can be via a tax on fossil fuels, a ration-and-trade system that limits impacts on people least able to afford an energy tax, or a combination of methods. This will make fossil fuels pay for environmental damage while stretching remaining oil and gas to accommodate sustainable economic growth. The certainty of a rising price will inspire indus-

tries to innovate and will reduce the incentive to exploit unconventional fossil fuels with high carbon dioxide emissions, such as tar shale.

In addition, we need real efficiency standards, for vehicles, buildings, and lighting. We must remove barriers to energy efficiency, such as the policy of most utility companies to promote energy consumption rather than conservation.

3. We must take steps to draw down atmospheric carbon dioxide. Farming and forestry practices that enhance carbon retention in the soil and biosphere must be supported. Biofuel power plants with carbon sequestration can draw down atmospheric carbon dioxide,[16] putting anthropogenic carbon dioxide back underground. Carbon dioxide can be sequestered beneath ocean sediments[17] and in other safe geologic sites.

4. We must take steps to reduce other, non–carbon dioxide forcings, especially black soot, methane, and ground-level ozone via stricter regulations.

International implementation of these steps requires recognition of responsibilities. Because of the long lifetime of carbon dioxide already emit-

ted, Europe bears a large responsibility. But the responsibility of the US is more than three times that of any other nation, and it will continue to be the largest for at least several decades, even though China will exceed the US in new emissions within a year or two.

Sadly, the requirements to avoid global disasters are not yet widely recognized: Germany intends to replace nuclear power plants with coal. But Europe, the US, and other developed countries should place a moratorium on new coal-fired power plants until carbon capture and sequestration are in place. This cannot wait until similar restrictions are practical in China and India. National responsibilities for climate change and per capita emissions are an order of magnitude greater in the US, Canada, and Australia than in India and China, and define moral obligations.

At the same time, China and developing countries should bulldoze old-technology coal power plants and build new coal power plants with *only* the latest technology. Storms and floods attending climate change will hit developing countries hardest because most megacities near sea level are in those countries. This should provide incentive for China and India to address climate change.

Efficiency of future vehicle power is also vital. California's requirement for 30 percent efficiency improvement has great value. In contrast, a pro-

posed national energy plan for 20 percent ethanol in vehicle fuels, derived in large part from corn, does more harm than good. It will do little to reduce emissions—because producing ethanol currently requires a lot of energy —and it would degrade carbon retention in soils. There are ways that renewable or other carbon dioxide–free energies may eventually power vehicles, but half-measures should not be dictated without sufficient scientific input to balance vested agribusiness interests.

That said, biofuels can play a major part in our energy future. As a native Iowan, I like to imagine that the Midwest will rescue compatriots threatened by rising seas. Native grasses, appropriately cultivated, and perhaps with improved varieties, can draw down atmospheric carbon dioxide. The prairies may contribute, if we get on with solving the climate problem before superdrought hits them. Biofuel investment should proceed with input from scientists and conservationists, because some industry and government biofuel production plans would clear more forest for plantations of oil palm and soy with consequences for wildlife and wildlands.

A Final Picture

Earth's paleoclimatic record tells us that atmospheric greenhouse gases are now near the dangerous level where tipping points become unavoidable.

Yellow-bellied marmots (*Marmota flaviventris*) advanced their emergence from hibernation by 23 days in the Rocky Mountains, presumably due to global warming.

We can choose a course to reverse greenhouse gas growth and promptly change our energy strategy. A step in the right direction was the April 2007 decision by the US Supreme Court that the Environmental Protection Agency can and should regulate greenhouse gas emissions. However, much more is needed.

In my view, special interests have undue sway with our governments and have effectively promoted minimalist actions and growth in fossil fuels, rather than making the scale of investments necessary.

US government complicity with special interests was clear when, at a practice press conference held by NASA on Arctic sea ice, a member of my group suggested that a reduction in greenhouse gas emissions could stem sea ice loss. His suggestion prompted a government "minder" to proclaim "that's unacceptable," on the grounds that it was a policy statement, when in fact it was scientifically based. While making policy is the right of our elected representatives, scientists had connected the dots of climate research and were prevented from communicating that information. In this case, vested interests posed a threat to our home planet and the fabric of life upon it.

It is worth imagining how our grandchildren will look back on us. The picture that I fear has the polluters, the utilities, and automakers standing in court demanding the right to continue to emit carbon dioxide for the sake of short-term profits. The disturbing part is that we, through our national government, are standing alongside the polluters, officially as a hulking amicus curiae (friend of the court), arguing against limitations on emissions. Is this the picture of our generation that we want to be remembered by?

We live in a democracy, and policies represent our collective will. If we allow the planet to pass tipping points, it will be hard to defend our role. The state of the wild is in our hands, and we can still preserve creation and serve humanity worldwide. A drive for energy efficiency and clean energy sources will produce high-tech jobs. Restoration of clean air will be universally beneficial. Rural life and the planet can benefit from intelligent development of biofuels and renewable energy.

At the front lines, observing the changes in the wild, conservationists serve as a voice for the plants and animals that have already started reacting to climate warming. To conserve as much biodiversity as we can, conservationists must unite with many others to push for a far more radical reduction in carbon dioxide emissions than has hitherto been considered practical. Otherwise, alpine and polar species, coral reefs, and species living in areas that become arid will be lost over the next century.

GLOBAL CONSERVATION NEWS HIGHLIGHTS

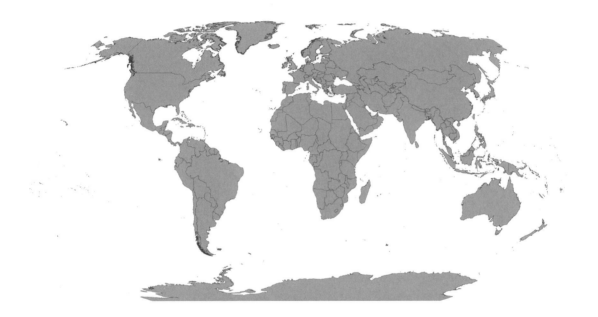

News regarding wildlife conservation is dramatic—bad news means extinction, and good news means survival. This section presents recent news from all continents since the last volume of *State of the Wild* was published in 2006. Some of the most important or interesting research, rulings, and events that have affected biodiversity and conservation serve as a global snapshot of recent developments that have altered the state of the wild.

Through these briefs, we seek to broaden awareness of recent global news events and major trends that are affecting wildlife and wildlands. We hope they will serve as a benchmark for conservation over the past two years, and as a reference for those wishing to learn more about a particular region.

Africa

Africa's forests and savannas are famed for the richness of their primate radiations and carnivore and ungulate guilds—from the cercopithecine monkeys of West and Central Africa to the white-eared kob and tiang migrations of southern Sudan. Recent years have seen some notable conservation successes: creation of protected areas in Madagascar and Central Africa, successful species conservation in southern Africa, and solid park management and rebounding tourism in East Africa. The moves to protect the Congo Basin rainforest from logging and the bushmeat trade continue to gather momentum.

Yet much of the continent's wildlife and great habitats face neglect and destruction, including West Africa's coastal forests, the antelopes of the Sahara and Sahel, and the continent's freshwater diversity. Because much global policy is focused on alleviating poverty and combating disease on the world's poorest continent, it has become ever clearer that wildlife conservation must be further reconciled with these social goals. That reconciliation is found in pioneering projects to stem illegal hunting by providing food security in Zambia's Community Markets for Conservation (COMACO); to share the proceeds of safari hunting equitably in Namibia's Living in a Finite Environment (LIFE); to build community development and ecotourism in Bwindi Impenetrable Forest, Uganda, and the Northern Rangeland Trust of Kenya; and to pioneer direct payments for ecosystem services such as carbon storage in Madagascar's Makira Forest. Africa's unique biodiversity and unusually poor conservation and development capacity are the context for some of the most recent successes and setbacks.

White rhino (*Ceratotherium simum*).

Africa: Northern rhino subspecies continue to face extinction in the wild, whereas southern subspecies are rebounding. A 2006 survey conducted by the African Rhino Specialist Group (AfRSG) found no signs of West African black rhino (*Diceros bicornis longipes*) in the subspecies' last refuge in northern Cameroon, suggesting that the subspecies may now be extinct. Northern white rhino (*Ceratotherium simum cottoni*) appear virtually extinct as well, with ground and aerial surveys finding only four in Garamba National Park in the Democratic Republic of Congo. Poaching for rhino horns for medicinal or ornamental purposes continues to be the main threat. Fortunately, some rhino subspecies are recovering: southern white rhino (*Ceratotherium simum simum*), reintroduced into many areas of southern and central Africa, have steadily increased from fewer than 100 animals to approximately 14,540, and, overall, black rhino (*Diceros bicornis*) numbers have increased by about 3.2 percent since 2004. www.iucn.org/en/news/archive/2006/07/7_pr_rhino.htm.

Western lowland gorilla (*Gorilla gorilla gorilla*).

Central Africa: The Ebola virus killed approximately 5,000 western lowland gorillas (*Gorilla gorilla gorilla*) over the past several years, wiping out more than 90 percent of the species in the region around the Lossi Sanctuary in the Republic of Congo and an unspecified number in neighboring Odzala National Park. Ebola causes a hemorrhagic fever resulting in internal bleeding and is fatal within two weeks to 80 percent of infected apes. (This is also the case in humans.) The recent study was based on carcasses found, sightings by local villagers, and lower populations of gorillas in the area. Ebola is moving at a rate of approximately 31 miles (50 km) per year in western Central Africa, and is second only to the bushmeat trade in the level of threat posed to wildlife populations. It is highly contagious between animals of the same species and between species, threatening the remaining western lowland gorillas, most of which live within 124 miles (200 km) of the current outbreak. *Science* 314:1522–1523; http://news.nationalgeographic.com/news/2006/12/061207-ebola-gorillas.html?source=rss.

Deforestation.

Congo Basin: The Congo Basin forest, the second largest moist tropical forest in the world, absorbs tons of carbon dioxide and stores it in wood, roots, and leaves. A crucial economic resource for the region, the forest is threatened by timber operations, agriculture, and charcoal production. Since launching the Congo Basin Forest Partnership with the Wildlife Conservation Society, the World Wildlife Fund, Conservation International, and the African Wildlife Foundation in 2002, the US Government has allocated more than $54 million to forest conservation, funds matched by France and other European partners. This could develop into a trend toward support for rainforest nations to avoid deforestation or to reduce carbon emissions from deforestation and degradation. New technology using infrared spectrum analysis is being developed to better assess carbon storage changes over large areas. Avoided deforestation and how it fits into existing conservation and climate change treaties will put global forests in the spotlight. www.cbfp.org/en/index.htm; *New Scientist* 2581: 10.

Greater flamingo (*Phoenicopterus roseus*).

Kenya: Lake Nakuru, home to Kenya's iconic flocks of greater and lesser flamingos (*Phoenicopterus roseus* and *Phoenicopterus minor*), is shrinking, and so is the flamingo population. Just six years ago 1 million flamingos fed in Lake Nakuru's shallow waters, but in October 2006, an estimated 500,000 were observed. Earlier in 2006, in the dry season, there were an estimated 30,000 to 40,000, and many flamingo carcasses were found near the lake. Lake Nakuru may have lost about half of its water in the past few years, leaving a salt-encrusted rim. Causes of the die-off are not well understood, and include deforestation in the watershed area and years of drought. Some birds are believed to have relocated to other lakes in the Rift Valley, meaning that the entire population, although now split, may still be strong. However, at Lake Bogoria, heavy rains swelled, creating less dense concentrations of lake algae, and flamingos were only consuming a tenth of their daily food needs, weakening that lake's population as well. Local communities around Nakuru have been replanting trees in the deforested areas around the lake in an effort to bring more flamingos back to the region. Declines in flamingo populations have negatively impacted Kenya's wildlife tourism industry. www.enn.com/top_stories/article/5472; www.enn.com/animals/article/6422.

Western red colobus (*Procolobus badius*).

Liberia: The first democratically elected president of Liberia, Ellen Johnson Sirleaf, brings hope for a country that is ending 14 years of civil war and which also has the largest remaining expanse of West African forest. Endemic and highly endangered species in the area include the lesser spot-nosed guenon (*Cercopithecus petaurista*), western red colobus monkey (*Procolobus badius*), and the heavily hunted Liberian mongoose (*Liberiictis kuhni*). President Sirleaf promised to bring stability to a country that has no functioning national road, telephone, or electricity network. Mass movements of refugees and internally displaced people have intensified pressure on Nigeria's forest resources, and stability could mean opportunities to study and conserve this part of the original Upper Guinean forest, a moist lowland forest that is one of the world's priority biodiversity conservation areas. At the same time, stability could translate into rapid road building and commercial harvesting of forest resources, including wildlife (bushmeat). www.biodiversityscience .org/priority_outcomes/west_africa/upper.html.

Ring-tailed lemurs (*Lemur catta*).

Madagascar: President Ravalomanana announced the protection of over 2 million acres (875,000 ha) of forest in three new protected areas, including Makira Forest, the largest block of forest in Madagascar. Madagascar is home to more than 200,000 species of plants and animals, three-quarters of which are found nowhere else in the world. Protecting this unique habitat is part of the long-term goal to bring 10 percent of the island country under protected management by 2008. The management will include sustainability planning for thousands of local people who live in and around the forests. Makira Forest, the Ankeniheny-Zahamena corridor in the east, and Anjozorobe in the central province are home to some of the island's most threatened species, including many of Madagascar's lemurs, such as the indri (*Indri indri*), ring-tailed lemur (*Lemur catta*), and black-and-white ruffed lemur (*Varecia variegata variegata*). www.cepf.net/xp /cepf/news /newsletter/2006/january_topstory.xml.

African wild dog (*Lycaon pictus*).

Sudan: In 2005, the Sudan People's Liberation Movement and the government of Sudan signed a peace treaty, resulting in partial autonomy for the government of Southern Sudan (GOSS). At their request, the Wildlife Conservation Society began aerial and ground surveys of Boma and Southern national parks, which are among Africa's half-dozen largest parks. The great white-eared kob (*Kobus kob leucotis*) migration, estimated in the 1980s to number more than 700,000 and second in size only to the wildebeest migration in the Serengeti, appeared to be intact. Elephants, too, were still present in several parks, including Boma, Southern, and Nimuleh, and there were anecdotal reports of African wild dogs (*Lycaon pictus*), one of the world's most endangered canids. The Jinjaweed, or northern Sudanese militias, continued to be implicated in human rights atrocities in Darfur and in the rhino horn and ivory trade from Sudan and neighboring Democratic Republic of Congo and Chad. www.sudantribune.com/spip.php?article7482.

Asia

The world's largest continent, Asia contains wildlife reflective of an astonishing diversity of habitats. In the west, gazelles cling to a precarious existence in the deserts of Iran. In the far southeastern reaches of Asia, garishly colored birds of paradise perform flamboyant courtship displays in the rainforests of Papua New Guinea. Marco Polo sheep nervously watch for snow leopards high in the Himalayas, and tigers and Asian elephants roam much of Asia's remaining tropical forests.

But with nearly 4 billion people, Asia is also the world's most populated continent, and the press of humanity is felt everywhere, as nearly every swath of level land is converted to agriculture, forests are logged, and rivers are dammed. Truly wild lands are few and far between, and only patches of mountainous or remote lands bear some resemblance to what they once were. Further compounding these troubles is the East Asian tradition of consuming wild animal parts for medicinal purposes. From seahorses to bears, much wildlife has at least one part with a purported medicinal property in traditional Chinese medicine, and as the demand grows, a complex web of hunters and traders scour Asia's last fragments of wilderness, leaving some forests eerily silent as even the smallest birds and frogs are targeted.

There are some encouraging signs, however: The Thai government banned logging and increased its commitment to protecting wildlife. In Tibet, local community groups have helped reverse the Tibetan antelope's decline. And Afghanistan's new government is writing new environmental laws and beginning to create its first-ever protected area network.

Marco Polo sheep (*Ovis ammon polii*).

Central Asia: The Pamirs, flanked by the Hindu Kush, Himalayan, Karakoram, and Kunlun ranges, are one of the world's most spectacular mountain regions. The borders of Afghanistan, Pakistan, China, and Tajikistan meet at this knot of mountains. The endangered Marco Polo sheep (*Ovis ammon polii*) and snow leopard (*Uncia uncia*) wander across the borders, meaning wildlife here can only be effectively protected through transfrontier cooperation of all four countries. In September 2006 the four governments met to discuss the development of a Pamirs Transboundary Conservation Initiative. Establishing four-country cooperation will enable better management of joint resources and encourage good neighborly relations, with an additional and substantial benefit to wildlife conservation. www.savingwildplaces .com/swp-home/swp-explorationandsurvey/239496.

Giant panda (*Ailuropoda melanoleuca*).

China: China is developing its industrial and energy capacity at a pace and scale more than double that of a decade ago. Wildlife is one of the casualties, particularly in the increasingly polluted and dammed Yangtze and Yellow rivers. The Chinese river dolphin, or baiji (*Lipotes vexillifer*), was declared functionally extinct in 2006. This long-beaked mammal may be the first cetacean to go extinct from human causes. Wildlife biologists are turning to save another Yangtze species of finless porpoise (*Neophocaena phocaenoides*) that is believed to number fewer than 1,000. Similar damage to the Yellow River led biologists to conclude that one-third of China's freshwater fish species are gone. Winding 3,350 miles (5,390 km), the Yellow River provides water for more than 155 million people and 15 percent of China's farmland. On the brighter side, the giant panda (*Ailuropoda melanoleuca*), a national icon, was afforded more protection. In 2006, Sichuan province's giant panda sanctuaries were designated a World Heritage site. Located in the Qionglai and Jiajin mountains, the sanctuaries cover 3,700 square miles (9,583 km^2) and harbor some of the last contiguous bamboo forest habitat, home to more than 30 percent of the world's pandas. Whereas logging, marble mines, and agricultural encroachment once threatened pandas, booming tourism in this region is now expected to become their biggest challenge. www.timesonline.co.uk/tol/news/world/article582811.ece; www.guardian.co .uk/china/story/0,,1993622,00.html; news.nationalgeographic.com/news/2006 /07/060718-pandas.html.baiji.

Snow leopard (*Uncia uncia*).

India: Wildlife trade has become the biggest threat to wildlife in Asia. Indian police recently arrested Sansar Chand, the kingpin of India's largest and most notorious wildlife trafficking gang. Chand's gang has been operating since the mid-1970s and is responsible for the deaths of hundreds of wild tigers and otters, hundreds or even thousands of leopards (*Panthera pardus fusca*), and an unknown number of snow leopards (*Uncia uncia*), foxes, and smaller wild cats. Chand operated in protected areas throughout India via a network of ties with family members and local people, including Nepalese smugglers who sell most of the animal skins and parts to Chinese traders in Tibet. Since his arrest, Sansar has provided information on his Nepalese clients and members of rival wildlife product purveyors to Indian authorities. http://timesofindia.indiatimes.com/articleshow/1162710.cms; http://www.wpsi-india.org/images/EIA-WPSI_Skinning_The_Cat.pdf.

Malayan tapir (*Tapirus indicus*).

Malaysia: Conservationists in Malaysia won an important victory in May 2007 when the Perak state government gazetted some 290,000 acres (117,500 ha) of the Royal Belum-Temenggor Forest Reserve as a state park. This move bans logging and makes the area a permanent forest reserve along Thailand's southern border. The Royal Belum is home to 270 bird species and may hold the world's greatest concentration of hornbills. More than 100 mammal species, including the critically endangered Sumatran rhinoceros (*Dicerorhinus sumatrensis*), Indochinese tigers (*Panthera tigris corbetti*), and the Malayan tapir (*Tapirus indicus*) are also found in the Royal Belum. The move came after a campaign led by the Malaysian Nature Society (MNS) collected over 80,000 signatures in support of protecting the entire Belum-Temenggor Forest Reserve. Continuing efforts to expand the state park are challenged by pressures to convert the forest to acacia plantations. www.mns.org.my/artabout.php?aid=79; www.birdlife.org/datazone/sites/index.html?action=SitHTMDetails.asp&sid=16003&m=021420&sec=mi_perak.

Source: Brian Smith/WCS.

Cast net fishermen signaling an Irrawaddy dolphin (*Orcaella brevirostris*).

Myanmar: In December 2005, the Myanmar Department of Fisheries protected 43 miles (70 km) of the Ayeyarwady River for critically endangered Irrawaddy dolphins (*Orcaella brevirostris*). This area supports one-third of the river's population of approximately 72 of these small, beakless dolphins, which have fostered a cooperative relationship with local fishermen: the dolphins voluntarily herd fish into nets when summoned by the fishermen, and feed on some of the catch in return for their services. Their range has declined by 60 percent, and incidental catch in fishing nets remains a serious threat to the species. Electric fishing and gold mining are now prohibited in the protected area to reduce dolphin injury from electrocution and mercury poisoning. The protected area will also foster public awareness of the dolphin and its unique role in supporting local livelihoods. www.wcs.org/353624/irrawaddydolphin.

Source: Robert Fournier/The Wild Lensman.

Gill net.

Philippines: Southeast Asian waters are highly biodiverse due to the convergence of several seas and the existence of many islands and reefs. A triangular region extending between Malaysia, the Philippines, and Indonesia has long been called Earth's "center" of marine biodiversity. Within the triangle of the Philippine islands of Luzon and Mindanao, more species exist than in any other subsection. According to researchers with Conservation International, the Smithsonian Institution, and the World Conservation Union (IUCN), about two-thirds of the known marine species of the Pacific can be found in these coastal waters. On November 8, 2006, President Gloria Arroyo declared the Verde Island Passage a new marine sanctuary and protected area. Philippine waters have long been highly threatened by pollution, agricultural runoff and erosion, and the use of poisons and dynamite by fishermen. www.odu.edu/ao/instadv/vol36issue5/news.htm#biologist.

Amur leopard (*Panthera pardus orientalis*).

Russian Far East: Two major oil and gas infrastructure developments were halted or rerouted due to their potentially severe impact on rare eastern species. The 2,565 mile (4,130 km) Siberia–Pacific pipeline would have had its terminal and liquefying facilities at Perevoznaya Bay on the Sea of Japan, cutting right through the habitat for the last remaining 30 or so Amur leopards (*Panthera pardus orientalis*). After a long battle with international and Russian conservationists, the plans for the terminal were rejected in February 2007, giving hope for the leopard and unique forests in this part of the Russian Far East. In December 2006, a Shell Oil Company project on Sakhalin Island was also canceled, because dredging and oil spills would have threatened the fragile western gray whale (*Eschrichtius robustus*) population, which numbers fewer than 100. www.amur-leop ard.org; www.panda.org/sakhalin.

Australia, New Zealand, and the Pacific Islands

The geographically diverse terrestrial and marine ecosystems of Australia, New Zealand, and the Pacific Islands span from the sub-Antarctic Chatham Islands to Hawaii's volcanic slopes, and from Western Australia's Ningaloo Reef to Micronesia. Many of the species evolved without knowing humans or mammalian predators, but they have been severely pressured since humans colonized the region and introduced rats, cats, foxes, and mustelids. As a result, scientists anticipate several imminent extinctions from Polynesian countries, New Zealand, and Australia over the next 20 years.

One of the main threats to these hundreds of islands, their wildlife, and people living at the edge of the sea is the potential of rising sea waters due to global warming. This will displace local people and move villages further inland, and cause reefs and mangroves to shift along the evolving coastal boundary, if possible. Although states like Tuvalu and Tokelau may disappear underwater, at the opposite extreme, climate change means Australia may become even drier.

Koala (*Phascolarctos cinereus*).

Australia: Depleted water reservoirs, successive hot, dry summers, and global warming have combined to give Australia one of the worst droughts in 1,000 years. Several regions experienced their fifth consecutive year of drought in 2006 and wildfires burned across the country, with up to 70 blazing at one time. In Western Australia's Kimberley and rangeland regions, a fire destroyed 30,000 acres (12,000 ha) of scrubland. The Environmental Protection Authority fears that the fires will lead to extinctions of small mammals in the northwest, due to the intensity of these fires, changing vegetation types, and lack of food sources for the surviving animals. In New South Wales, more than 204,100 acres (82,600 ha) of forest burned outside of Coonabarabran, including the Pilliga Nature Reserve, which contains one of the state's most significant koala (*Phascolarctos cinereus*) habitats. Wildlife department officials saw kangaroos, wallabies, and emus moving out of the forest but worried that slower-moving koalas may not have escaped the blazes. Bushfires are a regular feature of Australian summers and have killed more than 250 people over the past 40 years. www.guardian .co.uk/australia /story/0,,1941942,00.html.

Tasmanian devil (*Sarcophilus harrisii*).

Australia: Tasmanian devils (*Sarcophilus harrisii*), black, fox-sized scavengers endemic to Tasmania, are still plagued by a facial tumor disease that has already killed over 50 percent of their populations. The cancerous tumors are thought to be infectious and spread by the Tasmanian devils' biting behavior during fights and courtship. The large tumors protrude from the face and neck, sometimes pushing out teeth and invading eye sockets. Because the tumors interfere with feeding, the animals usually die within six months. As of December 2006, populations in the western third of the island remain healthy and viable. A comprehensive program to contain and understand the disease now includes isolating captive populations, monitoring wild populations, and searching for a vaccine for the cancer. http://news.bbc.co.uk/2/hi/science/nature/4674446.stm; www.dpiw .tas.gov.au/inter.nsf/WebPages/LBUN-5QF86G?open.

Buller's albatross (*Thalassarche bulleri*).

Australia/New Zealand: In November 2006, Australia and New Zealand joined with eight other countries as signatories to the Agreement on the Conservation of Albatrosses and Petrels (ACAP). More than half of the 28 species of seabirds covered by ACAP, including Buller's albatross (*Thalassarche bulleri*) and Cook's petrel (*Pterodroma cookii*), are native to New Zealand and Australia. The initiative launches a three-year plan to conserve some of the most threatened seabirds in the world, and includes sharing information and expertise to reduce the main threats facing albatrosses and petrels: accidental capture in longline and trawl fishing gear, pollution, and invasive species at breeding sites. Fishing operations are particularly challenging because they operate in the open ocean. When seabirds are attracted to the fish parts and bait around the boats, they often become hooked or entangled in the gear. Many albatross species lay only one egg per reproductive cycle, making their populations less resilient to unnatural mortality. www.acap.aq/; www.birdsaustralia.com.au/albatross/.

Palila (*Loxioides bailleui*).

Hawaii: In December 2005, seven extremely rare Hawaiian birds called palila (*Loxioides bailleui*) were released into their native habitat on the island of Hawaii. Hatched and reared at the Keauhou Bird Conservation Center, they are part of an effort to establish a new population of palila on the north side of Mauna Kea volcano. Palila are critically endangered finch-like honeycreepers that feed exclusively on the seeds of the native Hawaiian plant mamane (*Sophora chrysophylla*). They are threatened by habitat loss and introduced predators such as feral cats, rats, and mongooses. Fifteen types of honeycreepers have gone extinct in Hawaii in recent decades. Other bird reintroductions to the islands include 25 néné, or Hawaiian geese (*Branta sandvicensis*), released at the crater in Haleakala National Park on the island of Maui. Bolstering Hawaiian native bird conservation is part of a recent US Federal Recovery Land Acquisition Grant, which provided funds to acquire 3,148 acres (1,273 ha) of rare forest habitats within a core conservation region of the Southern Kona district of the island of Hawaii. This will help birds like the ʻakepa (*Loxops coccineus*) and ʻakiapolaʻau (*Hemignathus munroi*), and is also within the range of the ʻalala (Hawaiian crow, *Corvus hawaiiensis*) and ʻIo (Hawaiian hawk, *Buteo solitarius*). http://cres.sandiegozoo.org; www.fws.gov/southeast/news/2006/r06-062.html.

Great white shark (*Carcharodon carcharias*).

New Zealand: In December 2006, New Zealand banned the killing of great white sharks (*Carcharodon carcharias*) within the 200 nautical miles of its borders. The largest species of shark, adult female great whites can reach 22 feet (7 m) in length and weigh as much as 5,000 pounds (2,260 kg). They occur naturally in low numbers and, without protection, could be pushed to extinction. The Wildlife Act will protect great whites in New Zealand waters and will prohibit New Zealand–flagged boats from fishing them. Great whites are targeted as threats to humans and fisheries despite the fact that shark attacks are very rare. They are also killed for their teeth, jaws, fins, and meat, the last two of which are a delicacy in Asian countries. Great whites are solitary creatures and have been known to migrate thousands of miles. They are important predators in ocean systems and have remained little changed since the time of the dinosaurs. www.ens-newswire .com/ens/dec2006/2006-12-01-01.asp; http://marinebio.org /species.asp?id=38.

Hector's dolphin (*Cephalorhynchus hectori*).

South Pacific: In September 2006, nine South Pacific nations—Australia, New Zealand, Fiji, the Cook Islands, Niue, the Federation of Micronesia, France, Samoa, and Vanuatu—signed a regional agreement under the Convention on Migratory Species to protect whales and dolphins. Vanuatu was the latest to join in declaring a whale sanctuary in a zone stretching up to 200 miles (320 km) from its shoreline. The agreement recognizes that cetacean survival depends on conservation over a wide area and in a range of marine and coastal habitats and commits the group to an action plan to reduce threats to the mammals, protect migratory ocean corridors, and respond to strandings and entanglement in nets. Although the agreement may not counteract the resurgence in whaling by other nations in light of the erosion of the International Whaling Commission (IWC), it could enhance protection for dolphins, which do not tend to migrate as far as whales. www.iht.com/articles /ap/2006/09/14/asia/AS_GEN_New_Zealand_Whales.php.

Central and South America

L atin America is the least populated region in the world, with half a billion residents, including 28 million indigenous people who speak over 300 different languages. It has the most wilderness, particularly in the Amazon and Patagonia. Inequality and poverty remain major problems, and Latin American nations seek to increase revenue through infrastructure development and natural resource exploitation—particularly gas, oil, and other mineral resources concentrated in high biodiversity areas. As much as 70 percent of the Peruvian Amazon has been zoned for oil and gas exploration; only some strictly protected parks have been excluded. The agricultural frontier is also expanding due to increased global demand for soy and biofuels. The potential for biodiversity loss is very high.

In this region hunting and wildlife trade regulations exist but are not enforced effectively. Transcontinental efforts to establish and strengthen good governance are essential to help curb the depletion of wildlife. In the Upper Amazon, local stakeholders, including indigenous peoples, nongovernmental organizations (NGOs), and local authorities, are establishing management committees to provide timely guidance for protected area management. In Guatemala, local community groups are establishing *mesas de concertación* (consensus-building forums) to improve environmental safeguards around infrastructure development in the Maya Forest. Public–private partnerships also help improve conservation measures, as illustrated in Chile, Argentina, and the Brazilian Pantanal. Building strong alliances to save wildlife will open the path for long-lasting conservation.

Source: Todd Pusser/naturepl.com.

Pink dolphin (*Inia geoffrensis*).

Amazon/Orinoco: September 2007 marked the end of the first regional survey of river dolphins, led by the Omacha Foundation and Faunagua Foundation, with the support of a team of scientists and conservationists from the World Wildlife Fund, the Whale and Dolphin Conservation Society, and the Wildlife Conservation Society. The 14-month survey was an attempt to assess the population density of pink river dolphins (*Inia geoffrensis* and *Inia boliviensis*) and gray river dolphins (*Sotalia fluviatilis*), which are threatened by chemical and noise pollution, outboard motor propellers, and illegal fishing in the Orinoco (Venezuela) and the Amazon (Ecuador and Colombia) basins. The research team reported encouraging news for the Amazonian population: during a 183 mile (294 km) trek in the Amazon, Atacuari, and Yavari rivers, scientists observed more than 500 dolphins (321 gray and 199 pink), confirming that these species continue to survive. www.panda.org /news_facts/newsroom/index.cfm?uNewsID=96560; www.enn.com/animals /article/22913.

Source: Julie Larsen Maher/WCS

Jaguar (*Panthera onca*).

Central America/Mexico: At the Second Mesoamerica Protected Area Congress in Panama in 2006, environmental ministers from the nations of Central America and Mexico committed to support and implement the expansion of the Mesoamerica Biological Corridor, a network of parks and protected areas established to preserve the habitat and genetic diversity of jaguars (*Panthera onca*). The Central American Commission of Environment and Development (CCAD) is responsible for coordinating this project. Jaguar habitat, ranging from the southwestern US to Argentina, has become increasingly fragmented as a result of development. On-the-ground data collection activities began in 2007 at key jaguar habitat sites throughout the region. These data will inform the further selection and incorporation of important habitat into the Corridor. www.physorg.com /news67695492.html.

Hyacinth macaw (*Anodorhynchus hyacinthinus*).

Source: Eric Baccega/naturepl.com.

Brazil: A recent decision to split the Brazilian Institute for the Environment and Renewable Natural Resources (IBAMA) may weaken this government institution's ability to enforce environmental regulations and wildlife conservation. In theory, hunting and wildlife trade are banned in Brazil, but there are strong indications that wildlife trafficking is on the rise. A report by the National Network for Combating Wild Animal Trafficking (RENCTAS) claims that poaching and wildlife trade have become so profitable that some drug smugglers are shifting to the animal trade because of its higher profit returns and less stringent penalties. Monkeys and parrots are the most desirable wild animals in European and US markets: a hyacinth macaw (*Anodorhynchus hyacinthinus*) can sell for over $10,000. More than 50,000 illegally trafficked animals were confiscated in 2005 by police in the Atlantic Forest. www.mitpressjournals.org/doi/pdfplus/10.1162/itgg.2006.1.2.25.

Scarlet macaw (*Ara macao*).

Source: B. Levenson/WCS.

Guatemala: In October 2006, the US government joined with Conservation International and The Nature Conservancy to forgive a portion of Guatemala's $108 million in foreign debt. The largest debt-for-nature swap to date under the Tropical Forest Conservation Act of 1998 will provide significant financial support to Guatemala's most important reserves: the Maya Biosphere Reserve, which contains both Sierra de Lacandón and Tikal national parks; the Motagua/Polochic system, home to 80 percent of Guatemala's biodiversity; and the Sierra Madre volcanic chain, a critical bird migration route. The government of Guatemala will invest $24 million over the next 15 years to protect crucial forest habitat for scarlet macaws (*Ara macao*), jaguars (*Panthera onca*), ocelots (*Leopardus pardalis*), and harpy eagles (*Harpia harpyja*). www.nature.org/wherewework/centralamerica/guatemala/work/art19052.html.

Prairie dog (*Cynomys* spp.).

Source: Suzanne Bolduc/WCS.

Mexico: In June 2006 the federal government of Mexico created the largest protected area of continuous North American grasslands, comprising 1.2 million acres (500,000 ha) of continuous grasslands in the state of Chihuahua, including the largest remaining colony of prairie dogs (*Cynomys* spp.) in North America, one of the healthiest populations of reintroduced black-footed ferrets (*Mustela nigripes*), the southernmost wild population of bison (*Bison bison*), and the complete complement of the North American grassland ecosystem. Comisión Nacional de Áreas Naturales Protegidas. (2006) Estudio previo justificativo para el establecimiento del área natural protegida: "Reserva de la Biosfera Janos," Chihuahua, México.

Hawksbill turtle (*Eretmochelys imbricata*).

Nicaragua: Hawksbill sea turtle (*Eretmochelys imbricata*) populations around the world have declined severely, and the species is now listed by the World Conservation Union (IUCN) as critically endangered, meaning it faces an extremely high risk of extinction in the wild. One hope for the conservation of hawksbills lies off the east coast of Nicaragua on 18 small sandy islands called the Pearl Cays. These islands are one of the most important nesting areas for hawksbill turtles in the Caribbean, but, until recently, nests were poached for their eggs, which local people eat. In many instances, nesting females were also killed for their shells and meat. Since the start of a nest protection and education project in 2000, poaching has decreased to just 10 percent of nests. The total number of clutches laid in a season has increased by about 25 percent. Nesting success has gone from 155 clutches per year at the beginning of the project to a record 211 during the 2006 season. Project success is attributed to the extensive involvement of local community members in the collection of data and the guarding of nesting females. For the first time in living memory, local fishermen report seeing juvenile hawksbill turtles in the waters around the Pearl Cays. www.sciencedaily.com/releases/2004/01/040127083014.htm.

Giant armadillo (*Priodontes maximus*).

South America: The Guyana shield, the largest undisturbed stretch of protected rainforest in the world, was completed in December 2006 with the addition of 37 million acres (15 million ha) of Amazonian rainforest by Pará State, Brazil. This 2 billion-year-old granite formation spans most of French Guyana, Guyana, and Suriname, extending into Venezuela and northeastern Brazil. Over 5,000 species of plants thrive here, including pitcher plants (genus *Hemliamphora*) and kapok trees (*Ceiba pentandra*), both of which serve medicinal purposes for the indigenous peoples of the region. Rare species such as aracaris (*Pteroglossus aracari*), harpy eagles, giant armadillos (*Priodontes maximus*), and lowland tapirs (*Tapirus terrestris*) forage among the Guyana Shield's 960,000 square miles (2,500,000 km^2) of tropical forest habitat. Close monitoring will be necessary to control the growing threats of illegal logging, mining, agricultural encroachment, and poaching in this large area. http://seattletimes.nwsource.com/html/nationworld/2003462151_brazil05.html; www.conservation.org/xp/CIWEB/regions/neotropics/guianas.xml.

Europe

Europe has a long history of intensive agricultural land management. Visiting conservationists are often surprised to see nature reserves in which trees are cut, scrub is removed, and meadows are harvested for hay and grazed by sheep. Although it may seem attractive to stop such management and have more "natural" reserves, experience has shown that the species of interest are usually lost if populations and habitat are not actively managed. Much debate has ensued over the extent to which it is desirable (or realistic) to attempt to restore wilderness in some areas of Europe. The Oostvaardersplassen nature reserve in the Netherlands is the classic example; there, introduced species such as konik horses and Heck cattle provide ecological roles similar to their extinct counterparts, the tarpan (*Equus ferus ferus*) and aurochs (*Bos primigenius*).

European Union funding for agriculture has caused many of the conservation problems of recent decades by encouraging intensive agriculture and conversion of other habitat to farmland. At the start of 2006 a radical change in the subsidy system decoupled funding from agricultural production—a first stage toward an overall reduction of subsidies. European agriculture now depends more upon world prices and demand. Growing interest in biofuels further complicates conservation efforts in Europe, because production on marginal or fallow land—prime habitat for birds and small mammals—will presumably increase. It seems that Europe, despite being long settled and valuing conservation, is not immune from the pressures of agriculture and global connectivity facing wild places in the rest of the world.

Pied flycatcher (*Ficedula hypoleuca*).

Europe: Many long-distance migratory birds are rapidly shifting the timing of their migrations in response to the earlier arrival of spring temperatures in Europe. A team of scientists banded over 30 species of birds in Sweden, Norway, Finland, and the island of Capri in Italy, and found that some of the birds that winter as far away as Africa are arriving at their breeding grounds in Europe days earlier than they did in the 1980s, presumably in response to changing peaks in food availability. Birds that do not adapt well to climate change potentially face serious declines, as has been observed in European pied flycatcher (*Ficedula hypoleuca*) populations. *Science* 312:1959–1961.

Endemic Mediterranean sea grass (*Posidonia oceanica*).

Europe: A ban on bottom trawling below 3,000 feet (1,000 m) in the Mediterranean went into effect in early 2005. A study on the status of deep-sea fishing in the Mediterranean conducted by the World Wildlife Fund (WWF) and the World Conservation Union (IUCN) confirmed the need for the protection of little-explored deep-sea ecosystems, which are extremely vulnerable to commercial exploitation because of slow turnover rates and relatively high levels of endemic species. As shallow fish stocks are depleted, trawlers—many of them fishing for the red shrimp *Aristeus antennatus*—move into deeper waters, where juvenile shrimp nurseries and deep-sea corals thrive. http://iucn.org/places /medoffice/noticias/ban_fisheries_en.html; http://assets.panda.org/downloads /bookmeddeepsea.pdf.

Great white pelican (*Pelecanus onocrotalus*).

Bulgaria: In the spring of 2005, Bulgaria's minister of environment and water approved the construction of three wind-farm developments at Cape Kaliakra, which was declared a protected area in 1941. Over half a million migratory birds, including great white pelicans (*Pelecanus onocrotalus*), white storks (*Ciconia ciconia*), red-footed falcons (*Falco vespertinus*), and common cranes (*Grus grus*), fly over the northern Black Sea coast each year and will have to cross the path of at least 80 wind turbines at a height of 394 feet (120 m). www.birdlife.org/news /pr/2005/08/bulgaria_windfarm.html.

Iceberg calved from a glacier, Greenland.

Juvenile greater spotted eagle (*Aquila clanga*).

Greenland: A study conducted by scientists from the University of Colorado at Boulder between April 2002 and April 2006 reveals that the Greenland ice sheet is losing mass at an accelerating rate. Between 423 billion and 569 billion pounds (192 million and 258 million metric tons) of ice were lost during each year of the study. Particularly troubling is the fact that the rate of loss between 2004 and 2006 was more than double the rate of loss from the previous two-year period. In addition, temperatures in southern Greenland have increased over 4° Fahrenheit (15° Celsius) in the past 20 years and are projected to continue to increase. Shrinking ice sheets contribute to sea level rise and could affect climate by changing currents and albedo, or surface reflectivity, precipitating further warming and melting. *Nature* 443:277–278; 329–331.

Poland: WWF Poland, Central and Eastern European (CEE) Bankwatch Network, and the Polish Society for the Protection of Birds are among a number of nongovernmental organizations and European citizens concerned about controversial plans by the Polish government to construct a new segment of the Via Baltica (an international transportation corridor that runs from Portugal to Finland) through the city of Bialystok in northeastern Poland. The proposed road development plans cut through four sites designated as special protected areas, thereby violating EU environmental legislation. Biebrza Marshes National Park, Rospuda Valley in the Augustow Forest, Knyszyn Primeval Forest, and Narew River National Park have all been identified as Important Bird Areas (IBAs) by BirdLife International because they provide important breeding and nesting habitat for globally threatened birds, including the aquatic warbler (*Acrocephalus paludicola*) and greater spotted eagle (*Aquila clanga*). Construction of an expressway through these areas will contribute to further loss and fragmentation of habitat for lesser spotted eagles (*Aquila pomarina*), white-tailed eagles (*Haliaeetus albicilla*), black woodpeckers (*Dryocopus martius*), lynx (*Lynx lynx*), and moose (*Alces alces*), and will increase the odds of vehicle–animal collisions. The Polish government officially agreed to halt construction of the expressway through the Rospuda Valley in September 2007, and the European Court of Justice is expected to make a final judgement on the legality of the project by 2009. www.viabalticainfo.org/spip.php?rubrique2; http://bankwatch.ecn.cz/project.shtml?apc=147584-153973r=1&x=2039238.

North America

North America has a rich history of conservation innovation. In 1872, the very concept of national parks was established in the United States with the creation of Yellowstone National Park. This was followed by the first international peace park, Glacier-Waterton National Park along the US–Canada border; the first natural United Nations Educational, Scientific and Cultural Organization (UNESCO) World Heritage Site, Nahanni National Park in Canada; and the first designated wilderness area, Gila Wilderness in New Mexico.

Although such conservation mile markers have been critical to protecting ecosystems and species, these areas are frequently too small to maintain self-sustaining populations of wide-ranging species like wolverines and pronghorn. Many protected areas are becoming patches of remnant nature surrounded by human development. Furthermore, traditional models for designing protected areas have been based on assumptions that boundaries are static, but as temperature and climate variability increases, it is likely that wildlife range distributions will shift to higher elevations and more northerly latitudes. One practical approach to help wildlife and wildlands is wildlife corridors and connected landscapes that allow for adaptation and resilience in the face of dynamic events. Conservation of North American wildlife can no longer be relegated to parks and protected areas but has to be considered in the management of all land-use types and at all scales.

North America: A report by the US Geological Survey in November 2006 documented statistical and anecdotal evidence of increasing stresses on polar bears (*Ursus maritimus*) as a result of climate change. Declining sea ice cover and thickness, combined with thawing permafrost, is eroding Arctic coastlines in Alaska and Canada. Between 2001 and 2006, only 43 percent of cubs in Alaska's Beaufort Sea survived, compared to 65 percent 20 years prior. Adding to concerns are the first documented instances of bears drowning as they swim from shorelines to distant sea ice; of polar bears killing and consuming other polar bears; and of females apparently dying of starvation. In January 2007, the US Fish and Wildlife Service proposed listing the polar bear under the Endangered Species Act as threatened throughout its range. The Service will gather more information, undertake additional analyses, and assess the reliability of relevant scientific models before making a final decision about whether to list the species in early 2008. http://pubs.usgs.gov/of/2006/1337/pdf/ofr20061337.pdf; www.fws.gov/news /NewsReleases/showNews.cfm?newsId=E175D848-F85D-DEC6-CBC 1240B975C6F5B.

Source: Julie Larsen Maher/WCS.

Polar bear (*Ursus maritimus*).

Alaska: In September 2006, the US District Court of Alaska blocked US Department of Interior plans to open the area around Lake Teshekpuk in the 23-million-acre (9-million-ha) National Petroleum Reserve, Alaska (NPRA), to oil and gas development. The court found that the Bureau of Land Management (BLM) had not adequately considered the overall environmental impact of drilling on the 400,000 acres (162,000 ha) up for lease. Oil companies find the Lake Teshekpuk region desirable due to its proximity to Prudhoe Bay and the largest oil fields in North America. The Lake Teshekpuk region provides essential habitat for polar bears, caribou (*Rangifer tarandus*), musk oxen (*Ovibos moschatus*), wolverines (*Gulo gulo*), golden eagles (*Aquila chrysaetos*), Arctic wolves (*Canis lupus arctos*), snowy owls (*Nyctea scandiaca*), and migratory shorebirds. Drilling would lead to further habitat loss and fragmentation for these species. The US Department of Interior supports energy exploration elsewhere in the NPRA. www.enn.com/top_stories/article/5023; www.nrdc.org/land/wilderness/arctic.asp.

Source: D. DeMello/WCS.

Snowy owl (*Nyctea scandiaca*).

Grizzly bear (*Ursos arctos horribilis*).

Canada: In May 2007, scientists from over 50 countries submitted a letter to the government of Canada stating that at least half of Canada's northern boreal forest must be protected, and the rest carefully managed. This plan supports the Boreal Conservation Framework, a shared vision by governments and other stakeholders to conserve the natural and economic integrity of this important ecosystem. The 1.4-billion-acre (5.5-million-ha) forest, only 10 percent of which is currently protected, contains some of the world's largest populations of grizzly bear (*Ursus arctos horribilis*) and woodland caribou (*Rangifer tarandus caribou*) and stores more freshwater and carbon than anywhere else on Earth. Canada's boreal forest is increasingly targeted for logging, mining, and other development activities. www.ens-newswire.com/ens/may2007/2007-05-16-03.asp; www.birdday.org/resources /CBI_Framework_2006_NEW.pdf.

Hawaiian monk seal (*Monachus schauinslandi*).

Hawaii: In June 2006, the world's largest marine protected area was created, the Northwestern Hawaiian Islands (NWHI) Marine National Monument. This 140,000-square-mile (362,000 km^2) area is home to over 7,000 species, approximately one quarter of which are endemic, such as Laysan finches (*Telespiza cantans*) and critically endangered Hawaiian monk seals (*Monachus schauinslandi*). The ten islands and atolls serve as an important rookery for 14 million seabirds, including the black-footed albatross (*Phoebastria nigripes*), and are crucial breeding grounds for 90 percent of the threatened Hawaiian green sea turtle (*Chelonia mydas*) population. The waters are also home to the largest and healthiest coral reef system in the US. The reserve, however, is at risk from floating trash, especially plastic, that is pulled into the surrounding waters by ocean currents, and global warming, which may submerge some of the islands due to rising sea levels. Strict regulations prohibit unauthorized recreational activities, ship passage, and resource extraction within the boundaries of the NWHI, but they preserve access for native Hawaiian cultural activities and marine research. Commercial and sport fishing will be phased out by 2011. www.noaanews .noaa.gov/stories2006/s2644.htm; *Marine Pollution Bulletin* 54:6; http://news .nationalgeographic.com/news/2006/06/060605-hawaii.html.

Young moose (*Alces alces*) crossing road.

United States: In September 2006, the US District Court for Northern California ordered the reinstatement of the Roadless Area Conservation Rule, which had been repealed by the Bush administration in 2005. The publicly popular Roadless Rule was created in 2001 to prevent road building, logging, and mining on 58.5 million acres (24 million ha) of the last remaining wildlands in the US forest system, including portions of the Appalachian Trail and backcountry lands in the Rockies. The Rule preserves stretches of forest and grassland, critical for watersheds and habitat for more than 1,600 threatened, endangered, or sensitive plant and animal species, as well as public access for recreational activities such as hiking and fishing. www.earthjustice.org/news/press/006/court-reinstates-roadless-rule.html; www.nrdc.org/land/forests/qroadless.asp.

Bald eagle (*Haliaeetus leucocephalus*).

United States: Several iconic species have made substantial strides in graduating off the federal list of endangered species. The bald eagle (*Haliaeetus leucocephalus*), the country's national symbol, is one successful wildlife recovery story: The number of nesting pairs in the lower 48 states has increased from 417 to 7,066 in 43 years, and the species is now entering the final stage of the delisting process. Bald eagles were delisted in June 2007 and are now protected under the Bald and Golden Eagle Protection Act. After more than three decades on the list, the gray wolf (*Canis lupus*) population of the western Great Lakes has recovered to the point where the US Fish and Wildlife Service delisted those wolves in March 2007. In Minnesota, Wisconsin, and Michigan, the wolf population has grown to almost 4,000 animals. Also in March 2007, the US Fish and Wildlife Service removed the Yellowstone population of grizzly bears (*Ursus arctos horribilis*) from threatened status. This particular population increased from somewhere between 136 and 312 bears when they were listed in 1975, to more than 500 bears in 2007. Four other grizzly populations in the lower 48 states have not yet recovered and will continue to be protected under the Endangered Species Act. www.fws.gov/midwest/eagle/; www.fws.gov/midwest/WOLF/2007delisting/index.htm.

Brown pelican (*Pelecanus occidentalis*).

United States: Hurricanes Katrina and Rita struck the Gulf Coast in the late summer of 2005, devastating communities in Louisiana, Alabama, Texas, Mississippi, and Arkansas. The impact on wildlife and coastal wetlands was also significant, as the storm surge uprooted or crushed marsh grasses, and wetlands were converted to open water areas. In Big Branch Marsh National Wildlife Refuge, Louisiana, over 70 percent of the cavity trees used by endangered red-cockaded woodpeckers (*Picoides borealis*) were lost to the storms. Nesting habitat for brown pelicans (*Pelecanus occidentalis*) and Sandwich terns (*Sterna sandvicensis*) in Texas and southeastern Louisiana was severely impacted. Most of the dune habitat of the endangered Alabama beach mouse (*Peromyscus polionotus ammobates*) vanished, and about 50 sea turtle nests were destroyed. Scientists and engineers now face the complex task of determining how best to restore sediment to eroding wetlands, while protecting the Gulf Coast from future storms, floods, and rising sea levels. *Science* 313:1713; www.fws.gov /swlarefugecomplex/pdf/Impact.pdf.

Oceans

Humans have devastated ocean ecosystems to an extent previously imagined impossible, through increasingly effective fishing technologies, the steady loss of coastal habitats, and the inescapable fate of seas as the final repository for our wastes, whether or not we deliberately funnel them there. The greatest damage is from overfishing (catching fish faster than the population can replenish itself), which can trigger cascading effects throughout entire marine ecosystems as other species rise or fall in response to the imbalance.

The hope for marine conservation is that now more nations and coastal communities recognize the need to limit fishing activity and reduce other destructive activities. Marine protected areas (MPAs), areas in which human activities are managed to reduce adverse impacts on part or all of the designated sites, are finally coming into widespread use. When properly designed and managed, MPAs can be extremely effective in rebuilding overfished stocks and supporting the restoration of damaged habitats. There is also increasing evidence that by helping rebuild healthy ecosystems, MPAs can increase ecosystem resistance to the effects of climate change and other major stresses, and improve recovery when adverse events occur. Ocean ecosystems have proven remarkably resilient; if we make the right choices, oceans teeming with wildlife and capable of sustaining many human uses need not become a thing of the past. MPAs and improved regulation of fishing and trade in marine species show a way forward.

Source: ARC Centre of Excellence/Marine Photobank

Overfishing destroys ocean ecosystems.

Beluga sturgeon (*Huso huso*).

Source: Shannon Crownover/Marine Photobank.

Global: Human activities are accelerating losses of ocean biodiversity in estuaries, coral reefs, and coastal and oceanic fish communities. New research suggests that these losses undermine the stability, productivity, and resilience of ocean ecosystems, making them less able to provide services on which humans depend. Biodiversity losses in coastal ecosystems probably contribute to declining water quality and increasing incidence of harmful algal blooms, fish kills, oxygen depletions ("dead zones"), and beach and shellfish closures. Current trends suggest global collapses of all fished species by 2048 unless overfishing and other threats are reduced. *Science* 314:787–790.

Asia/United States: The year 2006 resulted in major conservation breakthroughs for sturgeon, the ancient fish that can reach over seven feet in length and lives in both salt- and freshwater. Sturgeon are among the world's most imperiled species, often caught as bycatch in ocean fisheries and long overharvested for their eggs (caviar). The Convention on International Trade in Endangered Species of Wild Fauna and Flora (CITES) regulates international trade in all species of sturgeon, and in 2006, its secretariat did not renew export quotas for black caviar for Caspian Sea nations Russia, Kazakhstan, Azerbaijan, and Turkmenistan because these countries did not provide sufficient information about their sturgeon stocks or adequate plans to prevent overfishing. The Caspian is home to three species of sturgeon: beluga (*Huso huso*), stellate (*Acipenser stellatus*), and Russian (*Acipenser gueldenstaedtii*). CITES also rejected export quotas for sturgeon in the Amur River, on the border between Russia and China. Iran was the only nation to receive an export quota for black caviar. A new Russian federal law is also in development; if put into place, the law will support sturgeon conservation by strengthening enforcement programs. In the US, Oregon and Washington reduced the maximum allowable size for green sturgeon (*Acipenser medirostris*) caught by commercial fisheries, thereby protecting the valuable adult breeders. www.cites.org/eng/news/press/2006/060413_caviar_quota.shtml; www.nmfs.noaa.gov/pr/species/esa.htm.

Source: WCS.

Walrus (*Odobenus rosmarus*).

Bering Sea: An ecosystem shift is occurring in the northern Bering Sea, with documented changes from Arctic to subarctic conditions. The amount and extent of sea ice are decreasing, affecting both wildlife and human populations. As the ice edge recedes, ice-utilizing species like walrus (*Odobenus rosmarus*) move with it. This can put them too far away for Inuit hunters, and it forces the animals to swim further between feeding areas. The geographic ranges of fish species also appear to be shifting, possibly in response to warming water temperatures, with species like pink salmon (*Oncorhynchus gorbuscha*) and pollock (*Theragra chalcogramma*) ranging further north. These changes may profoundly impact Arctic marine mammals, diving seabirds, and commercial and subsistence fisheries. *Science* 311:1461–1464.

Source: ARC Centre of Excellence/Marine Photobank.

Traditional fishing harvest.

Fiji: Fiji, which contains some of the Pacific's most intact and diverse reefs, has a system of traditional fishing grounds (known as *qoliqoli*) that are legally recognized and officially referred to as customary fishing rights areas. Traditional Fijian systems of marine resource management include seasonal fishery closures, limits on the number of users, catch quotas, and taboos on certain species or practices (such as using poison). Approximately 300,000 Fijian fishers make a living from the 385 marine and 25 river *qoliqoli*. In 2006, Fiji's first science-based marine protected area network was established within one *qoliqoli*, at Kubulau on the island of Vanua Levu. The network covers 37 square miles (97 km^2) and protects close to 30 percent of the area of the *qoliqoli*. A similar network is now being established at Macuata, also on Vanua Levu, with extensive input by local communities and the support of the government of Fiji. www.panda.org/news_facts/newsroom/features/index.cfm?uNewsID=55580.

Indonesia: Ecological assessments conducted shortly after the December 2004 Indian Ocean tsunami revealed some surprising results about reefs in the heart of the impact zone. Off the coast of Aceh in northwestern Sumatra, Indonesia, tsunami destruction to the reefs, while spectacular, was *less* damaging than decades of the destructive fishing practices of using dynamite and cyanide on or near reefs to kill or stun fish. A team of researchers from the Wildlife Conservation Society, Syiah Kuala University, and James Cook University found that reef health was clearly related to how effectively the reef had been managed prior to the tsunami, with corals in better condition in marine protected areas than in unprotected areas. Moreover, healthier reefs reproduce more effectively, meaning they are better at recovering from damage, whether from the tsunami or from other events, like bleaching. The team also discovered ecologically significant reef fish spawning aggregation sites in areas of high coral diversity and high current flows on the east coast of Weh Island and the southern coast of Aceh Island. As foreign aid rushes in to rebuild devastated coastal communities (providing new fishing gear and boats to replace those lost in the tsunami), protecting these areas is critical to ensure that rebuilding communities does not come at the cost of future fishing sustainability. www.coralcoe.org.au/news_stories/tsunamiimpacts.html.

Coral reef showing damage.

Kiribati/Pacific Islands: Kiribati announced the creation of the Phoenix Islands Protected Area (PIPA) in March 2006. At 73,800 square miles (184,700 km^2) and nearly uninhabited, it is the third-largest marine protected area in the world. The area's eight atolls, two near-pristine coral reef systems, and underwater mountains are home to over 120 species of coral and 520 species of fish, including two species of hawkfish, the arc-eye (*Paracirrhites arcatus*) and golden (*Cirrhitichthys aureus*), and the world's largest populations of Napoleon wrasse (*Cheilinus undulatus*), a fish threatened by high demand in Asia. The islands also serve as a key migration route for nesting seabirds, such as terns and frigatebirds, and provide essential habitat for green sea turtles (*Chelonia mydas*). In the PIPA, subsistence fishing and sustainable economic development activities will be permitted, but commercial fishing licenses will no longer be granted. http://depts .washington.edu/mpanews/MPA73.htm.

Coral reef, Pacific Islands.

Giant kelp (*Macrocystis* spp.).

United States: In April 2007, after years of negotiations among conservationists, fishermen, scientists, and government officials, California designated a network of 29 marine protected areas totaling 204 square miles (528 km²), about 18 percent of central coast state waters. This landmark decision was the first step in completing the first statewide network of marine protected areas directly on a US coastline. Fishing is prohibited in 85 square miles (243 km²) of the area and regulated elsewhere. This will provide important protection for rocky reefs, submarine canyons, estuaries, and kelp forests, and should allow many fish populations, including red snapper (*Lutjanus campechanus*), the chance to regenerate after decades of depletion to the point of population collapses. www.oceanconservancy .org/site/News2?abbr=issues_&page=NewsArticle&id=8731.

ACKNOWLEDGMENTS

The news was gathered from more than 20 environmental newsfeeds; *Oryx*, *Science*, and *Nature* magazines; and the field experience of Wildlife Conservation Society (WCS) staff and partner organizations. This section was researched and compiled with the invaluable help of Catherine Grippo at WCS. Insight and regional overviews were contributed by WCS's regional program staff and close partners: James Deutsch (Africa); Peter Clyne and Peter Zahler (Asia); Ross Sinclair (Australia, New Zealand, and the Pacific Islands); William J. Sutherland (Europe); Avecita Chicchon and Zach Feris (Latin America); Shirley Atkinson, Jeff Burrell, and Leslie Karasin (North America); and Cheri Recchia and Liz Lauck (Oceans). News for each region was vetted by an external expert, and we thank the following for their wise reviews: Helen Gichohi (African Wildlife Foundation), Kathy MacKinnon (World Bank), Craig Morley (University of the South Pacific), Gustavo Fonseca (Conservation International), Reed Noss (University of Central Florida), and Ellen Pikitch (Pew Institute for Ocean Science).

Discoveries

MARGARET KINNAIRD

Unveiling Saturn's rings; solving mathematical proofs; developing new technologies for transportation—new discoveries never fail to inspire us. It is hard to imagine that anything alive and large enough to be seen with the naked eye remains undiscovered. Yet natural scientists are still discovering species in the far reaches of our hyperconnected, present-day world. Previously unknown living species are being found, continuing the naturalist tradition embodied by Darwin's encounters on the Galápagos Islands. New species have recently been identified in Earth's remote corners and, unexpectedly, in the most densely populated areas. Sometimes species are unveiled with the aid of new technologies that allow us to see genes or that transport us to inaccessible ocean depths. Sometimes a discovery is the result of long, hard hours in the lab or field. Other times it is serendipity; we head out with one objective, perhaps to map a region, and stumble across a wildlife species unique and new to science. Admittedly, there is a vertebrate bias in this essay. There were probably hundreds of insects and microbes discovered over the past couple of years, but they were not selected for inclusion in this account. Whatever the phylum, new species allow us to ask some interesting questions about how species evolve and increase our knowledge base. However and wherever a new discovery occurs, it is heartening to know that much mystery remains in the world.

SEARCHING: DISCOVERIES FROM BIOLOGICAL EXPEDITIONS

**Wattled smoky honeyeater
(*Melipotes carolae*).**

THE MOST CELEBRATED DISCOVERIES OVER THE PAST FEW years arose from expeditions led by Conservation International's Rapid Assessment Program (RAP) to the Foja Mountains of Indonesia's easternmost province, West Papua. The cool, misty forests of the Fojas are touted as the "Lost World" because of their extreme isolation and lack of human disturbance. These remote forests have revealed a number of secrets, including the wattled smoky honeyeater (*Melipotes carolae*), a stylish black bird with bright-orange flesh that encircles the eyes and hangs down in paddle-shaped wattles on each side of the head.[1] This new honeyeater is the first new bird discovered on the island of Papua in nearly 70 years.

ANOTHER CONSERVATION INTERNATIONAL-LED TEAM FOUND A TROVE of discoveries while combing the waters off West Papua's Bird's Head Peninsula. Among the discoveries were two new species of epaulette sharks (*Hemiscyllium* spp. nov.), a group named for the distinctive spots near their head that resemble the shoulder ornaments of military uniforms.[2] These small, slender, bottom-dwelling sharks, also known as walking sharks, distinguish themselves by frequently scampering across the ocean floor on their fins. Their marine habitats are under intense threat from destructive fisheries, but conservationists hope the discovery will provide impetus for increased protection of this biologically rich seascape at the confluence of the South China Sea and Pacific Ocean.

Epaulette shark (*Hemiscyllium* spp. nov.).

Arunachal macaque (*Macaca munzala*).

INDIA, A COUNTRY WITH OVER A BILLION PEOPLE, is not a place where one would envision discovering a large unknown mammal. But a team of Indian researchers from the Wildlife Conservation Society, the Nature Conservation Foundation, the International Snow Leopard Trust, and the National Institute of Advanced Studies made just such a discovery when they sighted the Arunachal macaque (*Macaca munzala*) while conducting surveys in the country's remote northeastern state of Arunachal Pradesh.[3] The discoverers named the large, brown, stumpy-tailed macaque *mun zala*, meaning "deep-forest monkey" in the local vernacular. The macaque lives in rugged, forested mountains at elevations between 6,500 and 11,500 feet (2,000 to 4,000 m), making it one of the highest-dwelling primates in the world.

IN THE MIDST OF THE GLOBAL CRISIS IN amphibian decline caused by fungal infections, the nations of Laos and Vietnam have produced a

Rana cucae.

cache of new amphibian discoveries during recent years. American and Russian scientists have described six new frog species.[4] The three newest, *Rana cucae*, *Rana vitrea*, and *Rana compotrix*, are tiny creatures, with females measuring 1.5 to 3 inches (4 to 8 cm) in length. The frogs were discovered in three different regions of Laos and Vietnam, yet all of them have a preference for swift, rocky, mountain streams. The frogs have existed there, unknown, due to the impenetrable nature of the area.

Yariguíes brush-finch (*Atlapetes latinuchus yariguierum*).

A COLOMBIAN–ENGLISH TEAM OF ORNITHOLOGISTS DISCOVERED A COLORFUL new bird subspecies in a remote Andean cloud forest, Serranía de los Yariguíes, in Colombia. The bright yellow and red-crowned Yariguíes brush-finch (*Atlapetes latinuchus yariguierum*) was named for the indigenous tribe that once inhabited the mountainous area. The new finch is the size of a fist. In 2005, the Colombian government set aside a 193,698-acre (78,387 ha) area of grasslands and mountain forests as a national park in Serranía de los Yariguíes, helping to conserve the bird and other species.[5]

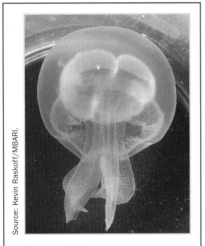

Source: Kevin Raskoff/MBARI.

**Deep-sea jelly
(Stellamedusa ventana).**

RESEARCHERS FROM THE MONTEREY BAY AQUARIUM RESEARCH INSTITUTE recently discovered an extraordinary deep-sea jelly (*Stellamedusa ventana*) off the Gulf of California. Its genus name, *Stellamedusa*, refers to the jelly's shimmering blue color and shooting star movements, and its species name gives attribute to the jelly's discoverer *Ventana*,[6] the submarine robot that videotaped the first images of the jelly at depths of 500 to 1,800 feet (150 to 550 m). The softball-sized jelly bears no tentacles but is armed with four trailing oral arms covered with batteries of stinging cells used to immobilize and hold prey. *S. ventana* has never been sighted by divers or hauled up in nets, and it is likely that the world would never have known of its existence without the aid of a deep-diving robot.

Source: Ifremer/A.Fifis.

Yeti crab (Kiwa hirsute).

WHILE TRAVELING WITH OTHER SCIENTISTS TO DEPTHS OF 7,200 feet (2,000 m) aboard the *Alvin* submersible craft, Michel Segonzac of the French Research Institute for Exploitation of the Sea (IFREMER) spotted a furry crustacean living near hydrothermal vents—cracks in the ocean floor that release hot gas from Earth's molten core, providing heat and nutrients to several deep-sea species—near Easter Island in the South Pacific. Nicknamed the Yeti crab because of its long, blond hairs, the blind deep-sea crab turned out to be not only a new species, *Kiwa hirsute*, but an entirely new family, Kiwaidae.[7] The wispy hairs, or setae, that cover the crab's appendages are loaded with bacteria—their function remains a mystery.[8]

Source: David Haring/Duke Lemur Center.

Mirza zaza.

TWO DISCOVERIES ON MADAGASCAR HAVE BOOSTED THE AFRICAN island's diversity of lemurs to an impressive 49 species.[9] Genetic decoding aided in their unveiling. German and Malagasy biologists believed they were studying two populations of the giant mouse-lemur (*Mirza coquereli*) until DNA analyses confirmed that the populations were actually two different species. The newest species weighs less than a pound (300 g) and was named *Mirza zaza*. *Zaza* translates to "child" in Malagasy, and is meant to remind the children of Madagascar of their responsibility for the future of their island's wildlife.

MARGARET KINNAIRD is a senior conservation scientist with the Wildlife Conservation Society and director of Mpala Research Centre, Laikipia, Kenya. She co-directed WCS's Indonesia Program for 13 years and has authored numerous popular and scientific articles, including the books North Sulawesi: A Natural History Guide *and* Farmers of the Forest: Ecology and Conservation of South East Asian Hornbills.

SERENDIPITY: UNEXPECTED DISCOVERIES

Barn owls in Europe led unsuspecting biologists down the trail of discovery when the owls regurgitated bones of an unclassifiable mouse during a feeding-ecology study. The questionable owl prey turned out to be a mouse new to science, the Cypriot mouse (*Mus cypriacus*).[10] This gray mouse hails from the crowded Mediterranean island of Cyprus. It has larger ears, eyes, and teeth than previously known examples. Biologists at the Cypriot Ministry of Interior claimed the discovery a first for the island and, as did others, expressed amazement that there are still undiscovered mammals in Europe.

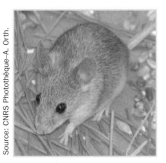

Cypriot mouse (*Mus cypriacus*).

Bugun liocichla (*Liocichla bugunorum*).

Who would expect an astronomer to make the most sensational ornithological discovery in India in recent memory? During a casual birdwatching jaunt in Arunachal Pradesh, Ramana Athreya glimpsed a peculiar, colorful warbler. Like most avid birdwatchers, Athreya knew his field guide by heart and puzzled over the lack of a good match: the closest fit to this strange bird occurred over 600 miles (1,000 km) away in China. When he netted the enigmatic bird, Athreya took pictures and released it, not harming the potentially rare find. Thus the description of the first new avian species in India in 50 years—bugun liocichla (*Liocichla bugunorum*)—was based on photographs and recordings.[11] In the absence of an actual specimen, the feathers left in the nets provide enough material for further study.

Two separate research teams working in Tanzania almost simultaneously stumbled upon the first new African monkey in over 20 years. One team, led by the Wildlife Conservation Society, was conducting wildlife surveys in the Livingstone Mountains when villagers began telling them stories of an unfamiliar mangabey, a type of forest monkey closely allied with baboons. The monkey has long brown fur, which stands in tufts on the sides and top of its head, and luxuriant whiskers. The monkey emitted low-pitched "honk-barks" instead of the "whoop-gobble" typical of other mangabeys. In the following months a second team of American primatologists, working 200 miles (350 km) to the northeast in the Udzungwa Mountains, serendipitously encountered this strange new monkey while on another search. The two teams joined forces and, based on photographs and behavioral observations, published their findings together, christening the new species the highland mangabey (*Lophocebus kipunji*).[12] Later, tissue samples taken from a specimen inci-

Kipunji (*Rungwecebus kipunji*).

dentally trapped by a farmer were analyzed at the Chicago Field Museum of Natural History and showed that the monkey belongs to a new genus.[13] Dubbed *Rungwecebus kipunji* for Mount Rungwe where it was first sighted, the kipunji immediately became one of the rarest and most critically endangered primates in the world.

The RAREST
of the *Rare*

Some of the World's Most Endangered Animals

CATHERINE GRIPPO

Rare species often have a small population size, limited geographic distribution, specific restricted habitat needs, or all of the above. Some that were once more common have become rare due to overexploitation, disease, or loss of habitat. The rarest wildlife are endemic species, found exclusively in a small region or a remote island, having specifically evolved in those conditions. Endemic species are particularly prone to extinction. Overexploitation, invasive species introductions, and habitat destruction contribute to species rarity.

Rare species capture our interest for many reasons. For ecologists, one of the great questions is why some species are naturally rare while others are widespread. For birdwatchers and natural historians, rare species are an exciting prize for their lists. And for conservationists, rare species pose immediate concerns and calls to action. These species often face extinction in the absence of conservation, and preventing extinctions is part of a strategy to reduce biodiversity loss. Each volume of *State of the Wild* highlights a number of the rarest species—those whose level of extinction risk is classified as critically endangered, endangered, or vulnerable

CATHERINE GRIPPO is program assistant for the Wildlife Conservation Society Institute. She served as photo editor for this volume of State of the Wild, *manages the production of the WCS Working Paper Series, and coordinates workshops that bolster communication between WCS and the larger conservation community.*

by the World Conservation Union (IUCN) in its authoritative IUCN Red List—and describes some of the threats they face.

The 2007 IUCN Red List revealed a continuing rise in the number of species threatened with extinction. Although only a fraction of all plant and animal species have been evaluated, the number of plants and animals listed as threatened currently stands at 16,306, an increase of 188 species since 2006.[1] Perhaps the most noticeable rise in the number of threatened species is reflected in fish, where nearly 400 additional species have been listed as threatened since 2004.[2] In recent years a third of the fish species in China's Yellow River have gone extinct, and nearly one-third to one-half of amphibian species are threatened with extinction.[3]

Concentrated efforts by zoos, conservation organizations, and government agencies to preserve biological diversity, however, have set several threatened species on the road to recovery. Of the 381 species reassessed by the IUCN in 2007, 74 have improved in status.[4] Across the globe, captive breeding and reintroduction programs attempt to stave off the extinction of the most threatened species; enforcement of sustainable use practices protects species from overharvesting; and public awareness activities inspire people to contribute to the conservation of the unique creatures that share their environment.

Abbott's booby: Christmas Island, a remote Australian island in the Indian Ocean, is the only breeding ground of Abbott's booby (*Papasula abbotti*), a large, black-and-white seabird of the gannet family that can live up to 40 years. In the 1990s, the island was infested by yellow crazy ants (*Anoplolepis gracilipes*), an introduced insect that decimated populations of red crab (*Gecarcoidea natalis*), the dominant species in the area, which ultimately altered the forest ecosystem. The ants have since been controlled, but Abbott's boobies remain endangered because of their limited nesting habitat and nest vulnerability.[5]

Addax: Well-adapted to the harsh arid climate of North Africa, the critically endangered addax (*Addax nasomaculatus*), an antelope species, lives primarily among the sand dunes of the Sahara desert. The only known significant population, around 200 individuals, resides in the Termit/Tin Toumma region in Niger. The addax is primarily nocturnal, with long, thin, spiral horns. Valued for its meat and leather, the addax has declined due to uncontrolled hunting. The addax is also threatened by desertification, mining exploration, habitat encroachment by pastoral and agricultural expansion, and the increased infiltration of more powerful firearms into the region. It is listed as critically endangered, meaning that it has an extremely high likelihood of going extinct in the wild.[6]

Source: Tony Palliser

Abbott's booby (*Papasula abbotti*).

Source: Mike Potts,/naturepl.com.

Addax (*Addax nasomaculatus*).

Angel shark: Once common throughout the Northeast Atlantic Ocean and the Mediterranean and Black seas, angel sharks (*Squatina squatina*) have become victims of benthic trawling, longlines, and fishing nets. These bottom-dwelling, nocturnal predators are now considered extinct in the North Sea and uncommon throughout most of their historical range. Two trawl surveys of the Mediterranean coastline conducted between 1985 and 1999 estimated that about 1,400 individuals were left, but additional surveys must be carried out. Fishing of angel sharks is prohibited within three marine reserves.[7]

Source: Brent Hedges/naturepl.com.

Angel shark (*Squatina squatina*).

Bengal florican: A comprehensive survey in the spring of 2006 concluded that fewer than 1,000 Bengal floricans (*Houbaropsis bengalensis*) remain in Cambodia, Nepal, Vietnam, and India. The largest population lives around Cambodia's Tonle Sap Lake. Whereas sport hunting, overgrazing by livestock, and flooding contributed to the florican's initial decline, agricultural expansion now threatens this critically endangered bustard with extinction, as the species' already fragmented grassland habitat gets converted to farmland. The government of Cambodia recently set aside over 100 square miles (260 km²) of grassland near Tonle Sap as a network of protected areas for the conservation of the species.[8]

Source: Allan Michaud.

Bengal florican (*Houbaropsis bengalensis*).

Black-faced lion tamarin: Deforestation for cattle ranching, the development of tourism, and harvesting of palm hearts threaten the black-faced lion tamarin (*Leontopithecus caissara*), a rare primate that was discovered on the island of Superagui, Brazil, in 1990. Small populations are also found in the provinces of Paraná and São Paulo. This diminutive arboreal species sleeps in tree holes dug out by woodpeckers and feeds on insects, fruit, and plants. The tamarins live in family groups, and females often give birth to twins. Approximately 400 individuals survive in the wild today.[9]

Source: E. Kellerman/WCS.

Black-faced lion tamarin (*Leontopithecus caissara*).

Burmese roofed turtle: The Burmese roofed turtle (*Kachuga trivittata*) is the most threatened of Myanmar's seven endemic turtles. Once abundant in the major rivers of central and southern Burma, the species has been hunted—and its eggs collected—to near extinction. Between 1935 and 2002, no specimens were reported, until, in 2002, one juvenile turned up in a Chinese market and several adults were found in a Buddhist temple pond. Subsequent surveys revealed small nesting populations on the Dokhtawady and upper Chindwin rivers, where damming for hydroelectricity has begun. A comprehensive recovery plan including captive breeding and release efforts has been established for this rare turtle.[10]

Source: Bill Holmstrom/WCS.

Burmese roofed turtle (*Kachuga trivittata*).

Dragonflies of Sri Lanka: Of the 53 endemic species of dragonfly found in Sri Lanka, at least 20—for example, the endangered *Tetrathemis yerburii*—are threatened with extinction, as rainforest habitat is destroyed and pollution seeps into streams and rivers.[11] Dragonflies are important indicators of environmental health because their larvae require good water quality to develop.[12]

Tetrathemis yerburii.

Golden arrow poison frog: Endemic to Panama, the golden arrow poison frog (*Atelopus zeteki*) has suffered an 80 percent decline over the past ten years. Chytridiomycosis, a highly infectious fungal disease, is primarily responsible for the dramatic decline. The frogs contract the disease through their skin when exposed to chytrid fungus spores (*Batrachochytrium dendrobatidis*) in water infected by other amphibians. Little is known about how the fungus kills the frogs, but possible causes include toxicity and diminished hydration and respiration functionality. In addition, water pollution and deforestation have led to major changes in habitat availability and suitability. These frogs are also collected for the pet trade.[13]

Golden arrow poison frog (*Atelopus zeteki*).

North Atlantic right whale: Once abundant, right whales (*Eubalaena glacialis*) are now almost extinct in the eastern North Atlantic Ocean. Weighing up to 220,000 pounds (100,000 kg), these slow-moving cetaceans have been hunted since the tenth century. North Atlantic right whales live in some of the world's busiest shipping waters and are frequently killed by collisions with ships and entanglement in fishing nets. The species depends on coastal habitat for breeding and is therefore vulnerable to the effects of pollution and oil development. An estimated 350 individuals remain.[14]

North Atlantic right whale (*Eubalaena glacialis*).

Ricord's iguana: Ricord's iguana (*Cyclura ricordi*) occurs in two isolated locations in the arid southwestern Dominican Republic: Valle de Neiba and the coastal lowlands of the Peninsula de Barahona. Drainage of wetlands, livestock overgrazing, limestone mining, and agricultural development, in addition to predation by introduced dogs, cats, and mongooses, has decreased the iguana's small historical range by over 60 percent. Illegal hunting of the species for food and trade has also caused the reptile's quick decline. An estimated 2,000 to 4,000 individuals remain.[15]

Ricord's iguana (*Cyclura ricordi*).

Pygmy hippopotamus: Endemic to a 2,000-square-mile (5,000 km²) area in the Upper Guinean Forest of four West African states—Liberia, Guinea, Ivory Coast, and Sierra Leone—the pygmy hippo (*Hexaprotodon liberiensis*) population stands at less than 3,000 individuals, including at least 800 hippos in captivity. Logging, agricultural expansion, and other human development activities have fragmented the hippo's habitat and made the animals increasingly vulnerable to poaching by bushmeat hunters. Although on paper this small hippo is fully protected as an endangered species, its protection is poorly enforced due to civil unrest and lack of resources in the region.[16] A recent camera-trap survey in Sierra Leone produced the first-ever photograph of a wild pygmy hippo, suggesting that there may be hope for the species' persistence in the war-torn country.

Source: Rod Williams/naturepl.com.

Pygmy hippopotamus (*Hexaprotodon liberiensis*).

Sumatran rhino: Fewer than 300 Sumatran rhinos (*Dicerorhinus sumatrensis*) survive in the wild today. The largest populations are found in the subtropical and tropical dry forests of Indonesia and Malaysia in Southeast Asia. Also known as the hairy or Asian two-horned rhinoceros, this species has declined by more than 50 percent over the last 15 years. These animals live in small groups and are increasingly threatened by forest loss due to the development of plantations, logging, and agriculture. Although the Convention on International Trade in Endangered Species (CITES) prohibits all trade of the species, illegal poaching of the rhino for its horns, believed by some Asian communities to have medicinal properties, continues to be a major problem. Breeding programs have been difficult and unsuccessful.[17]

Source: WCS.

Sumatran rhino (*Dicerorhinus sumatrensis*).

Road to Recovery

Antiguan racer: Once considered the world's rarest snake, the Antiguan racer (*Alsophis antiguae*) is strengthening its ranks. Thanks to the Antiguan Racer Conservation Project, a monitoring, public awareness, habitat restoration, and reintroduction program founded in 1995, this nonpoisonous endemic species' numbers have increased from 50 to over 250 individuals on three islands. The project worked to remove invasive Asian mongooses and rats from Antigua and its offshore islands, and garnered public support for the preservation of "Antigua's Friendly Snake" by putting its image on shirts, stamps, and phone cards.[18]

California condor: The decline of California condors (*Gymnogyps californianus*) primarily has been attributed to shooting and accidental poisoning from the ingestion of carcasses shot with lead bullets. Power line electrocution and habitat fragmentation also contributed to the bird's vulnerability. When the species' numbers reached an all-time low in the late 1980s, the last California condors were removed from the wild. Successful captive breeding and reintroduction programs, pioneered by the San Diego Wild Animal Park, the Los Angeles Zoo, and The Peregrine Fund's World Center for Birds of Prey, brought approximately 125 birds back to the wild, where some pairs are now breeding successfully.[19]

Source: John Cancalosi/ naturepl.com.

Antiguan racer (*Alsophis antiguae*).

Source: Chris Parish/The Peregrine Fund.

California condor (*Gymnogyps californianus*).

Alliance for Zero Extinction: Finding the Rarest—and Most Threatened—of the Rare

TAYLOR H. RICKETTS

A recent collaboration among 63 conservation institutions set out to identify and locate the rarest and most endangered of the rare. The goal of the Alliance for Zero Extinction (AZE) is to pinpoint centers of imminent extinction, where highly threatened species are confined to single sites. AZE examined five major taxa (mammals, birds, reptiles, amphibians, and conifers) for which global data are available and identified sites that (1) contain at least one highly threatened species, (2) represent essentially the sole area of occurrence for the species, and (3) permit management as a discrete unit. These sites represent clear opportunities for preventing extinction.

The analyses yielded 794 species in 595 sites, an immediate challenge for direct conservation action. When compared to the 245 recorded extinctions in these taxa in the last 500 years, it is clear that, in the near future, we risk losing three times as many species as have been lost. Also, the spatial pattern of extinction has shifted. Whereas 80 percent of previous extinctions occurred on islands, now the major proportion of imminent extinctions is occurring in mainland areas. About 50 percent of species currently facing extinction are found in the Neotropics, the world's richest biogeographic realm.

These sites are irreplaceable targets for a global network of protected areas, but 257 of them currently lack any legal protection (203 sites are within protected areas and 87 are partially included in a protected area). Regardless of management status, all sites are small and therefore highly susceptible to human activities in the

---

TAYLOR H. RICKETTS is director of the Conservation Science Program at the World Wildlife Fund. His research currently focuses on the economic benefits of conservation to people: the "ecosystem services" provided by forests, wetlands, and other natural areas.

surrounding landscape, or catastrophic events like storms, fire, or disease outbreak, and even small-scale land conversion. Near many of these sites, the human population density is high.

Preserving these species may prove difficult. However, several species are now recovering, like the Seychelles warbler (*Acrocephalus sechellensis*). This analysis helped mobilize conservation effort in unprotected areas. The Peruvian cloud forest—home of the long-whiskered owlet (*Xenoglaux loweryi*) and ochre-fronted antpitta (*Grallaricula ochraceifrons*)—was recently protected within the new 5,000-acre (2,000 ha) Abra Patricia reserve. Efforts like this can help prevent the extinction of species that took millennia to evolve.[20]

Rarest of the Rare Ecosystems

JONATHAN HOEKSTRA

Ecosystems sustain life on the planet and are inherently dynamic. Some ecosystems are common, but others become rare when habitats are degraded or when characteristic species disappear from the community. Among the rarest of the rare ecosystems are temperate grasslands, karst cave systems, and shellfish reefs, with only a few examples of these ecosystems intact and ecologically healthy.

Temperate grasslands once supported vast herds of antelope, buffalo, smaller

JONATHAN HOEKSTRA directs The Nature Conservancy's Emerging Strategies Unit, providing science leadership for conservation strategies regarding climate change, ecosystem services, agriculture, and energy and infrastructure development. He also maintains a faculty position in the biology department at the University of Washington.

prairie mammals, and grassland birds, providing prey for large carnivores and indigenous peoples. Today, most temperate grasslands have been plowed for crops or are used for livestock grazing. Fewer than 5 percent are protected for biodiversity. Some of the largest and wildest grasslands can still be found in Mongolia in Central Asia.

Karst ecosystems are as rare as they are mysterious. Systems of underground caverns and tunnels carved out by groundwater over the millennia support entire communities of animals uniquely adapted to dark, subterranean lives. These species, known as troglobiotic, are often blind versions of terrestrial species. There are also special bacteria that produce hydrogen sulfide, helping to carve out the caves themselves. Many of the world's karst systems, some as deep as 5,000 feet (1,500 m) and covering hundreds of miles of passages, are affected by pollution, invasive species, and diversion of groundwater for irrigation. Some of the best remaining karst systems are in Europe's Dalmation Coast and North America's Ozark Mountains.

Oyster reefs, like their coral counterparts, are made up of living organisms that create a marine structure, providing habitat for other species and protecting nearby shorelines from the sea. Once common in temperate estuaries, oyster and other shellfish reefs have been reduced to remnants by overharvesting, pollution, and coastal development. A large restoration effort is under way in Chesapeake Bay in the US.

Continuing to Consume Wildlife

An Update

ELIZABETH L. BENNETT

I wish I could say that the overall picture on global wildlife trade has improved in the two years since the first volume of *State of the Wild* was published in 2006. Sadly, I cannot. Commercial wildlife trade continues to deplete populations of many species across the world. The last two years have witnessed confirmation that tigers no longer occur in Sariska Wildlife Sanctuary in India, presumed to be a result of poaching, even though Sariska was one of the primary areas established to protect India's tigers in the 1970s. Surveys that look at impacts of commercial trade on wildlife populations paint a picture that is ever more grim.

On the other hand, there has been progress in the policy arena. Our understanding of how to balance the twin imperatives of wildlife conservation in the face of hunting while also supporting the livelihoods of rainforest peoples has advanced significantly. We have also seen some positive and exciting multigovernment initiatives to address the international wildlife trade, as the realization spreads that something must be done to save countless wildlife populations, and even whole species, from being extirpated by such trade.

New Data

The most striking new data produced in the past two years show that wildlife trade to East Asia affects more than just tropical species.[1] In Mongolia, the annu-

ELIZABETH L. BENNETT is director of the Wildlife Conservation Society's Hunting and Wildlife Trade Program. She has received many awards for her work, including the Pegawai Bintang Sarawak from the Sarawak state government in 2003, Member of the Most Excellent Order of the British Empire from Queen Elizabeth II in 2005, and the Wings World Quest Leila Hadley Luce Award for Courage in 2006.

al fur harvest is estimated to comprise 3 million Siberian marmots (*Marmota sibirica*), more than 200,000 Corsac foxes (*Vulpes corsac*), and 185,000 red foxes (*V. vulpes*), as well as snow leopards (*Uncia uncia*), wolves (*Canis lupus*), and many other species. The marmots, which once numbered more than 40 million, have

declined by 88 percent.[2] This hunting is mainly for fur exports to China. Once there, some furs are used locally, and others are processed and exported to Russia, western Europe, and the US.

Furbearers are not the only animals being overharvested on Mongolia's steppes. Saiga antelope (*Saiga tatarica*) are hunted for their horns for traditional medicines; within just five years, Mongolia's saiga population has declined from more than 5,000 animals to fewer than 800.

Wildlife also continues to flow into East Asia from tropical countries. The scale of the Asian turtle trade from Southeast Asia to China has been known for several years, and numerous efforts have tried to address it. In spite of this, the markets in China for wild-caught turtles remain vast. Surveys in a single evening in 2006 in Guangzhou recorded more than 5,600 turtles of 37 species being offered for sale. At a generous estimate, 2,500 of those, mainly red-eared sliders (*Trachemys scripta elegans*), were probably captive bred. But more than 3,000 of the turtles were wild caught, representing twelve endangered species and three critically endangered species.[3] With supplies of wild turtles in Southeast Asia apparently declining, animals are now being sourced from even further away, including Brazil and the US.

Additional information on the scale of the trade in East Asia has come from seizures by enforcement agencies. This might just be a glimpse of the actual overall amount of wildlife being traded, and it is also impossible to determine whether seizure data show that trade is increasing, or whether enforcement efforts are improving and intercepting more of the trade. But the scale of some of the recent seizures shows that the trade is vast.

Pangolins (*Manis* spp.)—scaly tropical anteaters—are listed on Appendix II of the Convention on International Trade in Endangered Species of Wild Fauna and Flora (CITES) and have a zero quota, which means that *no* international commercial trade is allowed. Yet on July 22, 2006, Hong Kong customs officers

Source: www.turtle-foundation.org.

A Chinese fishing boat carrying 397 dead endangered sea turtles was stopped by customs in Kalimantan, Indonesia, in May 2007.

Source: Elizabeth Bennett/WCS.

Turtles and their eggs are popular delicacies throughout East and Southeast Asia. Increasing demand has led to the emergence of a mainstream consumer market for farmed turtles.

seized 9,700 pounds (4,400 kg) of frozen pangolins coming from Indonesia and marked for re-export to mainland China. The pangolins were camouflaged by frozen fish. In 2006, the Vietnamese authorities seized 19 separate shipments of pangolins, accounting for more than 630 animals.[4] Pangolins are traded for their meat and leather, and also for their scales, which are used in traditional medicines.

In November 2006, 108 saiga horns were seized in Mongolia, heading for its southern border with China, and on January 19, 2007, Russian authorities seized 531 saiga horns near Russia's border with China. Hunting may impact wild saiga populations more broadly. Only the males have horns, and the selective hunting of males skews the sex ratio of remaining wild populations, in some cases leaving only one male per 30 to 100 females.[5] Given an estimated total world saiga population of 69,400 animals in 2006, and an optimistic adult male ratio of about 10 percent, the maximum estimate for the global population of male saiga is 6,940 animals. Those two seizures in 2006 alone accounted for 320 males or, at the most conservative estimate of sex ratios, 4.6 percent of the total male population of the species. In 2006, 50 percent of pharmacies surveyed in China were illegally selling saiga horn.[6] If this level of trade continues, the days of the bizarre and magnificent saiga roaming the steppes of Central Asia will soon be a fading memory.

Wildlife trade hits many more species than those mentioned here. In May 2007, a boat carrying wildlife to China was abandoned off the coast of the southern province of Guangdong with cargo containing 200 crates of animals, including 31 pangolins, in addition to 2,700 monitor lizards, 1,100 Brazilian turtles, and 21 bear paws.[7] In the largest bust of its kind in Russia in at least a decade, in addition to the saiga horn mentioned above, there were three Siberian tiger skins, eight tiger paws, 332 tiger bones, and 283 Asiatic black bear paws. Police had stopped a car that had its passenger seats removed and was stuffed full of bags that were ostensibly full of potatoes but, upon inspection, were found to contain animal parts.

Tiger bones are used in traditional Chinese medicine to reduce pain and inflammation. Tiger farming remains a controversial issue.

> In 2006, 50 percent of pharmacies surveyed in China were illegally selling saiga horn.

Commercial Wildlife Farms

One issue that has increasingly come to the fore in the past two years is commercial wildlife farms in Asia and their role in affecting traded wildlife species. This is extremely controversial because some governments and agencies see commercial wildlife farms as potentially supplying markets while reducing pressure on wild populations, whereas others, including many conservation groups, see them as exacerbating the problem. The primary critique is that farms can be a cover for laundering illegal trade of wild-caught animals, making it extremely difficult or impossible to enforce laws regulating wild-caught animals—it is simply not possible to determine if animal parts such as tiger bones are from a wild or a captive animal. In addition, farming of larger, slower-growing species is expensive, and it is inevitably much cheaper to poach an animal than to house and feed it for months or years in captivity. Poor economic viability increases the chances that farms may launder more cheaply available animals from the wild.

Another concern is that the output from farms can be negligible compared with demand, which means that pressure on wild populations would not be reduced. In China, approximately 2,000 musk deer in captivity produce 8.8 pounds (4 kg) of musk per year, but demand is up to 2,205 pounds (1,000 kg) per annum.[8] In addition, obtaining founder stock for farms can be a major drain on wild populations, and a continuing one if breeding is not successful or if new genetic material is needed. Demand for Siamese crocodiles (*Crocodylus siamensis*) for farms where they are reared for their skins has extirpated the species from much of its range.

Source: Robert Fournier/The Wild Lensman.

A third problem with wildlife farms is that, across much of East Asia where wildlife-derived medicines are consumed, products from captive-bred animals are sometimes deemed to be less efficacious than those from wild-hunted animals. This creates a two-tier price structure without significantly reducing the demand for wild-hunted products.

In spite of these concerns, the scale of commercial wildlife farms across East Asia is large, and growing rapidly. In 1997, China had 15,000 such farms, raising some 17 species.[9] That number is undoubtedly higher now, although the actual figure is unknown.

Crocodile skulls and snake bones in an illegal market in Cambodia. These items have both medicinal and spiritual value.

Some of the most commonly farmed animals are freshwater turtles, mainly the Chinese soft-shelled turtle (*Pelodiscus sinensis*). China currently has more than a thousand freshwater turtle farms, worth more than a billion US dollars.[10] Vietnam has 1,988 legally registered turtle farms housing more than a million animals. This is apparently leading to the emergence of a new consumer market for farmed turtles, often in mainstream restaurants, which increasingly view the farmed animals as "domestic." But traditional consumers still prefer wild turtles. Hence the farms are, at least in some parts of the market, failing to substitute for wild turtles.[11]

Farming of Asiatic black bears (*Ursus thibetanus*) started in China in 1984 when the practice was introduced from Korea. Farms in China and Vietnam hold an estimated 9,000 and 4,500 bears, respectively. The bears are kept for their bile, which is used in traditional medicine. The bile is extracted by draining the gall bladder through a permanent fistula and tube or by anesthetizing the bear about once a month and extracting the bile via syringe.

Most controversial of all within the past year have been tiger farms. Tiger farming was introduced relatively recently, and already there are thought to be more than 5,000 tigers in about a dozen farms in China. Selling of tiger bones has been illegal in China since 1993, yet increased pressure to sell the accumulating number of bones from the farms is resulting in fears that at least some aspects of the market might soon be legalized. Official statements on the issue have been ambiguous. In April 2007, Guilin's Xiongsen Bear and Tiger Park in southern Guangxi Province was alleged by a British television company, based on DNA tests, to be selling tiger meat in its restaurant; such tests were subsequently verified by a reputable third party. International criticism of the potential legalization of the tiger bone trade has been strong because sales of bones from captive-bred tigers would make regulation of trade in wild-caught tigers impossible. This has led to a coalition of 35 conservation and traditional medicine organizations opposing the trade. In June 2007, the triennial meeting of all CITES members passed a strong resolution stating that "parties with intensive operations breeding tigers on a commercial scale shall . . . restrict the captive population to a level supportive only to conserving wild tigers; tigers should not be bred for trade in their parts and derivatives." If the Chinese government continues to uphold its current trade ban, farms should eventually be phased out. However, the outcome remains unclear given the pressure from tiger farmers to legalize the trade.

Thousands of Asiatic black bears (*Ursus thibetanus*) are kept in small cages on wildlife farms in China and Vietnam, where their gall bladder bile is drained for use in traditional medicines.

Conservation and Rural Livelihoods

State of the Wild 2006 highlighted the controversy surrounding the wild meat issue, especially in the tropical forest regions of West and Central Africa, where wildlife conservation, wildlife harvests, and human livelihoods overlap in complex ways. This led to divergent views, depending on whether hunting was seen as an issue of conservation or of human livelihoods.[12] The controversy had stultified efforts to address the issue effectively in the policy arena as well as on the ground in Africa. To resolve this, people with interests in conservation and livelihoods met in Jersey, UK, in September 2005. The group examined the problem from their varying disciplinary perspectives—conservation science, social science, and environmental policy—and, by the end of two days, had reached a consensus.

Much of the controversy had stemmed from attempts to achieve both conservation and livelihood support within a single geographical area. The group recognized that, to accommodate different values, we must think about wildlife management at a larger spatial scale in heterogeneous landscapes with three different types of land uses:

1. *Strictly protected areas, the essential elements of any wildlife conservation strategy.* The primary aim here is biodiversity conservation, and no hunting should be allowed.

2. *Production forests, the primary role of which is natural resource production and harvesting.* The main focus here is generally timber but can also include nonprotected species of wildlife managed for sustainable use.

3. *Farm bush areas, which are mosaics of agricultural fields, tree crop plantations, fallow lands, and locally protected forests.* These areas are the primary source of cultivated and wild products, including wild meat. The role of such areas is to support local livelihoods. The species predominantly occurring here tend to be small, fast-breeding species, such as cane rats and the smaller duikers, so they are productive for wild meat and not of global conservation concern.[13] Nonprotected species should be managed locally, and local people should have the right to harvest them.

Hence no single area captures all values, but a well-planned, properly managed landscape can support both wildlife conservation as well as local livelihoods that include harvesting wildlife. When this consensus was reached, the wider policy debate moved forward with production of a unified paper on bushmeat and livelihoods for the Convention on Biological Diversity (CBD).[14]

The consensus has not yet brought about coordinated action in the complex real world of Africa. Turning ideas into practical reality involves many players, and improvements in legal frameworks, institutional strengthening, and governance. But the fact that reconciliation between the different aims seems feasible bodes well.

Government-Led Initiatives

Significant government-led policy initiatives to manage the international wildlife trade have emerged in the past two years. Two have been a response to the realization that wildlife trade can be a means of transmission for diseases such as highly pathogenic avian influenza, caused by the H5N1 virus. From July 2007, trade in wild birds has been permanently banned across the European Union (EU), replacing a temporary 2005 ban. Only captive-bred birds from approved countries are now allowed into the EU. Before the temporary ban was imposed, about 1.7 million wild birds were imported annually into the EU. The number of birds harvested for this trade was greater still, since about 60 percent of the birds caught for

> A well-planned, properly managed landscape can support both wildlife conservation as well as local livelihoods.

> Wildlife trade can be a means of transmission for diseases such as highly pathogenic avian influenza.

import died as a result of poor handling or disease before they reached Europe.[15] In the US, the Centers for Disease Control and Prevention (CDC) and the US Department of Agriculture have banned the import of wild birds and their derivatives from thirty-two countries, and parts of six others, where H5N1 might occur.

The past two years have seen three other major initiatives aimed at providing political and practical support to curtail the illegal wildlife trade.

First is the Association of Southeast Asian Nations (ASEAN) Regional Action Plan on Trade in Wild Fauna and Flora 2005–2010. This was adopted by all ASEAN countries in 2005 and has six objectives, with different countries taking the lead on each. The first, led by Indonesia, is to assist member countries to adopt effective legislation to implement CITES. The second objective, the Wildlife Enforcement Network, or ASEAN-WEN, aims to "promote networking amongst relevant law enforcement authorities in ASEAN countries to curb illegal trade in wild fauna and flora." Thailand is the lead country, and significant moves to increase enforcement training and networking efforts are being initiated by the Thai government, with the support of the Wildlife Alliance and TRAFFIC. The third objective is to promote research and information exchange, led by Malaysia. Objectives 4 and 5, led by Indonesia, focus on involving private industry and local communities in curtailing illegal wildlife trade, and on encouraging greater regional cooperation. Objective 6 is to seek technical and financial support for implementing the plan. To date, the only real action taken has been on objective 2, which is clearly critical, but the other objectives also require action to allow the agreement to fulfil its potential.

Another government-led step to tackle wildlife trade is the Coalition Against Wildlife Trafficking (CAWT), which was officially launched in Nairobi in February 2007. Initiated by the US Department of State, its aim is to form a coalition of partners from governments, nongovernment agencies, and private industry to "address the growing threats to wildlife from poaching and illegal trade." To date, the US, UK, India, Australia, and Canada have become members, as well as 13 organizations, including all of the main US-based international conservation groups. Because this is a new initiative, its outcomes are as yet unclear, but it has the potential to leverage significant political influence to address the illegal international wildlife trade.

At a national level, the UK government has set up the Partnership for Action against Wildlife Crime in the UK (PAW), with more than 130, mainly UK-based, organizations as members. PAW's aim is to promote the enforcement of wildlife conservation legislation across the UK. In addition, on October 20, 2006, the British police announced the formation of a National Wildlife Crimes Unit, which gathers intelligence on wildlife crime and provides support to police and customs officers.

I am often asked how I can continue to work on wildlife trade issues, when the news is so often grim. There is no simple answer, except to say that I cannot just sit by and watch the world's most magnificent wildlife disappear via shotguns and snares to be mere commodities in markets—passing shadows of their former wild magnificence—leaving increasingly tragic, empty wildernesses behind. Have the developments in the past two years done anything to stop these precipitous losses? No. At least not yet. The moves forward, especially on the policy fronts, however, are signs that people are becoming increasingly aware of the problem, and that addressing it is becoming a priority for certain senior government officials and agencies. The potential for consensus among those primarily concerned with human livelihoods and those primarily concerned with wildlife conservation is also critical, so that policy advisers are broadly pulling in the same direction. Nothing described here has rapidly translated into saved animals on the ground, but they are critical steps to ultimately reduce the intense pressure from the trade on wildlife populations across the globe. Only if this momentum continues and strengthens will elephants, tigers, gorillas, saiga, parrots, turtles, and multitudes of other species continue to roam the world's wild areas.

A Candid Conversation between Two Species

The Man: *I am the predilect object of Creation*
the center of all that exists . . .

The Tapeworm: *. . . You are exalting yourself*
a little. If you consider yourself the lord of Creation,
what can I be, who feed upon you and am
ruler in your entrails? . . .

The Man: *. . . You lack reason and an immortal soul.*

The Tapeworm: *. . . And since it is an established fact*
that the concentration and complexity
of the nervous system appear in the animal scale
as an uninterrupted series of graduations, where
are we cut off? How many neurons [nerve cells]
must be possessed in order to have a soul
and a little rationality?

SANTIAGO RAMON Y CAJAL
NOBEL PRIZE-WINNING NEUROANATOMIST
RECOLLECTIONS OF MY LIFE

PART II

FOCUS ON THE WILD

Emerging Diseases and Conservation: One World—One Health

ROBERT A. COOK AND WILLIAM B. KARESH,
SECTION EDITORS

It was once believed that disease, a natural phenomenon, posed little threat to the future of wildlife. Unfortunately, that is no longer true. Drivers of global change over the past century—population growth and agricultural production, animal movement and the wildlife trade, biodiversity loss, and global climate change—all degrade wild places and hence, disturb the balance of disease and health. Wildlife populations are fragmented, stressed, and exposed to novel infectious agents, setting the stage for those under pressure to be increasingly susceptible. People, domestic animals, and wildlife are threatened by changes in the environment that allow disease organisms to mutate, adapt, and spread. There is no doubt that the emergence of deadly infectious diseases—particularly zoonoses that can spread from animals to humans—has increased. If we hope

---

ROBERT A. COOK was appointed senior vice president and general director of Living Institutions, Wildlife Conservation Society, in 2007. Prior to that he was chief veterinarian and vice president at WCS. He received his veterinary degree from the University of Pennsylvania and has written extensively on the topic of wildlife health.
WILLIAM B. KARESH is director of Wildlife Health Sciences, WCS, and has directed the Field Veterinary Program for the Wildlife Conservation Society since 1989. He is leading efforts in the Congo Basin to reduce the impact of diseases such as Ebola, measles, and tuberculosis on endangered species and people. He co-chairs the World Conservation Union (IUCN) Veterinary Specialist Group, and is currently chief of party for the Wild Bird Global Avian Influenza Network for Surveillance (GAINS).

to meet the challenges presented by these changes, we must understand the connections between the alterations to our environment and health. The authors in this section, "Emerging Diseases and Conservation: One World—One Health," demonstrate the complex links between human, wildlife, and livestock health. The following essays speak to the value of a comprehensive approach to global health and the integration of knowledge across disciplines, what we call the "One World—One Health" approach.

Drivers of Disease Emergence and Reemergence

Current biodiversity loss is evidenced by extinction rates that are 50 to 100 times higher than those in the fossil record. In "Little Is Big, Many Is One: Zoonoses in the Twenty-first Century," zoonotic diseases crop up around the globe, with their roots in the disruption of ecosystems.

At the same time, the world's population is growing and is estimated to increase to 9.1 billion people in the next 50 years. The resulting forest fragmentation and rural development

bring ecological changes that alter the relationships of pathogens to host organisms. The essay "Land-Use Change as a Driver of Disease" outlines how change to land cover is a primary driver of human malaria emergence events.

Agricultural production, animal movement, and globalization, when not properly managed, serve to move pathogens around the world. By the year 2010, global output of meat is projected to grow to 283 million tons annually, with nearly three-quarters of this increase concentrated in developing countries (*UN Food and Agricultural Organization*). Reduced trade barriers have increased agricultural exports by over 50 percent since 2000 (*World Trade Organization*). What once were national health issues have become global concerns.

The essay "Transboundary Management of Natural Resources and the Importance of a 'One Health' Approach: Perspectives on Southern Africa" describes how the history of livestock interests and disease control efforts in southern Africa separated the landscape with fences, and how Transfrontier Conservation Areas

may set the stage for potential disease reemergence.

Intensified agricultural methods, when not performed under stringent biosafety criteria, lead to conditions ripe for disease outbreaks. Livestock may lose immunological traits, and crowded production systems may foster the rapid transmission and evolution of pathogens. The essay "An Ounce of Prevention: Lessons from the First Avian Influenza Scare," reviews how the relationship between domestic poultry production and distribution, live animal markets, and the environment facilitated the development and spread of highly pathogenic avian influenza.

The essay "Why Wildlife Health Matters in North America" describes diseases introduced via the movement of animals, how they spread between domestic livestock and wildlife, and how agencies try to control disease in these complex situations.

Climate change has always been a driver of ecological change and disease. Climate projections suggest an increase in global average surface temperature in the next 50 years. The essay "Warming Oceans, Increasing Disease: Mapping the Health Effects of Climate Change" examines the relationship between sea-surface temperatures and the onset of cholera epidemics. Climate change will also affect wildlife dis-

By the Numbers

Scientists estimate that over 170 amphibian species have gone extinct in recent years. Nearly half of all amphibian species are declining, and 30–50 percent of amphibian species are threatened with extinction, in large part due to chytrid fungus.

ease: Higher temperatures and changes in rainfall impact the geographic distribution of vectors (ticks and mosquitoes), and vector-borne diseases like Lyme disease, dengue fever, and West Nile virus. (*Intergovernmental Panel on Climate Change*, 2007)

With each new disease outbreak there is public demand for action, sometimes based on limited information. "Conservation Controversy: To Cull or Not to Cull?" weighs the pros and cons of culling wildlife to prevent disease spread.

Moving Forward

Public health and the safety of the food supply are fundamental to the future of humanity, and most nations invest in these goals through agricultural and public health authorities. However, there is no agency with significant global reach focused on the health of wildlife. We need well-funded, counterpart organizations with missions to protect the health of wildlife and their

habitats in order for the health of humans, domestic animals, and wildlife to be integrated in a balanced approach: One World—One Health.

> To better prepare ourselves, we must leverage concerns about human health to develop more holistic approaches to wildlife disease.

The challenge is daunting. West Nile virus, Severe Acute Respiratory Syndrome (SARS), Nipah virus, and avian influenza H5N1 are zoonotic diseases that caught society by surprise. To better prepare ourselves, we must leverage concerns about human health to develop more holistic approaches to wildlife disease. With timely information, regulatory and response mechanisms can better mitigate effects and make sound decisions about control. Responders and decision makers need high-quality information in every country, and

we must encourage open systems to share knowledge rapidly. We must foster new collaborative processes to bring together industry, government, and the nonprofit sector, allowing sovereign nations to realize the benefits of cooperation.

One step is the wild bird Global Avian Influenza Network for Surveillance (GAINS), established by a consortium of partners led by the Wildlife Conservation Society. It is the first system of global health surveillance of wild birds and could ultimately become a fully integrated surveillance and information management system for a range of wildlife species, livestock, pets, and people. This combines the strengths of government, the private sector, and civil society. The open, rapid sharing of information will help us move forward from a default approach of reaction to one of prediction in order to safeguard the health of the planet and all those who share it.

BY THE NUMBERS

Following the Severe Acute Respiratory Syndrome (SARS) outbreak of 2003, 838,500 wild animals were reportedly confiscated from markets in Guangzhou, China. Three species of horseshoe bat (*Rhinolophus* spp.) were found to be the natural reservoir host for closely related SARS-like coronaviruses.

The locks at the Pacific Ocean end of the Panama Canal. Globalization and the growing frequency of foreign and domestic travel has opened more pathways for the spread of infectious diseases.

Little Is Big, Many Is One

ZOONOSES IN THE TWENTY-FIRST CENTURY

DAVID QUAMMEN

Zoonotic disease is in the news again. Zoonotic disease is always in the news, of course, though most members of the general public wouldn't recognize the subject by that fancy label. They couldn't tell you offhand that a zoonosis is simply an animal disease that's transmissible to humans. They read alarming stories in their newspapers, they see garish images on their televisions, they hear radio reports about bird flu or SARS or West Nile fever, about Lyme disease in the Connecticut suburbs, about an Ebola outbreak among unfortunate African villagers, but they don't usually make connections. They tend to view these events as isolated dramas, some of which have the potential to affect them personally (*Will my child get bit by a Lyme-bearing tick?*) and some of which (*Africa and its diseases are far away, thank goodness*) seemingly don't. They might worry themselves with the question, Is this the Big One, the next global pandemic? But they seldom pause to consider that the prospect of a Big One (which might kill

DAVID QUAMMEN *is the author of 11 books, including* The Reluctant Mr. Darwin. *He is a contributing writer for* National Geographic, *and also writes for* Harper's *and other magazines, usually about science and nature. He has three times received the National Magazine Award for his essays and other work. His article on zoonotic diseases, with photographs by Lynn Johnson, appeared in the October 2007 issue of* National Geographic. *Although he has been a fulltime freelancer for most of his career, he presently holds the Wallace Stegner Chair of Western America Studies at Montana State University.*

millions of humans) and the increasing frequency of Little Ones (which claim only a few hundred people here or there, a few herds of livestock, a few flocks of poultry, and an uncountable number of wild animals) are parts of the same urgent and interconnected phenomenon.

Professionals know otherwise. Wildlife veterinarians, veterinary ecologists, health care workers, and conservation biologists deal variously with zoonoses and with anthropozoonoses (the converse: human diseases transmissible to other animal species) on a daily basis all over the world. They know that leaps of disease between species are common, not rare. They can cite stark statistics—that 58 percent of all human infectious diseases are zoonotic, and that 75 percent of all *emerging* diseases (read: new and scary ones) are likewise shared between humans and other species.[1] They understand that infectious disease is a natural part of biological systems, like predation and competition, like metabolism and senescence. And they recognize,

---

> The growing incidence of zoonotic disease outbreaks is one ramifying problem, not a series of disconnected calamities . . . it represents the consequences of things we are *doing* on the planet.

---

those experts, several other broad truths: that the growing incidence of zoonotic disease outbreaks is one ramifying problem, not a series of disconnected calamities; that it represents the consequences of things we are *doing* on the planet, not merely things that are *happening* to us; and that the whole situation will only get worse unless robust, well-informed measures are taken. The motto "One World—One Health" eloquently summarizes the goals and visions of the Wildlife Conservation Society in this realm, which include recognizing the essential linkage among humans, wildlife, and domestic animals, and the fact that practices involving land and water use, biodiversity conservation, and disease control and mitigation necessarily ramify from one kind of living creatures to another. But that positive phrase also suggests to the mind (at least to a mind as gloomy as mine) its own negative: one sickness. It *is* all one sickness, in the sense that our planet is suffering a systemic inflammation of *Homo sapiens*. The increasing frequency and increasing scope of zoonotic and anthropo-

zoonotic infections should be seen in this light—as a pattern, a set of interconnected effects, reflecting causes that are largely of human doing.

So, yes, the subject is in the news, and we can expect it to stay there. For one instance: Belgium is suffering its third consecutive year of epidemic-level hantavirus infection.

The strain of hanta afflicting Belgians is known as Puumala virus, prevalent throughout northern Europe. Its main reservoir (the species within which it lurks endemically) is the bank vole, (*Myodes glareolus*). Bank vole populations fluctuate in response to various factors, foremost of which seems to be the supply of acorns and beechnuts. Years of high mast production by oak and beech trees, combined with hospitable weather, seem to encourage earlier reproduction and higher survival rates among bank voles, thereby supplying more reservoir individuals for the Puumala virus and yielding more infections among people exposed to the virus-laden dust rising from all that vole feces and urine. Belgium had 160 cases in 2006 and, if the current rate continues, will record about 175 in 2007.[2]

In another report, this one from Colorado, state officials confirmed that a domestic cat recently died of plague. Presumably, the unlucky feline got hold of an infected rodent. The plague bacterium, *Yersinia pestis*,

---

BY THE NUMBERS

Of some 1,407 human pathogens, 58 percent (816) are zoonotic, and 177 are categorized as emerging or reemerging. Zoonotic pathogens are twice as likely to be in this category.

---

can travel from host to host in the blood of engorged fleas, which pass it by biting. There are other modes of transfer too, including direct contact with a victim's blood or pus; when a cat catches and eats a plague-ridden rat, fleas might be the least of its problems. Although every case of plague in a domestic kitty raises concern, according to John Pape, an epidemiologist with the Colorado Department of Public Health and Environment, "this is not an uncommon finding in areas where plague is circulating."[3] And where is plague circulating? More widely than you might want to think, if you're a Colorado resident. During the early months of 2007, within metropolitan Denver, 15 squirrels tested positive for *Yersinia pestis*, as well as a rabbit from City Park and a monkey from the Denver Zoo. The monkey died; the rabbit's fate is unknown. For the previous year, 2006, Colorado tallied 23 cats diagnosed with plague, and the disease was also found among wild animals in 25 counties.[4]

Advice from John Pape to cat owners: keep your pets away from dead squirrels and watch out for fleas, because the next victim could be your tabby or you. Advice from other experts, those who work on zoonotic diseases as a global problem: think about Puumala virus in Belgium and plague among urban squirrels when you contemplate certain simpler, per-

sonal matters, such as whether or not to take a walk in the woods or eat local venison or get a flu shot. Bear in mind that it's all connected.

How is it all connected? Scientists in recent years have made great progress charting the relationships, balances, and pathways involved in zoonotic and anthropozoonotic dis-

> Think about Puumala virus in Belgium and plague among urban squirrels when you contemplate certain simpler, personal matters, such as whether or not to take a walk in the woods or eat local venison or get a flu shot. Bear in mind that it's all connected.

eases. They have studied diseases caused by each of the six main types of pathogen: viruses, bacteria, protozoans, prions, fungi, and worms. They have identified a list of factors that combine to make the transmission of pathogens from species to species ever more likely and more consequential: bushmeat consump-

tion, intensive livestock operations that concentrate many animals closely together, extensive ranching operations that replace wild animals with domestic stock on natural rangelands, international trade in wild animals as food or as pets, ecotourism, unintentional transport of exotic species into vulnerable ecosystems, road building, habitat destruction, habitat fragmentation, climate change, and the very speed and ease of modern human travel, which allow a disease agent such as the SARS virus to distribute itself around the planet within days of its latest outbreak in, say, a market town of southern China. The common themes among all these factors are a dark yin-and-yang pair: disruption and connectivity. Disruption (of wild populations, of ecosystems) unsettles disease pathogens from their customary hosts and situations, putting them in search of new victims—and sometimes in search of new *kinds* of victims. Connectivity (through overly close juxtaposition of species or swift long-distance transport) delivers those

---

BY THE NUMBERS

In 2007, human demography hit the point at which now more of the global population lives in urban or semi-urban areas than in rural areas. By 2015 there will be at least 550 cities with populations over 1 million people, and the world population is expected to be 10 billion by 2050. China's population of 1.3 billion people is growing at a rate of 3.7 percent per year in urban areas.

pathogens to new opportunities. As we disrupt ecosystems around the world, shaking loose their resident pathogens from longstanding relationships, and as we invite those pathogens aboard our shipping containers and our passenger jets, we are globalizing some contagions that seemed troublesome enough when they were local.

Here is one more newsy instance of the connectivity problem: a dead crow, found recently beside a highway in York Region, Ontario, has tested positive for West Nile virus. Mosquitoes in that area are known to harbor the virus, and three human cases of West Nile fever were reported there last year.[5] York Region is a densely populated municipality of south-central Ontario, just north of the city of Toronto. It's a long way—as the crow flies or by any other method—from the West Nile district of Uganda, where West Nile virus was first identified in 1937. But the virus has made that journey and is still on the move.

By a strict definition, zoonotic diseases are those shared between *Homo sapiens* and other vertebrate species. Vector-borne diseases, carried be-

> Matters become more complicated in diseases that are both zoonotic and vector-borne, such as West Nile fever, which seems to be transmissible among various bird species, humans, and other mammals by several species of *Culex* mosquitoes.

tween humans by some sort of invertebrate, such as a mosquito, fall in a different category. Matters become more complicated in diseases that are both zoonotic and vector-borne, such as West Nile fever, which seems to be transmissible among various bird species, humans, and other mammals by several species of *Culex* mosquitoes. Such diseases, besides being wonderfully, fiendishly intricate, are paradigms of ecological interconnection. One group of researchers puts it this way: "Thus, infectious diseases are inherently ecological systems, involving interactions among small to large networks of species."[6]

Those words come from an interesting theoretical paper by Felicia Keesing, Richard S. Ostfeld, and R. D.

Holt. Much of what they know about complex ecological interactions is anchored in field data and hard won from the ground up: they study Lyme disease among small mammals and people in the forest patches of Dutchess County, New York. Ostfeld has led the study for 15 years, in the course of which he and his colleagues have trapped and examined thousands of mice, chipmunks, and other small mammals as well as an unholy abundance of ticks. Why ticks? Because they are the vector of Lyme disease. Ostfeld and his team have also examined landscape conditions—how many fragments of forest exist in the county, and how big is each fragment?—using Geographic Information System (GIS) maps combined with inspection on foot. Among their more significant findings is a relationship between biological diversity and disease risk. The relationship, at least in this case, is inverse—lower species diversity within a small patch of forest correlates with higher risk of Lyme disease for humans.

The dynamics of that relationship are complicated but intriguing. The disease agent is a spirochete bacterium, *Borrelia burgdorferi*. The vector, at least in the eastern United States, is *Ixodes scapularis*, sometimes known as the deer tick. Adult ticks climb aboard deer in autumn, each female tick seeking a final blood meal before winter, and each tick of either sex also

---

BY THE NUMBERS

The influenza epidemic of 1918–1919 would have an economic impact in today's dollars of $4.4 trillion. Over the past two years, the world has already spent almost US$2.5 billion on new flu vaccine development in preparation for avian influenza.

seeking mates. The deer, like a singles bar with tapas, offers both food and a good chance of sex. After mating, the females drop off the deer and hunker through the cold months; then, nourished by that gut-load of deer blood, they lay their eggs in spring. This has led some people to assume that deer abundance drives the system—that the more deer you have locally, the greater your chance of catching Lyme disease. Rick Ostfeld's research indicates otherwise. "I am something of a heretic about the role deer play in Lyme disease dynamics," he told me when I visited him in Dutchess County last year.

"Each adult deer can host thousands of adult ticks. And each adult female tick lays a clutch of about 3,000 eggs. So if you think about it," Ostfeld said, "it doesn't take that many deer to support an excess number of tick eggs in any given generation." What matters more, he explained, is the tick's dependence on other species in the earlier phases of its life history—when it's a newly hatched larva, free of bacteria, or when it's a nymph (a yearling adolescent). During those stages, no bigger than a poppy seed, an immature tick doesn't want the crowded, sexy circumstances of a tick-infested deer; it only wants warm, red blood. Accordingly, larval and nymphal ticks latch onto smaller hosts available closer to the ground. One recipient of their attentions—though not the only one—is the white-footed mouse (*Peromyscus leucopus*). Other small mammals, such as chipmunks,

A young tick may aquire the bacteria that causes Lyme disease from a white-footed mouse (*Peromyscus leucopus*). That tick may later pass the disease along to a human host.

shrews, and squirrels, are also attacked, and so are some ground-foraging birds, such as robins. So are people, if they happen to expose themselves by clambering through the underbrush where thirsty young ticks await.

In the course of these early meals, a tick either acquires or does not acquire the *Borrelia* spirochete from one of its vertebrate hosts. If a larval tick gets the infection from a mouse and becomes a carrier, then that tick can later pass it along to a human. If not, then that tick's bite will deliver annoyance . . . but no disease.

Now here's an important twist in

the system: white-footed mice are very hospitable to *Borrelia burgdorferi* and are likely to pass it along to any ticks that bite them. Chipmunks and robins are moderately hospitable as disease reservoirs. Other mammal and bird species are far less hospitable, or not at all. So the relative abundance of such small animal species makes a big difference to disease transmission. Two ecological factors are known to affect the local abundance of mice and chipmunks: size of the forest patch and presence of bounteous acorns. If the forest patch is large enough to include a rich community of species—weasels, foxes, raccoons,

By the Numbers

In 2005, 23,305 cases of Lyme disease were reported to the Centers for Disease Control and Prevention (CDC). Lyme disease is transmitted primarily by the deer tick (*Ixodes scapularis*) and is the most common vector-borne disease for people in the United States.

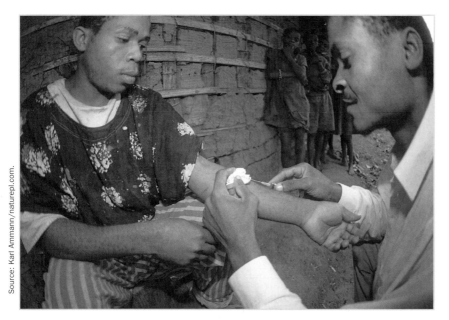

Ba'ka pygmy in Cameroon being tested for Ebola virus after eating infected gorilla meat. Genetic similarities between humans and apes means that many diseases can be transferred between them.

skunks, flying squirrels, gray squirrels, and shrews—then the mouse and the chipmunk populations will be relatively small, because of predation and competition, and the chance of a young tick getting infected will be relatively low. Result: reduced risk of Lyme disease for children who play in the woods. If the forest patch is small, though, and it contains oak trees that have lately produced a bumper crop of acorns, there will be many mice, many chipmunks, and a high risk of

tickborne disease.

The conclusion from Ostfeld's team is one that any conservationist is glad to hear: high biological diversity on intact landscapes can serve as a protection for human health. We all wanted to believe it, even without evidence, but we needed someone to count all those mice.

Ostfeld, Keesing, and Holt aren't alone in their search for broader ecological understanding of zoonotic disease dynamics. Recently, while

researching an article for *National Geographic* magazine, I've had the chance to talk with some farflung investigators in the same field. In the Northern Territory of Australia, I observed the work of Raina Plowright, a veterinary ecologist studying the ecology of a newly discovered virus called Hendra, deadly to humans and horses, that maintains its reservoirs in fruit bats, which have been displaced from their native eucalyptus habitat by land clearance and begun to congregate closer to cities. In Atlanta, I spoke with a dozen zoonosis experts at the Centers for Disease Control and Prevention. At a medical research institute in Franceville, Gabon, I interviewed Eric M. Leroy and Xavier Pourrut, two men at the forefront of efforts to discover the mysteriously elusive reservoir host of Ebola virus. And I spent many good days gazing over the shoulder of William B. Karesh, director of the WCS's Wildlife Health Sciences, as he did his routinely adventuresome work, investigating poultry health in a Cambodian village, then tracking gorillas in a region of the Republic of Congo where gorillas have been devastated by Ebola. My travels with Billy Karesh also allowed time for long conversations—around a campfire amid a Congo forest, in the prow of a small boat on the Mambili River, in the back of a jarring Landcruiser headed cross-country toward Gabon, and over icy martinis at the best bar in Phnom Penh.

One day I asked Karesh whether these famous cases of emerging dis-

BY THE NUMBERS

In the northeast part of Tasmania, where facial tumor disease has been observed for several years, there has been a 90 percent decline in populations of Tasmanian devil (*Sarcophilus harrisii*). An estimated 50 percent of the entire devil population has been wiped out. A lack of genetic diversity in the population is allowing the disease to spread at a rate that may lead to extinction within 20 years.

ease, Ebola and SARS and bird flu and others, represent many different subjects or a single big one. He replied by reminding me of nature's essential connectedness, within which all living organisms—predators and competitors, commensal and symbiotic species, parasites and pathogens of all sort— are each merely trying to make a living, but are each interdependent with numerous others. Humans too? Yes, we don't stand alone. In fact, Billy said, we have more microorganisms living within our bodies than we have cells. "Every living creature is a whole microcosm of other living creatures," he said. And sometimes those passengers move around, from individual to individual, even from species to species, adapting to new survival strategies in the process.

At the time, he and I were sitting on the veranda of a simple cabin at a base camp of the Seima Biodiversity Conservation Area, in eastern Cambodia. Billy wore a sleeveless T-shirt, leaving him cool in the tropical heat and showing large biceps such as you'd see on a middleaged wrestling coach. His salt-and-pepper beard was

> The goal isn't to eradicate all disease, as public health professionals have traditionally thought. . . . The goal is healthy systems, within which a richness of species, including native pathogens, have their roles.

closely cropped. His noggin top was bald. His eyes were pale blue. His voice was quiet and he spoke candidly, with muted passion, about variously controversial and technical aspects of the global disease situation, barely moving his jaw, as though he had no concerns about job security or political orthodoxy but was gently protecting his teeth. You know, he said, the goal isn't to eradicate all disease, as public health professionals have traditionally thought. It isn't the sterilization of the planet, the killing of every potentially infectious microbe. That's both impossible and undesirable. The goal is balance. The goal is healthy systems, within which a richness of species, including native pathogens, have their roles. "A lot of the problems that we *see* as problems," he said, "are from disrupting these systems and moving these organisms around to places where they shouldn't be."

I recognized the cardinal themes: disruption and connectivity. "We can't eliminate every disease or every organism in the forest," he added, "but we can stop some things from happening that are really simple."

Billy lay low through the sweltering afternoon, preparing his equipment. I took a nap and read a Victorian novel. And then, after dark, putting on black rubber boots and surgical masks, we went out to vaccinate chickens.

Land-Use Change as a Driver of Disease

JONATHAN A. PATZ, SARAH H. OLSON,
AND JILL C. BAUMGARTNER

To account for disease outbreaks, we often point to such drivers as economic and public health inadequacies, social crises, international travel, and sudden ecological disturbances. But we have been less attuned to the fundamental role that persistent human-induced changes to land use and land cover (LULC) have played in the spread of zoonotic and anthroponotic disease.

In fact, change to LULC and the disruption of balanced ecosystems is a primary driver of a range of infectious disease outbreaks and emergence events. Changes that especially influence infectious disease risk include destruction of or encroachment into wildlife habitat, particularly through logging and road building; changes in the distribution of water through dam construction, irrigation, or stream diversion; agricultural proliferation of both livestock and crops; chemical pollutants, including fertilizers and pesticides; and uncontrolled urban sprawl.[1]

Land-use changes can trigger key biological mechanisms of disease transmis-

---

JONATHAN A. PATZ is associate professor of environmental studies and population health sciences and director of Global Environmental Health at the University of Wisconsin–Madison. He is an affiliate scientist of the National Center for Atmospheric Research, and has served as convening lead author for the United Nations/World Bank Millennium Ecosystem Assessment. He is coeditor for the journal Ecohealth: Conservation Medicine and Ecosystem Sustainability.

SARAH H. OLSON is a joint Ph.D. candidate in Population Health and Land Resources at the University of Wisconsin–Madison. She studies land-use and disease ecology, with a focus on deforestation and malaria in the Amazon.

JILL C. BAUMGARTNER is a joint Ph.D. candidate in Population Health Sciences and Land Resources studying environmental epidemiology at the Center for Sustainability and the Global Environment, University of Wisconsin–Madison.

sion that facilitate the emergence or reemergence of some diseases, or they can facilitate the waning or disappearance of a disease. According to the 2005 Millennium Ecosystem Assessment, key disease triggers caused by changes in LULC include altered vector (or carrier) breeding sites, altered distribution of reservoir species, one species invading another's ecological niche, changes in the ability to host a disease, changes in biodiversity systems (such as increase/decrease in host population density), genetic changes of vectors or pathogens (such as pesticide-resistant mosquitoes or antibiotic-resistant bacteria), and the introduction of infectious disease agents into new environments. Often, several of these triggers can work in tandem.

Disturbing Intact Ecosystems

One form of land-use change that has been linked with the emergence of many diseases is conversion of tropical forests—with their high levels of biodiversity—to relatively homogeneous agricultural communities with high densities of humans, domestic animals, and crops. Forest encroachment increases opportunities for interactions between wild animals, livestock, and humans. In Malaysia, pig farming near fruit bat habitat was found to be the source of the emergence and spread of Nipah virus, a deadly hemorrhagic disease. Clearing forests for roads in central Africa is linked to the expansion of bushmeat consumption that may have played a key role in the early emergence of human immunodeficiency virus types 1 and 2,[2] and workers collecting chimpanzee meat have become infected with Ebola.[3]

Fragmenting forests alters biodiversity in ways that can change the fundamental ecology of infectious diseases, particularly those that involve multiple species in their life cycle. Because of the nature of food webs, predators at higher trophic levels exist at lower population densities and are often sensitive to changes in food availability. Forest patches may not supply sufficient prey, resulting in local extinction of predator species and a subsequent increase in the density of their prey.

Such dynamics are important if a species is a reservoir of disease, particularly if a disease becomes more prevalent when the host species increases. For example, people contract Lyme disease after being bitten by ticks carrying the bacterium *Borrelia burgdorferi*, which the ticks pick up from feeding on a variety of mammals that differ dramatically in their capacity to function as reservoirs: the chance that a tick will pick up *B. burgdorferi* from white-footed mice, the disease's main reservoir, is higher than from other forest vertebrates.[4] In woods with a diversity of mammals, the ability of the disease to spread from the main reservoir may

Lyme disease travels from tick to human when a tick that has bitten an infected small animal feeds on the blood of its human host.

be compromised. However, a near absence of predators in fragmented forest patches has allowed populations of two species in the ecological pathway of Lyme disease to soar: mice and deer have become overabundant in and around exurban developments. (Although deer are poor reservoirs of *B. burgdorferi*, they are adult ticks' food source and point of male–female interaction.) Indeed, habitat fragmentation that reduces biodiversity within the host communities may raise disease risk through the increase in both distribution and density of host and reservoir species. In fact, increased species richness in an ecosystem has been found to reduce disease risk.[5]

Similar conclusions apply to a number of other diseases, including cutaneous leishmaniasis and Chagas disease—both caused by parasites transmitted via biting insects—and tickborne diseases such as human granulocytic ehrlichiosis, babesiosis, louping ill, and tularemia. An instructive example of the relationship between LULC change and cross-species infectious disease can be found in the global spread of malaria.

Deforestation, Biodiversity, and Malaria

Since the beginning of the twentieth century, rates of deforestation have grown exponentially. The amount of rainforest lost annually now approximates an area larger than the state of West Virginia (or 28,000 square miles).[6] Driven by rapidly increasing human population numbers and industries, large swaths of species-rich tropical and temperate forests, as well as prairies, grass-

lands, and wetlands, have been converted to species-poor agricultural and ranching areas. Recent evidence from Africa, the Amazon, and parts of Asia now points to deforestation as one of the causes for the increase in malaria across the tropics.

Globally, malaria ranks first among vector-borne diseases and causes about 2 million deaths annually, mostly in children. It is responsible for 13 percent of global disability and mortality from infectious and parasitic diseases, according to the World Health Organization's (WHO) latest *Global Burden of Disease* report, and in Southeast Asia, Africa, and the Amazon, malaria risk is increasing alongside human population growth and environmental change.[7] In

Forest clearing for agriculture contributes to the spread of disease. Irrigation of farmland provides a watery environment for breeding insects.

2006, researchers at WHO estimated that environmental factors—including policies and practices regarding land use, deforestation, water resource management, settlement siting, and modified house design—contributed to 42 percent of malaria cases worldwide.[8] Yet malaria epidemiology research predominantly remains focused on individual, behavioral, population, and socioeconomic dimensions. Research on upstream LULC dimensions and pos-

Source: CDC.

A bi-plane sprays an insecticide during malaria control operations.

sible mitigation strategies remains limited, despite recent calls to address this knowledge gap.

We know that LULC changes have affected mosquito distributions for centuries. The draining of swamps surrounding Rome reduced mosquito populations and malaria in the city—much to the benefit of its residents. When agricultural practices spread across western Europe, the resulting social and land transformations contributed to the eradication of malaria. On the other hand, the removal of forests within the ancient Indus Valley may have shifted the habitat preferences of the mosquito *Anopheles stephensi* from the forest to urban areas and waterways and thereby contributed to the civilization's collapse circa 2000 BC. To this day, *A. stephensi* remains the most prolific vector for urban malaria transmission across the Middle East and Asia.[9]

For about 50 years following the discovery of malaria's transmission via mosquito vectors (over a century ago), malaria research and disease control was very ecologically minded. However, the rise of DDT and its efficacy shifted malaria research away from studying the influence of LULC

BY THE NUMBERS

Over the next 22 years, meat consumption in developing nations is expected to double. If the world's population today were to eat a Western diet of roughly 176 pounds (80 kg) of meat per capita per year, the global agricultural land required for production would be about 2.5 billion hectares—two-thirds more than is presently used. Livestock remains the world's largest user of land, but its use has shifted steadily from grazing to the consumption of feed crops.

on malaria risk. Instead, the primary goal of malaria programs became vector eradication via insecticides and clinical health interventions. If LULC was recognized as a risk factor, it was used mainly to focus the application of DDT to mosquito breeding sites.

An important exception during this time was a classic study in Trinidad, in the so-called bromeliad malaria epidemic. In the 1930s, economic pressures forced the nation's agricultural sector from subsistence farming into the international cacao industry. People surged into the forest, cropland was carved out of the Trinidad jungle, and the newly planted cacao trees created a lighter and drier environment. Tall flowering immortelle trees interplanted to provide shade for the cacao trees supported epiphytes, plants that live on trees and get water from rain and the air. In Trinidad, the immortelles supported a bromeliad tank species that naturally collects a small amount of water within its cluster of leaves—creating an ideal breeding site for *A. bellator*, a malaria vector that prefers drier areas and the subcanopy elevation of forests. Public health officials noted that splenomegaly (enlarged spleen, one symptom of malaria) among school children correlated with the areas cultivating cacao, and the vector, *A. bellator*, was not found outside the cacao-growing areas. Removing the bromeliads, both by hand and with herbicides, reduced *A. bellator* populations and returned malaria rates to prior endemic levels.[10]

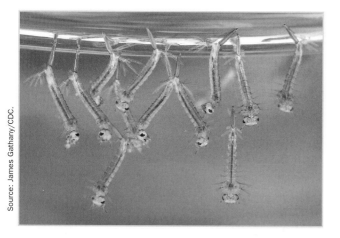

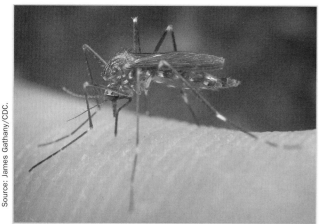

Top: Standing water is a breeding ground for mosquito larvae. The adult insects transmit diseases such as malaria and yellow fever.

Above: Mosquitos are vectors of a number of diseases, including West Nile and encephalitis.

This kind of longitudinal and interdisciplinary assessment of the link between LULC change and malaria risk provides vital clues to the mechanisms that alter the transmission dynamics of resurgent malaria. However, in place of generating comprehensive longitudinal data on complex drivers, we currently have narrower malaria studies that focus on one or two mechanisms.

A synthesis of narrow studies conducted in Africa suggests that altering breeding habitats—often pools of water where mosquitoes lay eggs—directly affects malaria risk. In one study, *Anopheles* breeding pools had significantly less canopy cover than breeding pools for non-malaria-carrying mosquito species.[11] Another study using artificial larval habitats showed that *A. gambiae* survivorship was 56 percent in open sunlit areas and 1.5 percent in forested habitats, meaning that deforested areas contributed to stronger populations of *A. gambiae*.[12]

In the Brazilian Amazon—a landscape undergoing unprecedented change—one particular species of mosquito preferentially seeks partially sunlit pools, sunlight being a by-product of removing canopy forests. *A. darlingi*, which is the most efficient and principal interior vector of falciparum, the most deadly type of malaria, was found in 13 of 14 human-altered sites studied and was absent from all five pristine sites.[13] During the study, 18 of 26 mosquito species had sampling patterns similar to *A. darlingi*, suggesting that human-altered sites accommodated a large niche invasion. Other findings documented increasing numbers of *A. darlingi* in newly urbanized areas of Belem, Brazil.[14] Similarly, in the city of Manaus, *A. darlingi* resurged in 1988 in suburban areas that were encroaching into the forest, sparking an epidemic of 20,000 cases of malaria.

In the region near Iquitos, in the Peruvian Amazon, *A. darlingi* had not been captured prior to the 1990s. A rare comprehensive study, incorporating human health data, mosquito biting, and larval mosquito collections at 56 sites along gradients of deforestation, sampled over 15,000 mosquitoes in the human biting component and 597 bodies of water that had *A. darlingi* larvae. The sites surrounded by deforestation had *A. darlingi* biting rates nearly 300 times greater than biting rates in forested sites. When researchers looked at land cover within a 1-square-kilometer area around the collection points, the sites surrounded by land that was more than 80 percent deforested had a mean mosquito biting rate of 8.33, whereas sites with less than 30 percent deforestation had a mean biting rate of 0.03.[15]

These studies suggest that environmental risk factors for malaria are related to the LULC changes associated with human expansion into forested areas. The Peru study suggests that reducing forest cover and overly disturbing intact, tropical ecosystems elevate malaria risk independent of human settlement patterns—that is, LULC has an effect on malaria separate from the location and size of human populations. This supports the frontier malaria theory, which holds that the initial stages of malaria emergence are "dominated by environmental risks, consequential to ecosystem transformation, that promote larval habitats," and that following "establishment of agriculture, ranching, and urban development," malaria risk is reduced.[16]

Land transformation near urbanizing areas is also a focus of malaria studies. The unprecedented high rate of urbanization, particularly in low- and middle-income countries, has substantial implications for the risk and transmission of malaria and other vector-borne diseases. Reduced vegetation, contamination of aquatic sites, urban farming practices, and water storage containers may all contribute to anopheline species density and longevity. For example, the highest larval productivity near medium-sized towns in Côte d'Ivoire was in rice paddies, agricultural trenches between vegetable patches, and irrigation wells.[17]

> The unprecedented high rate of urbanization, particularly in low- and middle-income countries, has substantial implications for the risk and transmission of malaria and other vector-borne diseases.

BY THE NUMBERS

Within endemic countries, malaria consumes 0.25 to 1.3 percent of per capita gross national product.

The latest remote sensing and mapping technologies enable us to identify patterns of land development and forest fragmentation that increase malaria risk.[18] As more isolated data points connect malaria risk to habitat, we can flag these potential mechanisms, follow up with more comprehensive studies (current indicators of LULC related to malaria risk remain to be tested across a broader region), and eventually begin to reincorporate LULC dimensions into malaria control.

Conclusions

We are now at a point where we can no longer focus solely on clinically based medicine to prevent malaria or other vector-borne diseases, but must look at the broader causative factors of disease emergence or resurgence, such as land-use and biodiversity change.

Recent developments in the science community give cause for optimism. First, the expanded International Association for Ecology and Health represents work being done at the intersection of ecological and health sciences and provides a gathering place for research that integrates knowledge about ecology, health, and sustainability, whether scientific, medical, local, or traditional.

Second, the conceptual framework developed by the Millennium Ecosystem Assessment is an integrative effort to address the causative factors of infectious disease. The framework enables us to optimize the relationship between ecosystems and human health by (1) identifying options that can better achieve human development and sustainable development goals; (2) allowing us to better understand the human health trade-offs involved in environment-related decisions; and (3) aligning response options where they can be most effective. The Millennium Ecosystem Assessment encourages policy makers to approach development and human and wildlife health at the levels of specific health risk factors, landscape and habitat change, and economies and behaviors.

Most clearly, we need to attend not only to our local environs but to entire ecosystems as we consider infectious diseases. Intact forests that support complex ecosystems and provide essential habitats for species are specialized to those flora. As the foregoing examples demonstrate, disrupting complex relationships by changing land use and land cover can produce unforeseen impacts on both wildlife and human health. And, although we may not live within a certain environment, its health may indirectly affect our own.

Transboundary Management of Natural Resources and the Importance of a "One Health" Approach

Perspectives on Southern Africa

STEVEN A. OSOFSKY, DAVID H. M. CUMMING,
AND MICHAEL D. KOCK

With the recent rapid growth in global tourism, the transboundary management of natural resources, particularly of water and wildlife, and the associated development of transfrontier parks and transfrontier conservation areas (TFCAs) has become a major focus of attention in southern Africa. At least 13 potential and existing terrestrial transfrontier parks and transfrontier conservation areas (also known as transboundary conservation areas) have been identified in the Southern African Development Community (SADC) region.[1] As opposed to the more discrete transfrontier parks, TFCAs often include national parks, neighboring game reserves, hunting areas, and conservancies embedded within a matrix of land under traditional communal tenure.

STEVEN A. OSOFSKY *joined the Wildlife Conservation Society's Field Veterinary Program in 2002 as the Society's first senior policy adviser for wildlife health and serves as an adjunct assistant professor at the University of Maryland. He was the first wildlife veterinary officer for the Botswana Department of Wildlife and National Parks, and a Science and Diplomacy Fellow of the American Association for the Advancement of Science serving as a Biodiversity Program Specialist at the United States Agency for International Development.*

DAVID H. M. CUMMING *has been working in wildlife research and conservation in southern Africa since the 1960s. He is an honorary professor at the Percy FitzPatrick Institute, University of Cape Town, a research associate at the University of Zimbabwe, and a consultant to conservation and development nongovernmental organizations, including to the Wildlife Conservation Society and the AHEAD program.*

MICHAEL D. KOCK *joined the Wildlife Conservation Society's Field Veterinary Program in 2003. He is a veterinarian who works as a conservation practitioner, with a particular interest in the issues of ecosystems and wildlife, and their relationships to human health and well-being.*

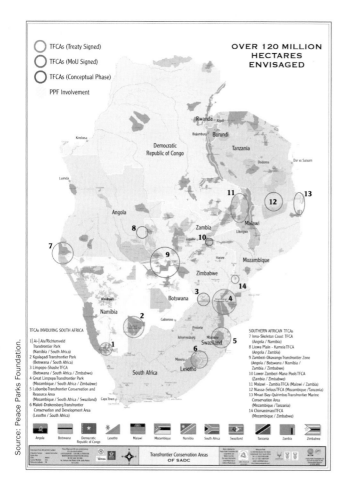

Figure 1. Terrestrial Transfrontier Conservation Areas (TFCAs) of the Southern African Development Community (SADC).

Altogether, the existing and proposed transfrontier parks and TFCAs cover more than 460,000 square miles (1,200,000 km^2), just shy of the area of Texas, California, and New York combined (see Figure 1). A dominant component of the TFCA vision is the reestablishment of transboundary movement and migrations of wildlife within and between larger landscapes. A key economic driver linking these conservation and infrastructure development initiatives is nature-based tourism[2] that seeks to maximize returns from marginal lands in a sector where southern Africa enjoys a global comparative advantage. Nature-based tourism (photographic, trophy hunting, etc.) now contributes about as much to the gross domestic product of southern Africa as agriculture, forestry, and fisheries combined.[3] However, the management of wildlife and livestock diseases (including zoonoses—diseases transmissible between animals and people) within the envisaged larger transboundary landscapes remains unresolved and an emerging issue of major concern to livestock production, associated export markets and other sectors, including public health, in the region.

One could argue that fencing that has separated wildlife and livestock, cutting back on disease transmission, has in many ways been the "simplest" approach to minimizing problems at this interface. But extensive cordon fencing, essentially a subsidy from governments (southern African and donor) historically favoring livestock agriculture as a primary land use, is far from ecologically benign. With fencing cutting-off key migratory pathways that wildlife had used for eons in times of thirst and hunger, real costs have been imposed upon the natural resources sector in many parts of the SADC region. Thus conservationists are excited about the possibility of more land under wildlife, and of expanded benefits-sharing and economic opportunity sustainably linked to sound stewardship of biodiversity. But this excitement is admittedly tempered by the recognition that much remains unknown. Proponents of TFCAs must thus proceed with caution, and perhaps humility, in the face of ecosystems and processes that are not fully understood.

Realities of the Wildlife–Livestock–Human Interface

Whatever the potential of wildlife-based tourism to generate wealth in areas zoned primarily for free-ranging wildlife, the current reality is that small-scale agropastoralists living in the adjacent communal lands depend greatly on livestock for their livelihoods, as of course do many rural people in sub-Saharan Africa. The need to balance their livelihoods and environmental security with the development of alternative land uses and opportunities gives rise to a very complex set of development issues. A central focus of these issues, and one that provides a unifying theme across sectors and disciplines, is that of animal, human and environmental health—"One Health." The concept of "One Health"—with a focus on the interface between human health and that of the environment—is not new.[4] During the 1960s and 1970s visionary attempts were made to construct a bridge between, for example, medicine and agriculture.[5] Innovative applications of these interdisciplinary concepts to disease and natural resource management are now urgently needed in the TFCA context, as TFCAs have the potential to have positive as well as negative impacts on sustainable livelihoods.

A Historical Perspective

The history of human relationships with wild and domestic animals in southern Africa is of course a long one. Livestock arrived in southern Africa between 2,000 and 1,500 years ago from East Africa and were present in the Limpopo Valley, an area shared among Zimbabwe, Mozambique, and South Africa, from about AD 600. Archaeological findings demonstrate that domestic livestock were present alongside wildlife within the area for at least 1,000 years before the introduction of alien/exotic livestock diseases approximately 150 years ago via European cattle.[6]

> Land use and tenure in southern Africa continue to be closely linked to livestock interests and disease-control efforts associated with the standards required for international (and highly subsidized) beef exports.

To this day, land use and tenure in southern Africa continue to be closely linked to livestock interests[7] and disease-control efforts associated with the standards required for international (and highly subsidized) beef exports—largely to Europe. Since the late 1950s, *disease control* has often meant fences to keep wildlife (particularly African buffalo) separated from livestock because of concerns about diseases like foot-and-mouth disease (FMD). A virus, FMD is among the most commercially important livestock diseases worldwide. It is important to note that FMD is associated with high morbidity yet low mortality (i.e., many susceptible animals may experience transient illness, but relatively few die), with most of its effects being related to trade restrictions and other secondary impacts. In other words, a small subsistence cattle farmer not dependent on export markets is certainly inconvenienced by FMD and its transient impacts on livestock productivity, but a variety of common diseases (such

---

BY THE NUMBERS

About half of southern Africa's 47 million cattle are under threat from transboundary animal diseases, despite improvements in regional surveillance and management.

Source: Michael D. Kock.

As carriers of diseases such as foot-and-mouth, African buffalo (*Syncerus caffer*) play a crucial role at the interface between wildlife health, livestock health, and human livelihoods.

as those carried by local ticks, for example) are more likely to affect his livelihood. FMD's impacts are more of an issue for commercially oriented livestock producers, as fears of the virus lead importing countries to close their markets to exporters from areas experiencing FMD.

Getting Off the Fence

Thus, the disease control (cordon) fences criss-crossing much of southern Africa run for thousands of kilometers—with major impacts on wildlife populations.[8] This is an important image as we start to think seriously about reconnecting wildlife areas across international boundaries. Since the 1950s, there is probably no region on Earth where animal health policies have had as tangible an effect upon the biotic landscape as in Africa, where land-use choices are often driven by perverse (domestic and/or foreign) incentives or subsidies that reinforce unsustainable agricultural practices instead of favoring more ecologically sound resource management schemes. This trend has been strengthened by the donor community, with pro-poor development portfolios often emphasizing livestock to the point of excluding wildlife-related options that could be components of a more balanced approach to risk diversification.[9] African nations, no longer able to subsidize the commercial agriculture sector with fences and extensive veterinary services (something colonial governments and later foreign aid had often enabled), should logically benefit from a more sustainable approach to land stewardship and the wildlife–livestock–human interface, as would small-holders and pastoralists: people who derive much of their subsistence directly from livestock as well as natural resources.

Wildlife and livestock diseases, including those that can directly affect people, will likely continue to have a significant impact on the development of sustainable land uses, transboundary natural resource management, biodiversity conservation, and human livelihoods in the marginal lands of southern Africa (see Figure 2).

Case Study: The Great Limpopo Transfrontier Conservation Area

The presidents of Mozambique, South Africa, and Zimbabwe signed the international treaty establishing the Great Limpopo Transfrontier Park in December 2002. Agreement has been reached on creating a TFCA that encompasses the Great Limpopo Transfrontier Park and the intervening matrix of conservancies and wildlife ranches on private land, together with the communal farming areas. The precise boundaries of this vast TFCA (approximately 39,000 square miles or 100,000 km²—almost the size of the state of Virginia) are not yet completely defined, but the primary land use is expected to be wildlife-based tourism with reasonably unimpeded movement of wildlife and tourists.

The Great Limpopo TFCA encompasses several land-

Source: Michael D. Kock.

Cordon fences such as this one in northern Namibia separate wildlife and livestock as part of national and regional disease control efforts.

Figure 2. Conceptual diagram of the linkages among the diseases of wild animals (WA), domestic animals (DA), and humans (H), and the potential implications of disease control strategies for livelihoods, economies at various scales, and conservation.

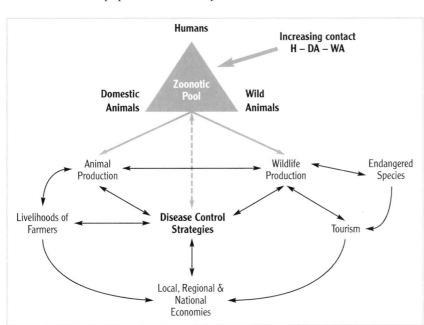

Figure 3. The Great Limpopo Transfrontier Conservation Area (GLTFCA), resulting from a recently internationally agreed land-use plan, brings together South Africa's Kruger National Park, Zimbabwe's Gonarezhou National Park, and Mozambique's Limpopo National Park (these 3 parks comprise the core of the Great Limpopo Transfrontier Park), along with Mozambique's Banhine and Zinave National Parks, and surrounding lands. The core area involved is almost 14,000 square miles (36,000 km²), with the broader GLTFCA matrix covering approximately 39,000 square miles (100,000 km²).

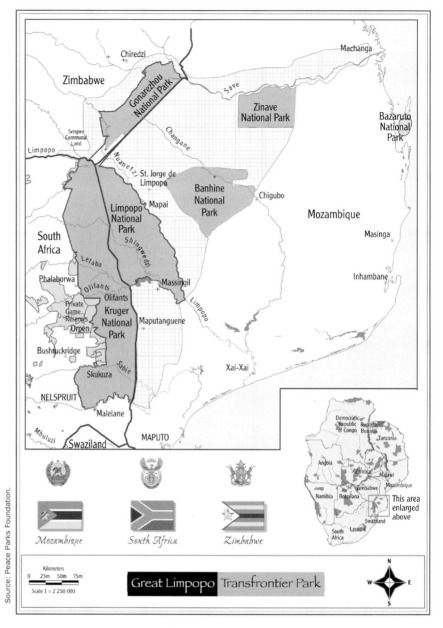

use/land-tenure regimes, including five national parks, state and private safari and hunting areas, conservancies and game ranches on private land, small-scale agropastoral farming areas under communal tenure, large-scale commercial irrigation schemes, and smaller irrigation schemes within the communal areas (see Figure 3). About 35 percent of the area comprises state protected areas and a further approximately 10 percent is private land under wildlife. Most of the remaining land, the matrix between the designated national parks, is under communal tenure with varying forms of small-scale agropastoralism.

The extraordinary conservation and economic opportunities represented by this transboundary concept are matched in magnitude by the management challenges such a land-use complex poses—not the least of which relates to the management of biologically and economically important diseases contagious between wildlife and livestock and, for some pathogens, people. The control and containment of livestock diseases have, in the past, relied heavily on fences and the control of domestic and wild animal movements and translocations. The prospect of removing barriers to wildlife and livestock movement therefore has major implications for animal health and disease control strategies within the Great Limpopo TFCA and will likely have broader implications for livestock disease control, livestock production, and export market access for the three countries involved.

Priority Animal Diseases in the Great Limpopo Transfrontier Conservation Area

Some of the animal health issues of greatest concern in the Great Limpopo TFCA include the following:

- The breakdown of controls for FMD related to ongoing political and economic chaos in Zimbabwe and the virus's spread (including novel strains of FMD) within the southeastern sector of the country.
- Evidence of a return of the tsetse fly to the Save-Rundi junction area of the Gonarezhou National Park in Zimbabwe. The southern expansion of the tsetse fly and trypanosomiasis is thus of concern, again, because official tsetse control programs in Zimbabwe have essentially collapsed. Apart from information on the control of tsetse flies during the 1970s, and some recent information on the spread of the fly, little published information is available on animal health and diseases in the Mozambique sector of the TFCA, although that is gradually changing. Trypanosomiasis here affects cattle and can affect some wildlife species such as white rhinos (*Ceratotherium simum*)—but fortunately not people (although human trypanosomiasis is an issue in more northern reaches of the SADC region). South Africa's Kruger National Park has not seen trypanosomiasis since 1903 and, with the largest white rhino population on Earth—doesn't want to see a resurgence of this disease.
- The northward spread of bovine tuberculosis (a zoonosis) across the entirety of Kruger National Park,[10] with buffalo and other species involved. Its possible entry into Zimbabwe and its status in Mozambique are of great concern.

It is critical to remember from history that many of the diseases affecting the Great Limpopo ecosystem are essentially alien invasive species, and are either already negatively impacting biodiversity or have the potential to do so. Today, bovine tuberculosis is found across South Africa's Kruger National Park but as yet has not been thoroughly studied in the wildlife of Zimbabwe's Gonarezhou

National Park. It has not been found in a preliminary survey of cattle in the intervening Sengwe Communal Land to the north of the Limpopo River, nor via initial wildlife and livestock disease surveillance in and around Mozambique's Limpopo National Park. Although hard data on the incidence of zoonotic diseases in Great Limpopo TFCA communities are largely unavailable, the high incidence of HIV/AIDS in the region increases the threat posed by zoonoses like bovine tuberculosis. Rabies is a serious public health problem in Mozambique's portion of the Great Limpopo TFCA (vaccination and stray dog control are inadequate, and children often suffer the consequences) but had never been reported in Kruger until 2006, when a side-striped jackal in the north of the park represented the first reported case, thought to be related to a deteriorating domestic dog rabies situation across the border in Zimbabwe. Canine distemper has not yet threatened the wild carnivores of the region.

Because the basic premise of the GLTFCA vision is reconnecting the various wildlife areas in this landscape, it is imperative not to allow any wildlife corridors we create to inadvertently become biological bridges for dangerous pathogens to utilize to travel to new areas where they can exploit naïve wildlife, as well as the livestock and people nearby—depending on the specific disease agent. This issue is not about interfering with nature—it is about the importance of trying to help a system already perturbed by diseases that in many cases don't belong there to reestablish a state wherein disease does not threaten vital conservation and development objectives.

Health as a Logical Entry Point for Conservation and Development Efforts

As in the Great Limpopo example, addressing disease challenges at the wildlife–livestock–human interface is critical to successfully facilitating wildlife as a socioculturally acceptable and economically rational land-use choice. If local people—whose very livelihoods are often closely linked to livestock-keeping at the household level—see expanding contact with wildlife as a threat to the health of their animals, or even to their own health in the case of zoonotic diseases, what hope do we have for building strong local constituencies for conservation, something the last several decades have hopefully taught us is sorely needed for sustained success?[11] Education and outreach efforts are critical in the face of disease threats that involve or are believed to involve wildlife: we ignore local perceptions at the peril of our conservation mission.

Addressing human health concerns in the context of our work should not be seen as diminishing the importance of critical conservation issues, but rather can actually be utilized to reinforce the value of maintaining biodiversity and the importance of respecting wildlife and wild places.[12] Done thoughtfully, linking human health with wildlife and environmental health can enhance the relevance of nature to a much broader constituency. Similarly, livestock disease control issues must be addressed within a broader environmental context that considers not only biodiversity conservation but, as importantly, the long-term provision of key environmental goods and services that the improvement of human livelihoods depends on.

Cross-Sectoral Approaches Critical

Too frequently, decisions focused on single resources have had multiple adverse resource and economic consequences. Examples include the control of foot-and-mouth disease via game fencing to support a subsidized beef export market in Botswana and the control of tsetse fly in the Zambezi Valley in Zimbabwe. In Botswana, inappropriately sited FMD fences decimated major wildlife populations[13] and preempted many sustainable wildlife tourism options. In Zimbabwe, subsistence farmers rapidly migrated into marginal areas cleared of tsetse fly where they overwhelmed the indigenous culture, displaced a rich wildlife resource, and developed an area that now depends on food aid in most years.[14] Tackling disease and designing pest control schemes within a framework of environmental and social impact assessments, coupled with the use of science-based epidemiological approaches, would contribute to more integrated and sustainable interventions. Utilizing extensive fences to control transboundary livestock diseases like contagious bovine pleuropneumonia, which does not actually involve wildlife at all, undermines potential options for other land uses that might rival livestock in terms of productivity per unit area and sustainability, particularly the types of land uses envisioned for TFCAs.

If those of us whose mandate is biodiversity conservation do not proactively address the threats that the politically and economically powerful livestock sector associates (rightly or wrongly) with wildlife and disease, our vision for protected areas (and TFCAs) in many parts of the world will likely fail. And if our job is to help make wildlife conservation a socioculturally acceptable and economically rational land-use choice, then leveling the playing field by identifying perverse incentives that support environmentally unsustainable agricultural practices becomes a critically important strategy. Southern African TFCAs may provide some excellent models within which to study and mitigate the pressures from and responses to the real political and socioeconomic tensions between biodiversity conservation and livestock agriculture (both commercial and smallholder) in the broader region. Given the economic importance and political clout of the livestock sector in much of southern Africa, proponents of biodiversity conservation ignore the livestock sector's concerns (and the policy constructs largely put in place at that sector's behest) at their own risk.

Recognizing and addressing issues emerging at an intensifying wildlife–livestock–human interface will be of critical importance to successful biodiversity conservation (as well as to public health and agribiosecurity). Conservation and development donors have been learning, over time, that biodiversity conservation does not occur in a vacuum but, rather, needs to be undertaken within a complex socioeconomic matrix that must be (1) recognized and (2) understood, not disregarded if said matrix does not fit with preconceived notions of how biodiversity's future can be secured. We all must continue to learn from disciplines with which we may not have communicated well (if at all) historically, and we must consciously work to break down sectoral barriers and the walls each discipline's technical language and vocabulary help to reinforce. Can the donor community, steeped in the traditions of monosectoral approaches, also make this integrative leap? We believe it can, but it will require a broadening of perspectives, an openness to ideas that, although potentially unfamiliar to many, are grounded in sound biomedical and ecological principles.

While challenges at the wildlife–livestock–human health interface are perhaps amplified by the scale and inherent complexity of TFCAs, these challenges are not unique to TFCAs or even new. These same issues of course impact conservation and development initiatives at a range of scales. Whether we are looking at a large, complex international land-use matrix such as a TFCA or at a small, isolated protected area surrounded by human-dominated activities, these issues simply merit more attention than either the conservation or development communities have given them to date. With a healthy respect for the complexity of the social-ecological systems we care about and adequate resources to fill key gaps in knowledge, a successful "One Health" approach in southern Africa and beyond is certainly within our grasp.

An Ounce of Prevention

Lessons from the First Avian Influenza Scare

WILLIAM B. KARESH AND KRISTINE SMITH

During the first years of the twenty-first century, most people on Earth learned that somewhere between 10 million and 200 million of us could die in an epidemic that would radically change how we work in the world. *Bird flu* suddenly became a common term from Europe to Indonesia, where villagers in the most remote areas could name the new disease, Flu Burung, that caused their chickens to fall dead at night.[1]

Governments and international agencies developed programs to prevent the spread of the disease or attempt eradication. Private industry moved from complacency to contingency planning. Thousands of scientists and journalists became overnight experts on pandemic influenza, and hundreds of millions of dollars were committed to fund new research. Wild birds—represented in the Old World by thousands of years of reverence in Chinese art, and in the Western Hemisphere by the works of John J. Audubon—suddenly became harbingers of pestilence. Governments in Asia and eastern Europe began inanely calling for the killing of wild birds to prevent the spread of the virus, even though 30 years of experience has shown that the only effective way to control

WILLIAM B. KARESH *is director of Wildlife Health Sciences (WCS) and has directed the Field Veterinary Program for the Wildlife Conservation Society since 1989. He is leading efforts in the Congo Basin to reduce the impact of diseases such as Ebola, measles, and tuberculosis on endangered species and people. He co-chairs the World Conservation Union (IUCN) Veterinary Specialist Group, and is currently chief of party for the Wild Bird Global Avian Influenza Network for Surveillance (GAINS).*
KRISTINE SMITH *obtained her veterinary medical degree from Tufts University School of Veterinary Medicine and completed a zoo and wildlife medicine residency at the Bronx Zoo. She is an international field veterinarian for the Wild Bird Global Avian Influenza Network for Surveillance (GAINS).*

the spread of the disease is to improve sanitation practices for poultry production and trade.

At a point in time when over 50 million US citizens described themselves as bird enthusiasts,[2] they heard that birds could spread a deadly disease around the world. Ironically, by 2007, the press in the Western Hemisphere had become less interested in avian influenza, even though more countries, more people, and more of the world's food supply were affected or at risk than ever before.

What have we learned from this experience?

The Nuts and Bolts of Avian Influenza

Influenza viruses are RNA viruses and hence, unlike DNA viruses such as herpes or hepatitis, they replicate without an internal mechanism that reduces mutation. As a result, genetic alterations occur continuously. These changes are selected by how successful the virus is at infecting and reproducing in new hosts. In the "r and K" terminology of ecologists, they are the r-selectors, producing millions of offspring with survival of only those with the best sets of genes. (K-selectors are like people, having relatively fewer offspring but investing heavily in the survival of each one.)

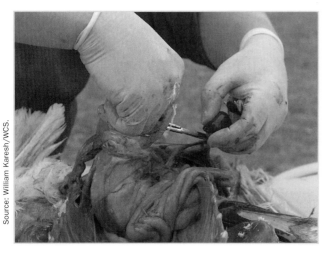

Source: William Karesh/WCS.

A field veterinarian necropsies a whooper swan (*Cygnus cygnus*) in Mongolia to determine whether any viral strains of avian influenza are present.

Influenza viruses are notable because they are segmented, and the genetic segments are interchangeable. Think how common General Motors cars would be if all the replacement parts fit any brand of car they made. Some of the gene segments affect how the virus attaches or sticks to the host cell it infects. There are 12 known types of these segments, and they are referred to as hemagglutinin segments. Other segments affect the ability of the virus to replicate and leave the infected cell to infect new cells. There are 16 known types of these segments, referred to as neuraminidases. The current avian influenza virus has the type 5 hemagglutinin and the type 1 neuraminidase, hence the name *H5N1*. In our lifetimes, we are all exposed to many of these influenza virus segments as they circulate around the world, and we develop at least partial immunity. Unfortunately, few people alive today have any immunity to H5N1 influenza because we have not been exposed to either H5 or N1 segments.

The 192 theoretical combinations (12 Hs times 16 Ns) of avian influenza viruses are called influenza A viruses. They can infect birds and mammals (including humans). Influenza B and C viruses infect humans but are not found in birds. Just as certain bacteria and viruses normally live in humans without causing major problems, avian influenza viruses have lived in relative harmony with water birds for thousands of years. Among wild migratory waterfowl of the Northern Hemisphere, which have the best-understood relationship with avian influenza viruses, the viruses are spread from bird to bird during the breeding season in northern latitudes, when millions of birds congregate. In humans, we would consider the effect of the virus akin to the "stomach flu" because avian influenza normally affects the intestinal tract.

Those of us who work with viruses keep them in freezers to preserve them for years. Arctic pools full of viruses freeze too, efficiently preserving the viruses until the thaw the following year when birds return to breed and raise their young. Individual birds get the flu, shed the virus, and then recover and stop shedding. But every year, millions of young birds hatch, contract the viruses in their environment, and help to perpetuate the strains. On top of that, an avian or mammal host can be infected with several strains of virus at the same time, and those interchangeable virus segments do what they normally do. Thus new strains are constantly being formed within hosts and being shed, infecting other animals immediately and contaminating pools of water for years to come.

Because this disease–host relationship has long existed, wild birds have adapted to avian influenza viruses. As a general rule, infectious organisms need living hosts in order to perpetuate themselves. However, when natural barriers are broken and avian influenza is transmitted from wild birds to an unnatural host like poultry, the virus is capable of, depending on the strain, causing serious disease. Because the poultry industry cannot afford to have severely lethal strains of avian influenza in its flocks, avian influenza viruses are categorized by the impact they have on chickens. They are termed highly pathogenic only if they cause greater than 50 percent mortality in domestic chickens (not domestic ducks, geese, or quail). With genetic analyses, we now can see that these highly pathogenic strains have two gene sites that allow them to reproduce, one requiring intestinal enzymes and the other not so specifically limited: that second gene allows highly pathogenic avian influenzas to grow in brain, lung, and liver tissues and causes rapid, massive infection. When the mutated highly pathogenic Asian strain of H5N1 spilled back to wild birds from poultry in China,[3] it killed wild birds, something not seen since 1962 when there was a mass mortality of wild terns in South Africa. Recent research suggests that some wild duck species may be resistant to this current strain of virus.

Spreading the Disease

Keeping birds for food is one of our oldest practices. Backyard chickens are still common in much of the world and, before rapid global movement of people and animals, were of little threat to global health even if they contracted a serious disease because they were confined or died before contacting other birds.

> Influenza viruses are notable because they are segmented, and the genetic segments are interchangeable.

BY THE NUMBERS

As of January 2008, there were 348 cases of avian influenza in humans, with 216 deaths.

> The international trade of animals and animal products, along with modern transportation, allows a virus that has long been constrained to one part of the world to suddenly appear in another place within a day or two.

Yet, over thousands of years, rare events of influenza jumping from chickens to people did occur, leading to global pandemics that are only now understood.

At the other end of the spectrum, well-run, large-scale poultry operations fastidiously control the movement of people, vehicles, equipment, and birds into their farms to prevent the accidental introduction of an errant virus or bacterium. Typically, workers change clothing before entering an area where poultry are housed, and all delivery and transport trucks for chickens or turkeys pass through a disinfecting car wash. Neither birds nor feed arrive unless they come from a certified pathogen-free supplier.

In between these two extremes of relatively safe poultry production falls the bulk of poultry raising in much of the developing world: large-scale operations with little to no disease-control mechanisms in place. In Asia, over 10 billion domestic chickens, ducks, and geese are raised every year in such systems. Here is where a fairly benign avian influenza virus of wild birds changed in domestic geese, ducks, and chickens into the current highly pathogenic H5N1 strain. In nature, a rapidly fatal disease will become extinct if it kills all of its hosts, but in artificial systems we can override this normal course by continually supplying new animals to give pathogens a place to reproduce, mutate, and contact more hosts to maintain the chain of infection, like continually feeding a fire when it would otherwise burn out.

By the first part of this century, tens of millions of domestic ducks and chickens were becoming infected with H5N1 and being allowed to move among farms and markets. Poor or poorly used vaccines suppressed the signs of the disease without eradicating the underlying infection, resulting in millions of domestic infected birds shedding and spreading the virus undetected as they were moved and traded. Worse yet, the production of ducks in Asia relies heavily on raising them on flooded rice fields, which led to contamination of these wetland areas and subsequent infection of wild birds.

Alongside the poorly secured poultry systems that fostered the creation of highly pathogenic H5N1 avian influenza, traditional marketing systems help spread the disease. In much of the world, particularly in places without refrigeration, people bring their birds to "wet markets" where the

Source: Tony Martin.

International trade—both legal and illegal—in poultry and poultry by-products plays a major role in the spread of avian influenza due to inadequate disease control mechanisms at many large-scale poultry operations.

animals are sold live. Vendors often return home with unsold stock, and infected birds may be purchased and leave the markets alive, either for consumption or to be added to another flock elsewhere. Uninfected animals easily contract the virus in the markets and can shed it for days before showing signs of illness.

Some of the markets to which infected birds are brought for sale are also filled with pet birds, reptiles, and wild mammals, frequently brought from other countries or continents through the illegal animal trade. In these markets, different species from far regions intermingle with each other, livestock, and humans. The international trade of animals and animal products, along with modern transportation, allows a virus that has long been constrained to one part of the world to suddenly appear in another place within a day or two.

Taken altogether, this unnatural contact between species defies natural boundaries and provides opportunity for infectious agents to infect new species. And because viruses and bacteria produce millions of offspring at hourly or daily rates, any of them with even the slightest genetic variation may adapt to thrive in a new host species, for example, humans.

Bar-headed geese (*Anser indicus*) suffered from an outbreak of H5N1 at Qinghai, China, in 2005.

Halting the Spread

Although eliminating wet markets would decrease the spread of disease, the economics and cultural traditions behind these practices make this solution impractical in the near future, particularly where the lack of electricity and refrigeration limits meat storage. But the risk of spreading disease could be significantly reduced by tightening trade, sanitation, and biosecurity regulations and by improving surveillance and law enforcement. Eliminating wildlife trade would also be a solution.

Furthermore, traditional methods of monitoring disease are no longer sufficient. Simple disease risk assessment models fail to address the complexity of a global animal trade that makes natural geographic and host barriers obsolete. Compounding the problem is poor communication. The study and management of zoonotic diseases involve people from many disciplines (livestock vet-

Illegal wild animal markets such as this one in Medan, Sumatra, showing ducks, quail, dogs, and rabbits caged closely together, contribute to the spread of H5N1. Infectious diseases can be transmitted easily from avian to mammalian hosts under stressed conditions.

Source: Peter Clyne/WCS.

erinarians, wildlife biologists, wildlife veterinarians, human physicians, epidemiologists, public health workers, government staff, and nongovernmental organization staff). Communication among these disciplines has historically lacked cohesion and timely information sharing; during the panics of outbreaks, communication often becomes nonexistent. No one organization or agency is mandated with, or currently capable of, addressing all of the infectious diseases that are shared among people, wildlife, and domestic animals.

An Ounce of Prevention

The biggest lesson learned from past disease outbreaks is that they should have been prevented. This is often forgotten over time, and resources invested on prevention inevitably come to appear of little value. The public health sector suffers from the fact that if it spends its money well, no one notices. A similar problem exists in animal husbandry. In the wildlife field, disease management is difficult because access to animals is so limited. Therefore, disease prevention is critical in protecting wildlife populations. Preventing the spread of H5N1 avian influenza from infected poultry into wild bird populations may be difficult, for example, but it is far more possible than trying to remove the disease from wild migratory birds. Because nearly a century has passed since the last global bird flu pandemic, it is probably natural that we have ignored prevention in recent years. But we are now in the midst of another avian influenza pandemic threat. Since 2005, billions of dollars have been spent on developing and stocking pharmaceuticals to treat humans if a pandemic occurs. Far less has been spent on eliminating the disease itself at the source, namely, controlling this disease in chickens and domestic ducks. If the same resources were applied to this source, infection of both humans and wildlife would cease.

We are powerless unless we reach across disciplines to fight global disease together. Both prevention and control start with communication and are empowered by cooperation. Thousands of individuals and groups are studying avian influenza, but unless the knowledge learned is shared rapidly, it will benefit few. Realizing this, many organizations are using technology to revolutionize science. Historically, scientific knowledge has been kept secret until publication, but that system—important as it is to evaluating and rewarding academic research—doesn't serve the global good when we are racing to stay a step ahead of disease. Academic institutions and granting organizations could contribute by rewarding faculty and researchers for quickly releasing information to publicly accessible systems. Further, prestigious journals such as *Nature* and *Science* should accept scientific submissions that include findings already made available to the public.

Fortunately, researchers, governments, and stakeholders are investing in information-sharing networks that collect scientific findings and make them available in "real time." Strides are also being made to become proactive in disease surveillance, testing humans and animals before a disease becomes endemic to an area. This is essential for preventing large-scale outbreaks and

Source: William Karesh/WCS.

A vendor in Bangkok, Thailand, selling birds for the Buddhist practice of "merit release," in which captive animals are set free as a peace offering. Releasing market birds back into wild populations may enable the transmission of avian influenza.

BY THE NUMBERS

Thirty of thirty-three provinces in Indonesia are infected with avian influenza. About 60 percent of Indonesian households keep chickens in their backyards or shared yards, and Indonesia has the highest number of H5N1 human fatalities, at 87 as of October 2007.

costly interventions. The threat of avian influenza has stimulated the creation of governmental preparedness plans, funding for surveillance efforts, and new diagnostic technologies, which are being shared among countries and continents at an unprecedented level. The Wild Bird Global Avian Influenza Network for Surveillance—which supports field and lab work on influenza in wild birds and provides mechanisms to manage and share research openly—is demonstrating that dozens of organizations and hundreds of scientists from a wide variety of disciplines can work together at a large scale to contribute to problem solving. The need to improve and sustain such multidisciplinary approaches to disease in the face of waning public interest could be one of the more significant lessons learned through facing bird flu in the twenty-first century.

But the main lesson of avian influenza remains the importance of dealing with major infectious diseases "upstream," before they reach epidemic proportions. Investments made to effectively control and prevent the spread of H5N1 in the early years of this century in Asia would have spared the world fear of a pandemic, saved human lives and human livelihoods, and prevented the slaughter of hundreds of millions of domestic birds and the needless death of tens of thousands of wild birds. Even now, focusing on control and eradication of this disease in poultry could protect humans and wild birds alike, preventing a pandemic and improving the lives of millions of people who rely on domestic chickens and ducks and quail for protein as well as income.

Finally, avian influenza's lesson is that poorly controlled human movement of animals, both domestic and wild, around the world, is a health threat. The lack of regulations, poor law enforcement, and inadequate inspection and testing can all lead to both the emergence of new diseases and rapid global spread. Humans have irreversibly altered the protective barriers between species and geographic separations that nature provided for millennia.

BY THE NUMBERS

Over 317 species of birds, as well as a small number of domestic and wild mammals, have been affected by West Nile virus. In 2007, there were 3,107 incidences of West Nile virus-related illnesses.

Why Wildlife Health Matters in North America

JOHN R. FISCHER

Many of the most significant diseases involving wildlife populations affect a trinity of players—wildlife, humans, and domestic animals—and involve a tangle of transmission routes. Wildlife may be a source of disease agents to poultry, livestock, and humans, but diseases just as easily spill over into wild populations from these sources. Unfortunately, people have released infected animals into the wild, provided feed and bait to wildlife, and owned and traded wildlife, which often elevates the risk of disease outbreaks. Wildlife health matters in North America because the disease interactions between wild and domestic animals are growing and disease can threaten human health, agricultural productivity, and rural economies in addition to valuable wildlife populations.

The Value of Wildlife

The substantial economic value of wildlife in the United States amply justifies increased attention to wildlife health issues. Although wildlife's aesthetic, ecological, nutritional, and educational values are difficult to quantify, there are useful proxies: every five years, the US Departments of Interior and Commerce survey how much Americans spend on consumptive and nonconsumptive wildlife-recreational activities to estimate the economic value of free-ranging wildlife. Consumptive wildlife recreation includes hunting, fur trapping, and scientific research, whereas nonconsumptive recreation includes feeding wild animals and viewing and photographing them. The two

---

JOHN R. FISCHER is professor of population health and director of the Southeastern Cooperative Wildlife Disease Study (SCWDS) at the University of Georgia's College of Veterinary Medicine. He has degrees in wildlife biology, veterinary medicine, and veterinary pathology.

A scrub jay (*Aphelocoma coerulescens*) gets up close to a birdwatcher. Nonconsumptive wildlife recreation activities like birdwatching and photography contribute to the economic value of wildlife.

forms of recreation can be viewed together because many people participate in both, and their combined economic value is indisputable. (Privately owned wildlife species, such as cervids [elk and deer] and furbearers, are not included in these economic assessments.)

The US *2006 National Survey of Fishing, Hunting, and Wildlife-Associated Recreation* reported that more than 38 percent of the population (87 million residents) participated in some sort of wildlife-related activity. Total expenditures for all wildlife-related activities were estimated to be $120 billion, representing approximately 1 percent of the entire gross domestic product.[1]

Hunting deserves additional attention because hunters spend approximately $23 billion per year, and many of the benefits serve rural areas. Taxes on hunting equipment also generate significant revenue through the Federal Aid in Wildlife Restoration Act (Pittman-Robertson Act of 1937). These funds are allocated to states based on land area and licensed hunters, matched with state dollars, and used to acquire, restore, and improve wildlife habitat. Pittman-Robertson currently provides $190 million each year for habitat and wildlife management,[2] including research important to conservation, such as the location, natural history, and population trends of species.

Nonconsumptive wildlife recreation is an even larger field. In 2006, US residents spent $45 billion to feed, observe, or photograph wildlife, generating additional economic benefits via travel and jobs in parks, refuges, and outdoor clubs.[3] Participation in most wildlife-associated recreation in the US has steadily increased and is projected to continue growing: there was a 155 percent increase in the number of bird watchers between 1982 and 1995, and noncon-

Hunter with elk meat. Hunting generates significant revenue for North American wildlife management agencies.

sumptive wildlife use such as viewing and photography is projected to increase 61 percent by the year 2050.[4]

Experience has shown that the presence of disease—whether real or perceived—in wild animals diminishes public enthusiasm for wildlife recreation and sets off economic ripple effects. In 2002, intense media coverage following the detection of chronic wasting disease (CWD)—a transmissible spongiform encephalopathy in the same family as mad cow disease—caused a 10 percent decrease in sales of deer hunting licenses, and a consequent decrease in revenue to the state of Wisconsin.[5] But this aversion can have further impacts: reduced hunting can hinder an agency's ability to manage game species populations as well as diseases, particularly when the disease management strategy includes public hunting to reduce host population density and decrease disease transmission opportunities.

Wildlife and Domestic Animal Health

Wildlife has often been implicated as a transmitter of disease to domestic animals. The spread of relatively benign avian influenza from wild birds to farmed poultry was widely reported. However, many domestic animal health problems are often the result of poor livestock and poultry husbandry. In North America, complex disease interactions now challenge traditional livestock management and jeopardize the hard-won successes of national disease eradication programs. For example, livestock diseases such as bovine tuberculosis (TB) and brucellosis that were inadvertently introduced to native populations of elk, deer, or bison have subsequently spilled back to livestock, with significant economic ramifications for meat and dairy producers. Unfortunately, the high commercial stakes increase political conflict between wildlife interests and domestic animal interests.

A veterinarian examines a bison calf. Bison are susceptible to many diseases that occur in cattle and other livestock, such as malignant catarrhal fever (MCF) and tuberculosis. Herds raised for meat must be carefully monitored.

Michigan's bovine TB experience illustrates the complexity of disease interactions when they involve wildlife, and, unfortunately, how human activities can exacerbate epidemiological risk factors. In 1994, bovine TB was found in a single free-ranging white-tailed deer in the northeast part of Michigan's Lower Peninsula. It was initially regarded as an isolated infection. However, in 1995, follow-up surveillance found 12 more infected deer, marking the first time that bovine TB had become established in the wild in the US.[6] It is widely believed that this disease emergence was precipitated by large-scale baiting and supplemental feeding of deer—for viewing and easier hunting—that artificially inflated the deer herd beyond the land's carrying capacity. Feeding stations also congregated deer that would otherwise have naturally dispersed, greatly enhancing disease transmission between deer. Thereafter, bovine TB was transmitted from the deer reservoir to numerous other species, including black bear, bobcat, coyote, raccoon, opossum, and elk.

By early 1998, bovine TB had moved to cattle, and Michigan subsequently lost its accredited TB-free status. Although one potential transmission route to cattle is direct contact with deer, TB does not require direct contact: the bacteria have been shown to survive on feedstuffs commonly fed to deer,[7] and calves became infected after exchanging pens with infected deer or consuming uneaten deer feed.[8] To date, 41 infected dairy and beef herds have been identified, and Michigan is now divided into two zones according to TB status, requiring extensive testing of cattle prior to movement.

> Disease agents do not distinguish between publicly owned game and nongame wild animals, or privately owned production animals.

The primary strategies to eradicate bovine TB have been to ban baiting and feeding of deer, reduce deer numbers in the affected area, detect and remove infected cattle, and physically separate deer and cattle. Since 1994, the costs are estimated to have been more than $100 million—incurred by testing more than 153,000 hunter-killed wild deer, indemnifying cattle owners for the destruction of their herds, testing cattle in the affected zone, fencing, and public education. In addition to the financial costs, Michigan agricultural and wildlife agencies lost significant public good will as they imposed stringent regulations to try to manage the disease. Although bovine TB has been reduced in wild deer, it will be many years, if ever, before it can be eliminated from all wildlife, and the continued presence of this disease reservoir poses a constant threat to the Michigan cattle industry.

Since late 2005, bovine TB has also been found in cattle herds and in wild deer in northwest Minnesota as well.[9] This strain of bovine TB is similar to strains found in cattle in the southwest US and Mexico, suggesting the disease may have been introduced to the area by human-assisted movement of animals, because neither wild nor domestic animals can travel that far on their own. The extent of infection in wild deer in Minnesota remains unknown.

One of the most problematic disease interactions between wildlife and livestock is bovine brucellosis in parts of Idaho, Montana, and Wyoming. Brucellosis has been recognized in bison since 1917 and in elk since the early 1930s, and was probably introduced via European cattle.[10] The disease was eradicated from cattle throughout most of the United States, but Wyoming lost

BY THE NUMBERS

US$16.1 billion: The global animal health product market in 2006 for wild animals and livestock. Europe, North America, east Asia, and Latin America held 97 percent, leaving 3 percent to all of Africa and south Asia.

its brucellosis-free status in 2004, and Idaho lost its in 2006 following transmission of *Brucella abortus* from infected elk to cattle.[11] The loss of brucellosis-free status increases regulation and costs for cattle producers, and fear of transmission naturally limits cattle ranchers' tolerance for elk or bison—the wildlife reservoirs of the disease—near grazing areas. Managing any disease in free-ranging wildlife is technically challenging. When state and federal animal-health and natural resource agencies, a national wildlife refuge, two national parks, and citizens' groups defending both the local cattle industry and wildlife all become involved, the complications multiply.

Wildlife management successes have helped elk and deer numbers rebound in much of North America, resulting in increased interactions among wild animals as well as between wild and domestic animals, and sometimes leading to contention between wildlife and livestock interests. However, livestock and wildlife advocates share substantial common ground. Both groups fear the introduction of foreign animal diseases, and both value population health management over individual animal treatment. Both groups are also losing farmland, grazing land, and wild areas to strip malls and subdivisions. Such shared interests call for enhanced cooperation on disease issues among wildlife and animal-agriculture agencies and the many related advocates. After all, disease agents do not distinguish between publicly owned game and nongame wild animals, or privately owned production animals. Transmission of diseases between domestic and wild animals will always be a two-way street—there would not be a concern about bovine TB and brucellosis moving from deer, elk, or bison to cattle today if these diseases had not originated from infected cattle in the past.

Human Health

Wildlife health matters because of the threat of new disease pathways to humans as well. Approximately 75 percent of emerging pathogens are zoonotic, and many are associated with wild animals. In North America, several reemerging or new zoonotic pathogens pose threats.

Bovine TB, for example, is fully capable of infecting humans, and two human infections have been documented in Michigan, one the direct result of a hunter field dressing a tuberculous deer.[12] Another disease that can afflict humans is rabies. A raccoon-associated strain of rabies virus was endemic to the southeastern corner of the United States. However, in the 1970s this strain was introduced to the mid-Atlantic region via illegal translocation of raccoons for hunting. Since then, it has spread throughout the eastern US and into the Midwest and Canada, resulting in tens of millions of dollars spent on animal testing, oral vaccination of wild raccoons, post-exposure treatment of humans and pets, and at least one human fatality.[13]

In another instance, over 70 people contracted monkeypox virus introduced into the US via imported African rodents in 2003. This virus—which had already

BY THE NUMBERS

Whirling disease affects fish in the trout and salmon families, and has been found in 24 US states, either in wild fish or in hatcheries. The parasitic disease damages cartilage and causes fish to swim in an uncontrollable whirling pattern, rendering them unable to properly function.

People often facilitate wildlife/human disease transmission, as was the case when African rodents imported to the United States for the pet trade infected native prairie dogs (above) that were sold as pets.

killed many people in Africa—spread to native prairie dogs assembled at an exotic pet distribution facility.[14] Fortunately, monkeypox does not appear to have spread to free-ranging rodents, although there were numerous opportunities for it to do so. Although previous outbreaks of zoonotic disease, such as tularemia and plague, in pet prairie dogs did not precipitate regulatory changes,[15] the monkeypox episode was well publicized and resulted in new regulations prohibiting the import, transport, sale, and release of prairie dogs and six species of African rodents.

These cases highlight that wildlife disease matters directly to human health and that people often facilitate wildlife-associated disease. The trend for artificial "management" practices is on an upswing and includes deer farms, shooting enclosures, animal translocation, and wildlife feeding stations. People in the US seem to be more willing to pay for and less willing to work for gratification, whether by watching wild animals at a feeder, shooting a deer over bait, or hunting exotic species like nilgai (*Boselaphus tragocamelus*) in Texas or wild swine in Michigan. We can expect to see more health problems in humans, wild, and domestic animals as a consequence.

Managing Wildlife Health for Everyone's Benefit

The threats that diseases pose to wildlife, domestic animals, and humans warrant the dedication of increased time and resources. Unfortunately, even though agencies try to prevent outbreaks, disease management is often put into effect after an outbreak has started. The most frequently applied disease control technique is population reduction—culling. Additional methods include remote delivery of oral vaccine for rabies in wild carnivores, or separating wild and domestic animals. The limited management tools available makes developing innovative protocols extremely challenging. There have been recent successes in epidemiological research and disease monitoring. These increase our understanding of disease behavior in wildlife and population responses and allow us to better predict what might occur in a given scenario, particularly when management of the disease is not possible.

Among state wildlife management agencies, some wildlife health programs are excellent, whereas other states have only rudimentary wildlife health services. The tide does seem to be turning, however, and wildlife health programs have been created in states that previously had no dedicated resources: wildlife veterinarians have been added to at least seven states' agencies.[16] Some state agencies have also pooled resources to form regional wildlife health cooperatives that promote information-sharing and a more uniform approach to common disease problems affecting several states, which has helped standardize protocols and leverage limited resources. For example, the midwestern and western wildlife health cooperatives are consortia of individual state and provincial wildlife health programs, several of which are strong because they have dedicated infrastructure and staff to disease issues for many years.

> People in the US seem to be more willing to pay for and less willing to work for gratification, whether by watching wild animals at a feeder, shooting a deer over bait, or hunting exotic species like nilgai in Texas or wild swine in Michigan. We can expect to see more health problems in humans and wild and domestic animals as a consequence.

The oldest of the cooperative wildlife health programs is the Southeastern Cooperative Wildlife Disease Study (SCWDS). Founded in 1957 at the University of Georgia's College of Veterinary Medicine, this cooperative provides wildlife health services to agencies in 16 states and Puerto Rico, and to the US Department of the Interior (DOI) and the US Department of Agriculture's Animal and Plant Health Inspection Service (APHIS). Through this cooperative approach, funds from individual SCWDS member states are combined with funds from DOI, APHIS, and faculty grants and then leveraged to develop and disseminate much more up-to-date health and disease information to all involved.[17]

BY THE NUMBERS

In northern Canada, 40 percent of the former range of the wood bison would be available for wood bison reintroductions if it were not for the presence of brucellosis and bovine tuberculosis in the current herds in Wood Buffalo National Park.

Source: William Karesh/WCS.

Field veterinarians weigh a radio-collared pronghorn. The health of this animal is a reflection on prey availability and the overall quality of its environment.

Recognizing the uneven capability among states to effectively address wildlife health, the Association of Fish and Wildlife Agencies has developed a National Fish and Wildlife Health Initiative. This will build capacity among state fish and wildlife management agencies to address disease issues and to minimize the impacts on wildlife. Through the lens of wildlife health, this initiative will combine policy, resources, information sharing, and training, disease surveillance, research, and management strategies. Adequate and sustained funding is also essential, as is better public outreach to gain the acceptance and assistance of stakeholders and the public for programs to prevent or reduce disease problems involving wild animals. Finally, a continent-wide health plan is being drafted in coordination with Mexico and Canada; such coordination will cover a vast continent with porous borders.

Disease diminishes wildlife numbers and the value of wildlife to our economy and society. Funds generated through wildlife-associated recreation are substantial, and game and nongame species enhance our quality of life in North America. This is more than enough reason to champion the best possible management of wildlife health. Indeed, responsible stewardship of all wildlife resources mandates attention to disease: the increasingly complex disease interactions between domestic animals, wildlife, and humans mean that wildlife managers and the policymakers who approve their budgets should prioritize increased research, surveillance, and management of disease agents in North American wildlife.

Warming Oceans, Increasing Disease

Mapping the Health Effects of Climate Change

RITA R. COLWELL

Climate change is a current focus of extensive discussion nationally and internationally, notably on the potential effects it will have on societies and the environment. However, complex factors associated with climate change and human health—specifically the influence of climate change on infectious diseases—are rarely included in predictive models.[1] Although the problem is complicated and the interactions involved are both multidisciplinary and interdisciplinary, human health must be considered if the global effects of climate change are to be understood. Ocean and land surface annual temperatures have increased, with sea surface levels predicted to rise accordingly.[2] These two factors, sea temperature and rising sea levels, will likely exacerbate infectious diseases in some warmer, wetter places, but also in parts of the world that are currently considered relatively disease-free.

A US surgeon general's report in the mid-1960s declared the war on infectious disease to be over, claiming that new, powerful antibiotics rendered infectious diseases remnants of human history. However, infectious diseases today are an even more serious threat to global health, mainly because of the multiple antibiotic-resistant strains of many disease agents, such as the various bacteria causing tuberculosis and staphylococcal infections. Acute respiratory infections, including pneumonia and influenza, are the leading killers. For children under the age of five, waterborne infections—notably the diarrheal

RITA R. COLWELL is Distinguished University Professor at the University of Maryland and at Johns Hopkins University Bloomberg School of Public Health, and senior advisor to Canon US Life Sciences, Inc. Her focus is on global infectious diseases, water, and health. A geological site in Antarctica, Colwell Massif, was named in recognition of her work. She acknowledges colleagues in Bangladesh at the International Centre of Diarrhoeal Diseases Research.

diseases—remain a serious concern, especially for developing countries.

Cholera, a diarrheal disease caused by bacteria native to the aquatic environment, has afflicted humankind over the ages, evidenced by reference to what most probably was cholera in ancient Sanskrit writings. Pandemics began occurring in India and Bangladesh in the early 1800s. Until the nineteenth century, the disease was generally confined to the Indian subcontinent, but it erupted in Europe and the Americas with the first recorded pandemic in 1817. The second North American pandemic occurred in 1832 and included New York,

> Cholera had been believed to be transmitted only by person-to-person contact, but the bacteria are now recognized to exist naturally in the environment.

Philadelphia, and Washington, DC. Altogether, seven global pandemics of cholera have occurred over the past 200 years, spreading illness and death. They continue today, with serious consequences in many countries, including Latin America and Africa.

In 1977, *Vibrio cholerae*, the bacterium that causes cholera, was isolated from the Chesapeake Bay in Maryland.[3] This finding was the first report of the cholera vibrio in the environment of a non-cholera-endemic geographical area: no major cholera outbreaks had been reported in Maryland since around 1900. Subsequently, the cholera vibrio has been shown to be a native inhabitant of the Chesapeake Bay and other bays, estuaries, and rivers of temperate and tropical regions, and these waters are now known to be reservoirs of these bacteria. That discovery of an environmental source of cholera shifted the medical community's understanding of the disease—cholera had been believed to be transmitted only by person-to-person contact, but the bacteria are now recognized to exist naturally in the environment. They have been observed to have a dormant stage in the environment between epidemics.[4]

Vibrio cholerae populations peak twice annually (in the spring and fall) in association with plankton blooms. A relationship between sea-surface temperature and onset of cholera epidemics was discovered in the 1980s, with the seasonal pattern of cholera following the seasonal rise and fall in sea-surface temperature and sea height.[5] The concomitant relationship between the cholera bacteria and plankton populations was also discovered: in the spring, with warmer surface

BY THE NUMBERS

Mexico identified 27,000 cases of dengue fever in 2006, more than four times the number in 2001. Dengue viruses are transmitted between people or between monkeys through mosquitoes of the genus *Aedes*. Dengue fever is the most common vector-borne disease of humans, infecting some 50 million people in tropical and subtropical regions of the world each year.

water and sunlight, phytoplankton become abundant. The surge in phytoplankton is followed by blooms of zooplankton feeding on the phytoplankton. Zooplankton blooms are associated with increases in cholera bacteria because the vibrios actually make up the natural flora of the copepods (microscopic crustaceans that are a major component of the zooplankton bloom). Thus a definable relationship between sea-surface temperature, sea-surface height, and cholera epidemics was established for Bangladesh.[6]

In 1991–1992, an unprecedented cholera epidemic occurred in Peru, resulting in approximately 200,000 cases and 5,000 deaths. Cholera had not been reported in South America for nearly 100 years, and, notably, the epidemic occurred during an unusually strong El Niño cycle (which is associated with a warmer-than-usual Pacific Ocean and changing wind and rainfall patterns). When the next El Niño was predicted in 1997–1998, scientists prepared to study the relationship between cholera and El Niño events. In 1997, as El Niño caused the sea-surface temperature off the coast of Latin America to rise, cholera bacteria appeared, associated with plankton. The numbers of the bacteria increased from spring to summer in South America (September 1997 to March 1998), and cases of cholera increased, with a slight lag (late November through the summer of 1998), showing significant correlation with sea-surface temperature and clearly indicating an influence of El Niño events on cholera epidemics.[7] The complex interactions of sea-surface temperature, sea-surface height, zooplankton populations, and related environmental parameters such as El Niño now provide a predictive model for cholera epidemics that draws on data obtained from climate monitoring via satellite sensors and environmental field data.

Given our new perspective of biocomplexity, global warming can be expected to profoundly change the pattern of infectious disease. Cholera, which is so strongly influenced by the environment, is but one example. Climate change is also likely to influence the geographic range and intensity of diseases that are vector-borne, particularly those carried by mosquitoes or other insects. Both traditional vector-borne diseases and cholera may pose public health threats in many parts of the world that have not seen them for centuries, and their resurgence may undo global efforts to eradicate them.

Global warming may allow more—and varied—vector pathways for those diseases that thrive in warmer weather, for example, malaria, hantavirus, and dengue fever. In temperate climates, winters may no longer be cold enough to kill insects that carry parasitic diseases. Most vector-borne diseases exhibit a distinct seasonal pattern, suggesting their carriers are weather sensitive. Another vector-borne disease that may spread in response to changes in climate is Rift Valley fever, a mosquito-borne disease of sub-Saharan Africa. Heavy rains are associated with its onset, and the disease can persist in reservoirs of wild and domestic animals.[8] Although disease transmission by vectors is complex and unique for each disease—and actual epidemics are dependent on human

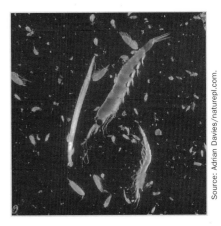

Marine zooplankton blooms are associated with increases in cholera bacteria.

BY THE NUMBERS

Both drought and flood can trigger malaria epidemics: During El Niño years, the death toll from malaria increased by 36 percent in Venezuela, and in northwest India, malaria epidemics increased by 500 percent.

Cholera epidemics often occur in poverty-stricken areas, such as this slum in Indonesia. The disease spreads via contaminated food or water.

Source: Curt Carnemark/The World Bank.

populations, health care, and ecological factors—it is safe to say that if parts of the world receive increased rainfall or flooding, human populations near those areas could experience increased waterborne bacterial outbreaks like cholera, rodent/fleaborne diseases, and mosquito-borne diseases.[9]

Climate change is already significantly affecting Earth's biological systems, with even more severe effects predicted. The climate models developed to date, however, do not include human factors such as global infectious disease. Human health cannot continue to be omitted from predictive models. The complex interaction of humans, cholera bacteria, plankton, and other environmental factors provides an example and can offer a reasonable prediction for future cholera disease outbreaks. Climate-driven diseases, in general, may prove similarly measurable. Thus, understanding and modeling the role of climate change on infectious diseases is paramount for a holistic understanding of the consequences of global climate change and, certainly, for establishing policies that address societal needs related to global change.

BY THE NUMBERS

Lassa fever, occurring in northern and central Liberia, has caused five deaths as of April 2007, and at least 13 people have been infected. The disease is transmitted by the saliva of rodents and by the excrement and urine of the multimammate mouse (*Mastomys natalensis*).

Conservation Controversy

To Cull or Not to Cull?

BARRY ESTABROOK

From a common-sense perspective, it seemed like a workable, albeit controversial, disease-control program. At least that's what British wildlife officials and farmers thought back in the early 1970s when they embarked on a massive campaign to eradicate badgers from large areas of the UK. Bovine tuberculosis was rampant in the country and getting worse. Badgers were susceptible to tuberculosis. Cattle grazing near setts—the large communal tunnel systems in which European badgers live—could catch the disease from badgers, who foraged for earthworms in the same fields where cows grazed. Wherever infection-carrying badgers lived, you would inevitably find afflicted cattle, and vice versa. The solution? Eradicate all badgers in an area, or as many as you could, in order to eliminate the reservoir for the disease.

Even though the badgers (*Meles meles*, a different species from North American badgers) are beloved by the British public, the government bowed to the demands of farmers who were losing money because of the disease—which can also spread to humans who consume unpasteurized milk. At first, cyanide gas was pumped into setts. But eight years into the program, when a pair of badgers were exposed to the gas in a laboratory experiment, it became clear that they suffered horrendously in the process, so the government switched tactics. Badgers were caught in cage traps and shot. It was more humane, but no more effective. Over the course of two decades, upward of 30,000 badgers were killed. It wasn't until the mid-1990s that officials asked whether the culling program, so clearly effective in theory, was

BARRY ESTABROOK is a contributing editor at Gourmet *magazine. He contributes regularly to the* New York Times *and is the author of two crime novels published by St. Martin's Press. His work has been anthologized in* The Best American Food Writing.

actually working. Were cattle in the culled areas catching TB at a lower rate?

In the past, few wildlife managers bothered to ask themselves that question, even as culling was used in programs to control disease in such diverse animals as bison, elk, deer, skunks, foxes, raccoons, wolves, lynx, bats, African buffalo, and wildfowl. Both politicians and the public saw culling as a crude but necessary weapon against epidemics in animal populations, especially those that could spread to domestic animals or humans. Often, culling was the only "cure" at a manager's disposal.

To analyze the tuberculosis-control program, Britain's Department for Environment, Food and Rural Affairs called Rosie Woodroffe, a specialist in badger behavior who is now at the Zoological Society of London. She and her associates did what no one had done before. They designed what is perhaps the largest controlled experiment in wildlife conservation history. In it, certain rural areas underwent complete eradication of badgers, while in other areas, badgers were only killed in specific localities where tuberculosis was prevalent. Most importantly, in certain control areas the badgers were left unharmed to go about their business, whether they had TB or not. In all, the 30 different experimental sites covered 7,400 acres (3,000 ha). After seven years, the results proved a shock to many. Around culled areas, the incidence of tuberculosis in cows was 25 to 29 percent *higher* than in the areas where badgers were left alone. "If you understand badger behavior," says Woodroffe, "you can see how culling was making matters worse."

The flaw had nothing to do with the neat logic behind culling as a general strategy and everything to do with English badgers' specific living habits. According to Woodroffe, undisturbed groups of badgers are extremely territorial. Because they ferociously fend off trespassers from other colonies, undisturbed badgers rarely have contact with outsiders, and therefore outbreaks of tuberculosis tend not to spread from one sett to another. But if the social balance is disrupted by culling many badgers, something akin to a land rush results, as badgers from surrounding areas move in and compete with each other over turf. In the process, the disease spreads far afield, not only to more badgers, but to cattle as well. And the more you cull, the worse the situation becomes. "Every time we went back to repeat the culling, the prevalence went up," says Woodroffe. "By the fourth cull, we had doubled the prevalence of infection. From first principles, culling made perfect sense. But unfortunately it failed to take into account the real importance of badger behavior. It wasn't something that anyone other than a behavioral ecologist would have predicted."

Animal behavior is only one of the obstacles that make

Source: Andrew Parkinson/naturepl.com.

Tens of thousands of European badgers (*Meles meles*) were culled during the 1970s in an effort to prevent the spread of tuberculosis between the badgers and cattle.

> Politicians and the public saw culling as a crude but necessary weapon against epidemics in animal populations, especially those that could spread to domestic animals or humans. Often, culling was the only "cure" at a manager's disposal.

Pile of red deer carcasses (*Cervus elaphus*), waiting to be airlifted by helicopter after culling, Scotland. Hunting of red deer has been used as a method of population control.

culling impractical. The reproductive biology of a species is another. In Europe, there have been attempts since the 1980s to control rabies in foxes through extensive hunting, trapping, and poisoning, yet there is no evidence that the widespread effort has actually reduced the disease. Marc Choisy, of France's Institut de la Recherche pour le Développement, has created a theoretical model that offers explanations for this apparent contradiction. His work may even explain why across-the-board culling could be making rabies outbreaks worse. "Birthrates and death rates often depend on the density of a species' population," he says. "When the density is lowered, and in culling this is usually through killing older, mature animals, the survivors have more resources at their disposal, and the birthrate rises. You end up with a lot of young animals." Choisy points out that it's easy to create a vicious circle: the more animals you cull, the more offspring are born and survive, so you have to cull even further to maintain the same level of population.

It's the older members of the group that often have immunity to viral diseases (like measles or chicken pox in humans). Unexposed young animals are highly susceptible. So what might have happened in the European rabies program was that an older population of animals with resistance was replaced by a young population. "Basically, it appears that in cases like this, culling is

Major eradication programs have been implemented in an effort to control the spread of diseases such as rabies. Red foxes (*Vulpes vulpes*) were the victims of one such attempt.

a good way to increase the susceptible part of the population," Choisy says.

The bottom line, according to Choisy and other wildlife experts, is that there is very little scientific data showing either positive or negative results from culling campaigns. "We don't know if they will work," says Dr. Gary Wobeser, a professor of veterinary pathology at the University of Saskatchewan. He undertook an exhaustive search for data on the subject for his comprehensive book *Investigation and Management of Disease in Wild Animals*. "The whole basis of culling is usually the assumption that the spread of disease is dependent on the density of the population. If you reduce the population by half, there should be half as much transmission of disease. But that's not generally applicable. Diseases are all different," Wobeser says. For a correlation in human health, measles is a density-dependent disease. Unless you have a population of 250,000 to 300,000 people coming into contact with each other in an area, measles will die out.

Wobeser's research did provide a clear idea of the sorts of culling programs that definitely do not work, such as those conducted over expansive geographic areas. One problem is that it's very difficult to kill a large enough percentage of animals to have an effect. Fruit bats are thought to be a reservoir for the Ebola virus that has decimated gorilla populations in western Africa. Some well-meaning gorilla advocates have proposed culling the bats by gassing their roosts. But how are you going to find and kill a mean-

> It also makes little sense to cull a species that has a high birth rate. Such animals have evolved to take advantage of drops in their numbers by filling the gaps with huge numbers of offspring.

ingful number of mobile bats scattered throughout equatorial jungles? Even if you could, the cost would be prohibitive and there is the likelihood that other "collateral" species could also be killed by poison gas targeted at bats.

It also makes little sense to cull a species that has a high birth rate. Such animals have evolved to take advantage of drops in their numbers by filling the gaps with huge numbers of offspring. And animals that live in herds are also poor candidates. Research on bison shows that when overall numbers are reduced over a large area, the remaining bison find each other and congregate at the same density of animals, just in fewer herds, leaving the rate of exposure to each other unchanged.

That said, Wobeser has come across a couple of examples where it appears that culling may have been successful. "If you can use culling in a localized situation where you can put very high pressure on a population for a long enough period of time against a disease that hasn't established itself in the area, that may be effective." He points to Ontario's efforts to prevent the spread of raccoon rabies from the United States. When the disease appeared there in 2001, biologists immediately launched what amounted to a full-court press. Whenever a single case of raccoon rabies came to their attention, the officials killed all raccoons and striped skunks found within a 3-mile (5 km) radius of the infected animal. This amounted to nearly 90 percent of the entire raccoon population in the areas hit by rabies. In a radius between five and fifteen kilometers of the outbreak, raccoons and skunks were trapped, vaccinated by injection, and released. Oral baits containing vaccine were dropped from airplanes over an even larger area, and in cities and towns where aerial distribution was impractical, baits were set out manually. In all, more than 600,000 baits were distributed from Ottawa to the US border. More than 10,000 animals were culled, and although the program succeeded in stopping the spread of the disease, the cost was enormous, CAD$1,500 per hectare, or at least CAD$2 million per year.

Culling may also work as a way to prevent the spread of epidemics that move slowly and in one direction, rather than in all directions from a central point. When rabies broke out in skunks in Saskatchewan, Alberta created a 20-mile-wide "fire line" against the approaching virus from the east by killing skunks along its border with the neighboring province, an approach also called "barrier

African fruit bat (*Rousettus aegyptiacus leachi*). Fruit bats are suspected carriers of the Ebola virus, but culling them would be strategically complicated and costly.

BY THE NUMBERS

Ghana reported its first case of H5N1 outbreak in May 2007, after 100 chickens died each day for three days. In response, 1,700 chickens were slaughtered to prevent further spread. In September 2007, 32,600 ducks were culled in Panyu district of China to prevent the spread of H5N1. In October 2007, 50,000 chickens were euthanized in Saskatchewan, Canada, to prevent the spread of H7N3.

Wood bison (*Bison bison athabascae*), Wood Buffalo National Park (WBNP), Canada. Culling of wood bison has been a controversial issue. Proponents claim that the kills will help to eliminate brucellosis and tuberculosis throughout the herds, but opponents feel that disease management is much more complex.

depopulation." Similarly, geographic barriers or bottlenecks, such as steep mountainsides, helped officials to concentrate culling efforts against a rabies outbreak that was advancing toward a Swiss valley.

But attempts to control rabies through culling have produced some truly horrific eradication programs. Wobeser describes an attempt to control rabies in Alberta in the 1950s that resulted in the gassing, poisoning, and shooting of an estimated 50,000 foxes, 100,000 coyotes, 4,200 wolves, 7,500 lynx, and 1,850 bears. These animals seem to have died for no reason: during the same outbreak, Saskatchewan and Manitoba did no culling, and yet the epidemic disappeared from those provinces just as quickly as it did in Alberta.

Despite such evidence, wildlife managers still find themselves under pressure to cull at the first sign of disease, especially if it is a malady that can spread to livestock or humans. Avian influenza epitomizes this difficulty. Even in view of evidence that it won't work, governments in several Asian countries stand ready to use widespread culling of wild birds and waterfowl to stop the spread of avian influenza. "Culling is clearly not the right solution there," says Dr. Damien Joly, a wildlife epidemiologist with the Wildlife Conservation Society. "We don't know what bird species carry the disease. We don't know what effect density has on transmission of the disease. And there are concerns that the act of culling could help disperse the disease—when you start firing shotguns, the ducks in a pond scatter far and wide."

Still, Joly understands how wildlife managers come under heavy pressure to cull. "Governments or the public decide to do something, and culling may be the only tool available." But the public often sends contradictory messages. A prime example is the plight of bison that roam outside Yellowstone National Park, many of which have brucellosis, a disease that can spread to cattle. Ranchers want any errant bison shot to protect livestock from possible contact with the disease. Environmentalists say that the open range is public land and bison are a natural part of it. Emotions run high, so wildlife biologists find themselves caught in the crossfire. "A lot of culling efforts are aimed at species that are not hugely popular with the public—animals like skunks and vampire bats," says Wobeser. "But if you are trying to reduce the populations of animals people like, then you run into problems."

> Wildlife managers still find themselves under pressure to cull at the first sign of disease, especially if it is a malady that can spread to livestock or humans.

Joly ran into precisely that problem working with a state management team to control chronic wasting disease (CWD) a contagious illness that eventually kills. The disease appeared in deer in 2002 in south-central Wisconsin, and just as the Ontario officials had done when faced with rabies, the CWD management team singled out areas surrounding cases of CWD for extensive culling campaigns to reduce the numbers of deer and thereby transmission of CWD.

And that's where Joly encountered his people problem. Science notwithstanding, some landowners didn't share his interest in determining whether culling could be an effective way to control CWD and signed a petition protesting intensive deer reduction. Many had an emotional attachment to the deer on their property or simply felt that hunting was cruel. Others had a visceral dislike of the thought of hordes of hunters and government sharpshooters swarming over their land for extended open seasons, gunning down fawns and does as well as bucks. Because of patchy participation, it remains to be seen whether the culling worked.

Any culling program is bound to be met with vociferous resistance from animal advocacy groups. "I strenuously oppose culling," says D. J. Schubert, a wildlife biologist who works for the Washington, DC–based Animal Welfare Institute. "Using culling as a method of wildlife management is a shortcut. Let's face it, it's much cheaper to buy a bullet or hire a sharpshooter than it is to solve the complex ecological problems that have caused a disease.

"In some cases, such as when you are dealing with serious diseases that can be transmitted to humans, you can't afford to take a lot of time. There's going to be a public outcry if you wait. But in other cases, brucellosis for example,

> "The act of culling could help disperse [avian influenza]—when you start firing shotguns, the ducks in a pond scatter far and wide."
> —Dr. Damien Joly

you are not dealing with a disease that's all that serious."

Most wildlife managers feel that there is a middle ground, that careful, extremely focused culling efforts do have a place in disease management in wildlife and are sometimes the best chance they have. "There is certainly an irony here," says Joly. "We all care about individual animals, and the idea of culling can be distasteful. But sometimes—especially in an environment that humans have so drastically altered—you have to put the needs of the group above the needs of the individual. The science of controlling wildlife diseases is in its infancy—these are the early stages of our discipline. To be frank, we have had only limited success controlling wildlife disease with other strategies. Nobody wants just to let diseases go rampant. It's a societal decision of whether the cure is worse than the disease."

By the Numbers

The economic impacts of the Nipah virus outbreak in Malaysia in 1997–1998 was estimated at US$350 to $400 million. The 2001 foot-and-mouth disease outbreak in England and Europe was estimated to have cost markets almost US$20 billion.

This

has been the time of the finishing off of the animals.

They are going away—their fur and their wild eyes,

their voices. Deer leap and leap in front

of the screaming snowmobiles until they leap

out of existence. Hawks circle once or twice

around their shattered nests and then they climb

to the stars. I have lived with them fifty years,

we have lived with them fifty million years,

and now they are going, almost gone. I don't know

if the animals are capable of reproach.

But clearly they do not bother to say good-bye.

HAYDEN CARRUTH
ESSAY

PART III

EMERGING ISSUES IN THE WILD

Each species we discover, learn about, and protect helps preserve the richness of our planet. The Wildlife Conservation Society, other organizations, and the authors here dedicate their efforts to understanding and conserving wildlife and wild places. To do so, they take many avenues. One is careful wildlife science, highlighted in the section, "Conservation of Wildlife." We must also understand habitat needs and protect landscapes, as the section, "Conservation of Wild Places," illuminates. Another avenue toward conservation is working with people, via education and by understanding natural resource needs of local communities, as shown in the section, "People, Culture, and Conservation." But even if we get all this information right, actually putting conservation into action depends on the political and social contexts created by many other compounding factors, illustrated in the section, "The Art and Practice of Conservation."

The global nature of pressing conservation emergencies requires efforts in all these facets of work. For example, the conservation of amphibians, whose numbers are being decimated by chytrid fungus, requires rescuing vulnerable populations, research on the fungal disease, captive breeding at zoos, education, and conservation of frog habitat around the world. Similarly the conservation of the last 3,000 to 5,000 wild tigers requires work across eight countries, science, habitat preservation, work with local communities, and addressing the illegal trade in tiger parts. The following sections detail emerging issues in the conservation of wildlife, wild places, human culture, and the art and practice of execution to provide lessons for future conservation.

Conservation of Wildlife

This section covers emerging issues in the conservation of some of the world's lesser-known wildlife. They are not necessarily "flagship" species, yet the challenges of conserving them provide fascinating lessons. Taken together, the essays in this section illustrate our deep cultural connection to these species and highlight the importance of long-term field conservation.

The first essay, "The Last of the Great Overland Migrations," lays out the broad-scale conservation needed to sustain long-distance ungulate migrations, whether of determined pronghorn in the US or saiga antelope in Mongolia.

Every volume in the *State of the Wild* series highlights one particular species, and vultures are this year's "Species in Focus." "Downward Spiral: Catastrophic Decline of South Asia's Vultures" describes how wildlife scientists responded to vulture declines in Asia.

The third essay provides a lesson on the evolving state of ecosystems threatened by invasive species, focusing on reptiles, in "Conserving Cold-Blooded Australians."

Finally, "Settling for Less: Disappearing Diadromous Fishes" documents journeys of salmon, sturgeon, and eel through rivers and coastal waters, and how our amnesia constrains their conservation.

The authors, all dedicated wildlife biologists at the tops of their fields, have taken conservation stories that are local in scope and broadened them to reflect common threats and shared challenges in the global conservation of wildlife.

The Last of the
Great Overland Migrations

JOEL BERGER

Before dawn, I awoke to a star-studded sky. Sound travels further in the cold, and, in my semiconsciousness, I thought I heard soft shuffles passing somewhere near my Alaskan cabin. My watch read 4:00 a.m. Perhaps it had been a dream. I snuggled back into my sleeping bag. After first light, I stepped outside and scanned ridgelines. The eastern mountains were already awash in pink, and Square Lake was not the same as yesterday. Slicing across its frozen surface was a swath of freshly churned snow. Nearly half a mile long, the path flared in and out, like an accordion stretching with each note.

The first caribou of spring had arrived. By afternoon others trundled past, concave hooves clicking on ice, snorts and grunts bringing the frozen lake to life. Within a few weeks, 50,000 more would arrive. The migration would be in full swing, completing a cycle that has replenished the tundra since the melting of the Talkeetna glaciers in this part of central Alaska. Called *xalibu* by Micmac Indians of the Canadian Maritimes, the name *caribou* means pawer or shoveller, which aptly describes the feeding behavior of this gregarious hoofed mammal. This population had traveled day and night and was heading farther into Alaska.

To many people, long-distance migrations bring to mind gray whales swimming from Mexican to Arctic waters, or Arctic terns that fly more than 20,000 miles (32,200 km) annually. Across much of the planet, species use migration—

JOEL BERGER is a senior scientist based in the Northern Rockies Field Office of the Wildlife Conservation Society in Missoula, Montana. He is also the John J. Craighead Chair in Wildlife Biology at University of Montana. His current efforts concentrate on the development of conservation strategies to protect long-distance migration and wide-ranging movements in terrestrial mammals both in Mongolia and in western North America.

seasonal treks that require moving away from a home area and back again—as an ecological strategy. Among land mammals, these treks also arise as variants of a common theme: survival. In mountainous areas, it is often the progressive greening of grass that spurs animals upward in elevation and the snows of autumn that force them down. In arid regions, patchy rains attract animals to areas of new plant growth, a dynamic well known among the big herds of wildebeest and zebra in eastern and southern Africa. Several species migrate to find safer calving grounds. But these ecological strategies do not tell the whole story of overland migrations. For many species, we know that they migrate, but not why.

Caribou from the Central Arctic herd, migrating near Franklin Bluffs and the Sagavanirktok River, south of Prudhoe Bay, Alaska.

Alongside the sheer strain of traveling great distances, overland migrators face significant perils. Not unexpectedly, wolves hunt caribou, and hyenas follow wildebeest, targeting their young. Some species can outdistance predators, but the round-trips still require crossing open spaces, swimming rivers, and—most importantly in our modern world—navigating fences and other challenging structures.

Freeways, railway tracks, cities, large agricultural areas, and suburbs bisect lands that were prime pathways for ungulate migrations not long ago. It is these increasingly numerous structures that make scientists believe we will lose many of the world's long-distance migrations over the next 20 years.[1] Once lost, migrations are rarely regained. Traditional tools of habitat restoration and species reintroductions will likely not succeed in re-creating a wildlife migration generations after it has stopped.

Migration routes usually map both inside and outside of national parks and protected areas. They also span international boundaries—elephants from Namibia cross into Angola, pronghorn from Mexico into Arizona, and caribou between Alaska and Canada. The maintenance of transboundary movements is politically thorny, and regulation of a species can differ on either side of a border. Because conservation of long-distance migrations can be geographically complex, only innovative conservation efforts—planned and implemented on the largest of scales with the collaboration of scientists, conservationists, wildlife enthusiasts, hunters, ranchers, herders, and politicians—can combat the attrition of these marvelous wildlife spectacles.

More than 95 percent of large mammal migrations and routes have disappeared in the last 100 to 150 years. Notable among these were the migration of thousands of springbok and perhaps a quarter million wildebeest roaming freely from the Kalahari, Karoo, and Etosha pans of Botswana, South Africa, and Namibia.[2] These populations plummeted to just 10 percent of their former abundance in part because of fencing, mining, and slaughter for food. It is unclear how reduced numbers translate to loss of migration impetus. It may be that populations reduced beyond a certain point do not migrate simply due to a loss of knowledge.

In North America, the 20 to 40 million bison that once moved across the plains are gone. Although remnant herds still dot the landscape in isolated parks such as Badlands and Yellowstone, no bison migration routes into and out of Yellowstone National Park remain. Similarly, pronghorn antelope once migrated throughout the 22,000-square-mile Greater Yellowstone Ecosystem (GYE). Based on historical journals and altered landscapes, it is estimated that pronghorn have lost 80 percent of their migration pathways, and elk tread less than half of their historic routes.[3]

These losses have occurred in the GYE despite the fact that this area includes a fair amount of protected land: two national parks, six national forests, and four national wildlife refuges. In less protected regions throughout the Great Plains and Rocky Mountains, corridors and preferred paths used by wildlife were lost more quickly.

Although it seems like an era of animal history is winking out, what remains is still inspiring. A 2004 global analysis of 103 migratory populations representing 29 species of mammals from all continents (except Australia) shows that the greatest overall movement is performed by barren-ground caribou (*Rangifer tarandus*).[4] Caribou inhabit tundra and woodland regions of North America, Europe, and Asia, with many populations descending to less snowy regions in winter. They are the world's true long-distance overland migrator. Some groups cover more than 1,800 miles (2,900 km) per round-trip, a distance equivalent to

> Some species can outdistance predators, but the round-trips still require crossing open spaces, swimming rivers, and—most importantly in our modern world—navigating fences and other challenging structures.

Source: Julie Larsen Maher/WCS.

Pronghorn antelope (*Antilocapra americana*) obstructed by fencing. In the developed world, fences, roadways, and residential areas block pathways that not long ago served as routes for migratory species.

marching from Mexico into Canada. Those from Alaska's Arctic National Wildlife Refuge move more than 2,400 miles per round-trip. The caribou's migration is far longer than that of another hardy long-distance migrant, the Serengeti's wildebeest (*Connochaetes taurinus*).

The average distance of all wildebeest migrations is about 270 miles round-trip, but those in the Serengeti traverse 420 miles. The movement of more than a million animals, creating clouds of dust, is rivaled by no other current wildlife spectacle on Earth. However, outside the Masai Mara and Serengeti, unregulated poaching and agriculture pose significant interruptions to this phenomenon.

Around the world, the diversity of overland migrators and the magnitude of their treks are striking. In Africa, elephants average 120 miles a trek, and some zebras travel up to 200 miles. In Tibet, the beige and tan antelope of the alpine steppe known as chiru (*Pantholops hodgsonii*) migrate seasonally across the high plateaus, moving an estimated 360 miles from areas around Xizang to birthing grounds near Shar Kul. Having already experienced a 90 percent population decline in the past century, the chiru now face fencing and grazing encroachments on their migration paths. Out on the eastern steppes of Mongolia, white-tailed gazelles (*Procapra gutturosa*) push 500 miles per year. Another antelope, the small, timid saiga (*Saiga tatarica*), with their large probosces, migrate across the steppes of Kazakhstan and the desert of Mongolia. Although their trek in the Gobi desert remains a mystery, one radio-tracked adult female marched 150 miles in less than two weeks. Other saiga move through a narrow (less than 5 km wide) suture zone that connects two subpopulations.[5]

Source: Julie Larsen Maher/WCS.

The small southern pudu (*Pudu puda*), found only in Argentina and Chile, migrates short distances in search of vegetation.

South America, too, has many unique, though less well traveled, migrating species. These include mountain tapirs, two native members of the camel family—guanacos and vicuñas—and two relatively unknown deer, the taruca and the smallest deer in the world, the pudu (*Pudu puda*). Tarucas (*Hippocamelus antisensis*) are speckled yellow-brown animals of open environments now restricted to the far south, in the central Andes, that move about their home ranges according to the seasons. These five species all travel modest distances, none more than fifteen miles round-trip. (Europe's only long-distance migrators are Scandinavian moose [*Alces alces*]—known locally as elk—and they average 100 miles.)

Most people are aware that caribou, bison, and zebra herds migrate, but few realize that nonherd mammals also get the travel bug. In North America, the solitary sojourns of moose into the northern boreal forests take them nearly 180 miles as they seek out safe birthing grounds or food. Alternately, one might assume that musk ox (*Ovibos moschatus*), being hoofed and northern, migrate. They do not; known as a residential species, they remain in areas of decent food and light snowfall throughout the long Arctic winter. And, surprising to most, Utah's little black-tailed jackrabbits (*Lepus californicus*) seasonally shift ranges by up to seven miles.

Opportunities to witness the spectacle of migration are quietly vanishing, not just from Yellowstone or southern Africa, but from virtually every region of the globe. If conservationists are to protect the last of the great overland migrations, long-term studies of animal movements are critical to influence land-use planning and to guide wildlife management.

Among the challenges is documenting migratory routes in Asia, South America, and Africa, where funds spent on wildlife research pale in comparison to efforts in the US, Canada, and Europe. The disparity becomes clear if we compare the American West, where we have extensive data sets on migration movements, to central Asia, where chiru and saiga were only first radio-collared in 2006. In the American West there are at least 15 studies of radio-collared bighorn sheep (*Ovis canadensis*) moving between deserts and mountain areas, 30 studies of elk (*Cervus elaphus*), and at least a dozen of pronghorn (*Antilocapra americana*). Yet, during the first effort to radio-collar saiga in far western Mongolia, thirteen saiga were captured and eight radio-collared. Collar failures and mortality due to golden eagle predation and unknown causes reduced the sample to six. This reflects the inevitable challenges of highly remote fieldwork and the fact that resources to undertake such research in less-developed countries simply do not exist. Finally, a challenge in any country is discovering more about smaller species' migrations—like that of the black-tailed jackrabbits. Efforts to document the more diminutive terrestrial migrants are only just beginning.

Monarch butterflies (*Danaus plexippus*) migrate farther than any other butterfly species. Every year, three successive generations of Monarchs make a single round-trip journey of over 2,000 miles, from the first generations' birthplaces across the US and Canada to wintering grounds in central Mexico and back north in the spring.

Source: Julie Larsen Maher/WCS.

Greater Yellowstone Ecosystem Migrations

Yellowstone is known for distinct geothermal geysers, grizzly bears, and, more recently, reintroduced wolves. But what has slipped the notice of park and tourism planners is that the GYE harbors the greatest remaining migrations of four large ungulates in the Western Hemisphere. Moose from Grand Teton undertake longer round-trip travels than moose elsewhere in the contiguous US (approaching 60 miles), as do elk (130 miles). Mule deer (*Odocoileus hemionus*) that winter in Wyoming's Upper Green River Basin move almost 200 miles to their summer ranges.

Most surprisingly, we now know that pronghorn antelope in southwestern Wyoming have the second-longest land migration in the Western Hemisphere after caribou. Although the average round-trip journey for the species is about

67 miles, pronghorn in the southern GYE can move four times as far—from wintering grounds in the Upper Green River Basin to summer grounds in Grand Teton National Park, and back again—making them the marathoners of the pronghorn world; they even outdistance many African ungulates. They migrate in part to get to birthing grounds in Grand Teton, but their other reasons remain unknown. Their 300-mile route weaves through a corridor that they and other species have used for 6,000 years. However, natural gas wells, access roads, and more than 175 fences around ranches and subdivisions now force the animals to pass through increasingly narrow topographic bottlenecks, some no wider than 350 feet—a challenge for a 1,000 pronghorn to file through. These obstructions threaten to turn them around partway through their journey, and eventually destroy their annual migration.

Long-distance migrations are still relatively intact in the GYE because it is one of the few large ecosystems in the continental US where suites of prey and predators still interact. Mule deer, moose, elk, and pronghorn have moved for millennia in this landscape and thereby serve to delineate the boundaries of the ecosystem, just as the boundaries of the Serengeti ecosystem are defined by its wildebeest.

Sadly, and perhaps understandably, given economies that thirst for energy, both the pronghorn and mule deer migrations are being squeezed by poor, short-term, or nonexistent land-use planning. Although public lands are just that—lands for multiple public uses—there seems to be an indifference to protecting wildlife migrations for public enjoyment. With each passing year, development intensifies in and around the public lands that anchor the Greater Yellowstone system, eroding opportunities to establish permanent protection. In the southern portion of the GYE, the number of existing gas wells is currently fewer than 1,000, but is expected to quadruple over the next decade.[6]

> Given economies that thirst for energy, both the pronghorn and mule deer migrations are being squeezed by poor, short-term, or nonexistent land-use planning.

Wildlife science can help influence land-use planning. In Wyoming, Governor Dave Freudenthal supports the protection of migration corridors, and conservation organizations such as the Wildlife Conservation Society and local groups like the Greater Yellowstone Coalition and Jackson Hole Conservation Alliance are working to create a permanently protected corridor for pronghorn migrating through the precarious bottlenecks linking summer and winter areas. Without that corridor, local pronghorn populations in either or both the Upper Green and Grand Teton will become geographically isolated and, over time, dwindle to extinction.[7] Additionally, the Western Governors Association, which represents 18 states, recently proposed to remove the Energy Policy Act's "categorical exclusions" for environmental reviews for oil and gas development on some federal lands. If this proposal goes forward, it

would allow for appropriate site-specific analysis and conditions for approval that would help protect habitat corridors.[8]

Pronghorn lay massacred by the roadside. Roadkill incidents are on the rise because roads are being constructed across migration routes.

Long Distance Migrations around the World

Other regions, too, must address impediments to migratory movement. White-tailed gazelles (*Procapra gutturosa*) in Mongolia walk many miles along the fenced railroad tracks that connect Ulaanbaator to Beijing, searching unsuccessfully for ways to cross to access the nitrogen-rich grasses on the other side. Caribou in western Canada panic as massive transport vehicles roll by at high speed, sometimes smashing four animals in a single collision.

Innovative approaches have been developed at the small scale. In Alberta, highway overpasses laden with earth and shrubs enable bears and other species to cross the Trans-Canadian Highway. Corridors for elephants are being planned to connect isolated reserves and to maintain healthy populations in Zimbabwe, Ghana, Kenya, and southern Asia.[9] In Patagonia, a recent guanaco (*Lama guanicoe*) corridor between two reserves may protect the world's largest population of the animal.[10]

But the overarching conservation question remains urgent: are authorities in charge of wildlife comfortable with the prospect that a species will become extinct from protected areas due to current inaction? If not, then conservation steps to save long-distance overland migrations must be implemented soon. More and more wildlife science studies prove that connectivity is important to maintaining genetic resilience; that populations will decline below recoverable numbers if they cannot reach appropriate summer or winter range for food, calving, and mixing with other populations; and that migration plays a crucial role in the dynamics of healthy ecosystems. However, the real solution involves far more than wildlife science.

Saving long-distance migrations requires a broad conservation picture and bold action. Conservationists need to reach out to people who live in the lands where these wildlife spectacles occur and those whose pressures constitute the main threat—farmers, ranchers, local communities, oil and gas companies, and road infrastructure planners all have the potential to be part of the solution. Government agencies must stop bickering and work together, and elected officials must lead the way.

Although long-distance migration is not a phenomenon that most people think about, and *saiga* and *chiru* are hardly household words, we must make known that real conservation extends beyond parks and their resident species and includes protecting life-history phenomena that those species depend on, and that inspire us with their scale and determination.

> No one will ever see millions of bison migrating across unfettered prairies. But there are still places one can go . . . where the poignancy of odors, the din of grunts, and the pounding of hooves capture the cadence of movement; where the sheer number of animals propelling forward . . . strikes awe.

When I sit alone at the cabin on the shores of Square Lake, I worry little about human pressures. I enjoy the moment—caribou, bald eagles, wolves. I am fortunate. But when friends and others who will never visit Africa or Alaska ask why they should care about migrations, I pause. I consider the answer steeped in science—that connectivity is important for population viability and that species' natural history moves them to return to places that have provided sustenance and safety for thousands of years. However, I opt for an answer more visceral.

I tell them that we all know the clock can't be turned back. No one will ever see millions of bison migrating across unfettered prairies. But there are still places one can go—whether rural or urban, cowboy or banker, Asian or African—where the poignancy of odors, the din of grunts, and the pounding of hooves capture the cadence of movement; where the sheer number of animals propelling forward—all following groups of herd leaders—strikes awe. It is here that my dreams take me, the tireless harmony of a long trip out and back, and it is something that we should save for the next generation, and the one after that.

Downward Spiral

Catastrophic Decline of South Asia's Vultures

TODD E. KATZNER

The sight of circling vultures has long been regarded as an omen of death. Few of nature's signs are as universally recognized as the slow, spiraling flight of these giant scavengers. Many times I have seen these birds soaring— at carcass dumps in India, above highways and fields in North America, through mountain passes in the Caucasus, and over prairie and alpine mead-

ows in the Tian Shan range of south-eastern Kazakhstan. Their languid movements presage their patience even as they exhibit a remarkable purposefulness.

Since the new millennium, the sight of vultures circling has taken on a new meaning—signaling one of the world's greatest wildlife catastrophes. The spiraling omen now portends not the death of some poor creature on the ground, but that of the vultures

themselves. A plague has sprung from human hands, reaching into the sky and turning each of these magnificent fliers into a sun-struck Icarus.

About 15 years ago, an Indian ornithologist named Vibhu Prakash was the first to notice that something was wrong at his favorite nesting colony at Keoladeo National Park in Bharatpur, Rajasthan. Vultures were dying of

Vultures die of kidney failure within 2 to 3 days after feeding on the carcasses of livestock that have been administered the veterinary drug diclofenac.

TODD E. KATZNER is director of conservation and field research at the National Aviary in Pittsburgh, Pennsylvania, and a Wildlife Conservation Society research associate. He maintains active research programs on ecology and conservation of eagles and vultures in North America and abroad, especially in the former Soviet Union.

unknown causes and in an unusual manner: Vibhu saw them sitting listless in trees, their long necks hanging down, until they eventually fell from their perches to the ground.[1] These birds, whose digestion is so highly evolved that they can eat anthrax-tainted meat and suffer no consequences, were found to suffer from visceral gout, a symptom of kidney failure. Like a strongman besting Hercules, whatever was killing Keoladeo Park's vultures attacked them where they were strongest—in their remarkable internal organs.

> Vultures were dying of unknown causes and in an unusual manner: Vibhu saw them sitting listless in trees, their long necks hanging down, until they eventually fell from their perches to the ground.

Vibhu's observations spawned a series of scientific papers and no shortage of academic drama. Two teams strove to solve the problem, testing different hypotheses, giving competing talks at conferences, working in different countries, each pursuing its own line of clues, and each pushing the other to succeed. Eventually the team from The Peregrine Fund, the diagnostics led by Lindsay Oaks, reached an end point and, in a dramatic fashion, announced its findings at a scientific conference in Hungary in 2003.

What was killing vultures was diclofenac, a simple nonsteroidal anti-inflammatory drug (NSAID) much like ibuprofen.[2] Diclofenac had been developed for use in humans, but in India and Pakistan, local drug companies could produce it cheaply, and it quickly became a staple in veterinary medicine. In India, cattle are treated with great respect and not eaten by Hindus. When cows die, their carcasses are taken to dumps on the outskirts of residential areas where they have been historically consumed by vultures. So numerous were cows and so benign were India's people that vultures had become omnipresent. Some say that the most common species, the Oriental white-backed vulture (*Gyps bengalensis*), may

Once abundant throughout southeast Asia, Oriental white-backed vultures (*Gyps bengalensis*) are now critically endangered. The extremely high death rate of this species in the late 1990s led some to believe that the vultures were suffering from an epidemic.

Source: The Peregrine Fund/Martin Gilbert.

have once numbered 40 million. Yet the vulture's dependence on livestock also made it vulnerable. Cows treated with diclofenac may die with the drug in their system. It turns out that diclofenac is toxic to vultures, and any bird that eats tainted meat is almost certain to die. Because many vultures may feed off a single carcass, one contaminated cow can kill many birds.

Conservation only works when solutions address the root cause of population declines. The discovery that diclofenac is toxic to vultures was a victory, but only the first battle in confronting this great wildlife problem. Soon after, an international conference in India evaluated the current state of knowledge and began establishing research priorities for conservation actions.

On the research front, several aspects of the diclofenac story needed to be further understood. Although Oaks's identification of diclofenac as a mortality agent for vultures was a significant breakthrough, it was also necessary to establish that diclofenac was present in enough cow carcasses to have caused the observed vulture population declines. In addition, having observed the extent of the threat to three vulture species—the Oriental white-backed vulture, the long-billed vulture (*G. indicus*), and the slender-billed vulture (*G. tenuirostris*)—it was critical to identify other bird species at risk. Finally, because diclofenac was important as a veterinary drug in India, a vital step to solving the problem lay in identifying an effective and inexpensive alternative so that diclofenac could feasibly be removed throughout South Asia.

The British Royal Society for the Protection of Birds (RSPB) has, in many regards, led the charge on the research front. In fairly short order, scientists were able to show that large numbers of dead vultures in India had clear signs of diclofenac poisoning,[3] and they used mathematical models to show that the observed declines in vulture populations could have occurred even if less than 2 percent of bovine carcasses were tainted with diclofenac.[4]

RSPB scientists also tackled the other side of the problem, researching diclofenac's effects on other species and finding a replacement drug. In 2004–2005, they surveyed zoos and other institutions about observed impacts of NSAIDs on their birds.[5] They found that: first, diclofenac did kill other species of birds, especially other vultures; and second, meloxicam, another NSAID, was likely a safe and effective alternative to diclofenac. Subsequent fieldwork and controlled experiments conducted with international collaborators verified both the toxicity of diclofenac to other vultures and the safety of meloxicam to these and other birds.[6]

> What was killing vultures was diclofenac, a simple nonsteroidal anti-inflammatory drug (NSAID) much like ibuprofen.

This research identified a clear path to manage the crisis, and on the conservation front things have moved forward relatively quickly. Conservation priorities were to take stopgap measures to slow the 50 percent mortality rates from diclofenac poisoning and to work with the Indian, Pakistani, and

Nepalese governments to ban diclofenac use. Another priority was establishing captive breeding programs to build reservoir populations. Throughout the region, conservationists are now working to provide feeding stations with "clean" food for vultures. Although this is an imperfect way to protect them, it has lowered the rate at which they are being poisoned. At the same time, captive breeding has begun in order to safeguard the future of the species while diclofenac-laden cattle carcasses are removed from the environment. There are now two breeding facilities in India thanks to work by the RSPB, their Birdlife partners at the Bombay Natural History Society, and various government agencies. In 2006, a center in Pakistan was created by World Wildlife Fund–Pakistan with assistance from the Pakistani government and The Peregrine Fund. Another is planned for Nepal as a cooperative effort between the Zoological Society of London and the Nepalese government.

Perhaps the most impressive achievement, however, has been the progress made toward removing diclofenac from the environment. This, more than any other action, is essential if vultures are to survive in South Asia. In a remarkable show of unity, conservation groups from around the world have worked together with local governments on how to phase out diclofenac and substitute meloxicam as a safe and reasonable alternative drug. International conservation agreements are always a challenge to enact, often more so when they run contrary to financial interests. It is therefore all the more impressive that diclofenac has now been banned in India, Pakistan, and Nepal.

Source: Allan Michaud.

"Vulture restaurants," sites where diclofenac-free food is provided for vultures, serve as a conservation tool for these slender-billed vultures (*Gyps tenuirostris*). This stopgap method will help reduce vulture mortality until diclofenac is no longer used in livestock.

If success in conservation were measured by the effort expended and the quality of science produced, then the case of the South Asian vulture would be one of the world's most successful conservation efforts. Unfortunately, effective conservation has only one metric—halting the loss of biodiversity. By this measure, the vulture effort has yet to be judged. Vulture populations have been reduced by more than 95 percent throughout the region and the birds can now be counted in only the thousands. In Mumbai, where vultures used to breed at incredible densities, there are none to be seen. Few biologists hold out hope that vulture populations will ever return to their former millions, but some of us, particularly those who believe in the usefulness of captive breeding, dream of a day

Source: Allan Michaud.

With so few vultures left in the wild to consume them before they rot, livestock carcasses are increasingly devoured by other scavengers, such as rats and dogs, that could potentially spread rabies and other diseases to both human and wildlife populations.

when diclofenac and other unsafe NSAIDs are gone from the environment, and captive vultures can be released to circle again.

Until then, much remains to be accomplished. Progress is being made on removing diclofenac from the environment, and vulture populations are now closely monitored. But conservationists are distressed that it took a near-total decline of one of the most abundant, visible bird species in one of the most populated parts of the world before an alarm was raised.

Protecting vultures in other regions of the world is equally important. Many potentially vulnerable populations are smaller and more isolated than those in South Asia, making undocumented but catastrophic declines possible for those species. For example, two other *Gyps* vultures in Asia are vulnerable to diclofenac, and their population status is unknown.

In Cambodia, relict populations of *G. bengalensis* and *G. tenuirostris* (two of the endangered South Asian species) exist geographically cut off from the populations in India. Diclofenac is not heavily used in Cambodia for veterinary purposes, so, although these populations are small, they are likely the most stable Asian populations remaining in the wild. However, Cambodia's vultures face other threats, most importantly habitat loss and a scarcity of food sources. The Wildlife Conservation Society is working to protect them by providing safe food and by conducting public education programs.

> In a remarkable show of unity, conservation groups from around the world have worked together with local governments on how to phase out diclofenac and substitute meloxicam as a safe and reasonable alternative drug.

Source: Allan Michaud.

A juvenile red-headed vulture (*Sarcogyps calvus*) reluctantly shares his meal with a crow. Food scarcity and habitat loss threaten vulture populations across the globe.

The decimation of South Asian vultures has been a remarkably high-profile conservation story. As a consequence, biologists in other regions have looked more closely at their own local vulture populations, revealing more about the state of their birds than was previously recognized. In Cambodia, for example, virtually no vultures remain at some sites, yet a recently discovered breeding colony of slender-billed vultures (*G. tenuirostris*) may be one of the largest remaining in the world. In the former Soviet Union, populations of griffon vultures (*G. fulvus* and *G. himalayensis*) have seen significant declines.[7] In Africa, vulture populations appear to be suffering throughout the continent, from the northern sub-Saharan areas to the extreme south, where diclofenac is known to be present. The news is especially grim from West Africa, where transect surveys have documented 45 to 95 percent declines in all species, with little conclusive knowledge yet as to the causes.[8]

To help conservationists gain a better picture of vulture numbers, the Wildlife Conservation Society and the US National Aviary are developing an innovative technique to help provide accurate counts of vulture populations. Vultures are among the most difficult vertebrates to census accurately, and their population status is often indeterminate. Although they are thought to be reasonably faithful to colony sites, individual vultures breed irregularly, nonbreeders are itinerant, and all individuals can travel hundreds of miles to feed. At present, the only way to reliably estimate population size is by marking and recapturing individuals—a process that requires exceptional effort. The technique we are developing involves using DNA taken from feathers found at livestock carcasses to identify the individual birds present, allowing birds to be "captured" without ever trapping them or even seeing them. This approach allows us to generate reasonable estimates of population size and other demographic parameters for birds. It is being tested in the Caucasus Mountains in the Republic of Georgia, in the Tian Shan Mountains of Kazakhstan, and in Cambodia—all with less effort and expense than previous methods. This will allow for more accurate and frequent monitoring even in remote areas, which is essential for management, for it is practically impossible to allocate conservation effort effectively without knowledge of the species' population status.

Some hope for avian scavengers exists in the Americas, where populations seem robust. In North America, turkey vultures (*Cathartes aura*) have adapted well to more human-dominated environments, and their populations have grown so numerous that they are almost becoming a nuisance. Continuing a hundred-year trend, turkey vultures are expanding their range farther and farther northward. Populations of related species (black and yellow-faced vultures) appear stable, although in some cases our knowledge of these species is too limited for an accurate conservation assessment. Condors, the America's largest bird, appear to be relatively stable in South America, although component populations are sometimes misguidedly persecuted on the assumption that the big birds are predators on livestock. California condor (*Gymnogyps californianus*) populations are also growing, through reintroduction and other means, in the American Southwest.

Humans have deliberately caused the extinction of many species; the story of how we have *inadvertently* brought about the imminent extinction in the wild of three species of Asian vultures is therefore particularly poignant. It is also an inauspicious start to a century that many conservation biologists fear will someday be viewed as one of humanity's worst. In the Americas and a few other regions of the world, we can still see large numbers of vultures circling in search of carrion or thermals. These giant masters of the air, flying effortlessly on slotted wings, are both a reminder of how rare their kin have become in other areas and a signal of hope for the conservation of remaining vulture populations. The next time you see vultures, watch them carefully. Know that sometimes even scavengers must fear death, and know that when enough deaths move a population to extinction, we, as the drivers of that extinction and the dominant force on the planet, have a moral obligation to do all we reasonably can to ensure their survival.

Conserving Cold-Blooded Australians

RICHARD SHINE

Australia is a land of lizards. A single sand ridge in the central Australian desert can contain up to 42 species of lizards,[1] and the continent as a whole has far greater reptile biodiversity than anywhere else on the planet. Reptiles flourish in the land down under due to—not in spite of—the harsh, uncertain climate and poor soils on much of the continent. Long droughts make the search for food and water difficult, yet cold-blooded, or ectothermic, animals need very little energy to survive: a lizard requires only 10 percent as much food as a mouse of the same weight,[2] and a lizard can go without feeding for months at a time, especially because it can lower its metabolism during cool months. As a result, ecological niches occupied by warm-blooded mammals in other parts of the world are taken up by lizards and snakes in Australia.

A casual tour around Australia's magnificent wild places reveals an abundance and diversity of reptiles. Venomous front-fanged snakes—such as tiger snakes and brown snakes—dominate most habitats in the cooler southern half of the continent. In the tropics, harmless species like pythons or nonvenomous colubrids are more likely to slither across your path as you walk through the woodlands at night. Surprisingly, as many other Australian species have been lost, the only Aussie reptile known to have come close to the brink of extinction is the pygmy bluetongue lizard (*Tiliqua adelaidensis*), a medium-sized skink that was not seen for decades and was then "rediscovered" in the belly of a road-killed snake.[3]

Yet Australian reptile habitats are under increasing pressure, the most obvious

RICHARD SHINE is a professor of biology at the University of Sydney and holds a Federation Fellowship from the Australian Research Council. He is best known for his long-term ecological studies on Australian reptiles, but has also worked extensively on many other systems, from garter snakes in Canada to pit vipers in China.

involving agriculture in the semiarid zone that occupies much of the country. Poor soils and erratic rainfall make farming only marginally viable here, and environmentally damaging in terms of water use and soil salinization. Cattle and sheep grazing has eliminated much vegetation critical for native lizards, snakes, and frogs that now cling to a precarious existence in relict patches of scrubby trees. Carpet pythons (*Morelia spilota*)—heavy-bodied snakes that grow up to 10 feet long and conceal themselves in leaf litter and fallen logs to ambush native rats and possums—have happily expanded their diet to include feral rabbits and now use hiding places in human-made structures. But even their adaptability is being challenged by the broad-scale clearing of vast areas of the inland plains that leaves little ground cover for even a tiny lizard to conceal itself, let alone an 11-pound python.

> Reptiles flourish in the land down under due to—not in spite of—the harsh, uncertain climate and poor soils on much of the continent.

Given reptiles' resilience and ubiquity, it is all the more puzzling that they remain poorly studied. Australia has more species of reptiles than birds or mammals (850 vs. 794 and 296, respectively[4]), yet far more resources are invested in the study and conservation of warm-blooded Australians. (The same conservation bias is true around the world.[5]) However, reptiles merit closer study because populations of many ectothermic vertebrates can tolerate ecological disruptions that would imperil their warm-blooded counterparts. How are they able to do this? The high reproductive output of many ectothermic species may help them to evolve rapidly to counter ecological threats. Therefore, the study of reptiles presents an opportunity to observe adaptive advantages that will serve wildlife conservation well.

Source: Mark Hutchinson/South Australian Museum.

Ploughing for agricultural purposes has destroyed much of the pygmy bluetongue lizard's (*Tiliqua adelaidensis*) native grassland habitat.

The reptile conservation issue that arouses the most interest among the Australian public relates to invasive cane toads (*Bufo marinus*). These large anurans, native to South and Central America, were introduced to tropical northeastern Australia in 1935 to control beetles in the sugarcane crop. Their usefulness to agriculture proved limited, but the toads thrived and rapidly spread to the north, south, and west. They now cover more than 385,000 square miles (1 million km²) of Australia, and the "invasion front" progresses westward at more than 31 miles (50 km) per year.[6] One of their worst threats lies in their toxicity to predators; the specialized poisons, called bufotoxins, in their skin are not found in any native Australian frogs, so most native predators have little defense against them. Some birds overcome the problem by picking out only the nontoxic toad parts, but snakes have no such option. Even a toad egg or a tiny tadpole is likely to be a fatal meal for a naïve lizard or snake.

For this reason, most researchers have assumed (and the public fervently believes) that the cane toads are catastrophic to native Australian fauna. Their arrival often inspires vigorous public campaigns to eradicate them in every way imaginable: they have been run over by vehicles, caught in traps, and attacked with golf clubs. So far, these attempts have done little to slow the warty invaders. It is true that, due to Australia's eons of isolation, invasive species have disturbed this continent's ecosystems more dramatically than they would in other parts of the world. Intuition suggests that because cane toads attain high population densities (up to 2,000 per hectare[7]), they *must* negatively affect native animals. Voracious eaters, they do deplete insect numbers. We know that toads live in similar habitats as frogs, so we expect them to compete with native anurans. And we expect that the toads' poison dooms the many frog-eating predators that mistakenly grab a cane toad as their (last) meal.

Habitat clearing leaves carpet pythons (*Morelia spilota*) with fewer hiding places from which they can stalk their prey.

But what is the effect on toad-eaters over the long term? Reports show that predators such as varanid lizards, snakes, and quolls (marsupial carnivores) die in huge numbers when the toads first arrive in an area, but these populations gradually recover and, in at least some cases, return to "pre-toad" levels within a few decades.[8] And, although *B. marinus* has been introduced to more than 40 countries worldwide, few ecological disasters have been reported (perhaps reflecting the presence of native Bufonidae family members—nonexistent in isolated Australia—in many of those places). Most Australian predators succumb to toad toxins, but a few species do not: colubrid snakes that arose in Asia, for example, have retained a genetic legacy of physiological resistance to the poisons of Asian toads that stands them in good stead.

Figuring out the true long-term ecological effects of toads is also important economically. Millions of dollars of public money have been spent to develop a "magic bullet" (such as importing natural amphibian diseases from South America or genetically engineering toad viruses) to eliminate cane toads. So far these strategies have failed.

Faced with undeterred introduced species, our scarce conservation resources may be better spent on understanding the enemy rather than on developing weapons of destruction. A group of scientists at the University of Sydney has set out to discover exactly how the toads are affecting Australian wildlife over the long term by studying whether local wildlife populations have an opportunity to adapt or develop toad-resistant characteristics after decades of cohabitation with the toxic amphibian. If predators can adapt to the toad's presence, cane toads may inflict less damage on Australian ecosystems than has been believed, and instead serve as a dramatic force for coevolution.

Our current work covers the entire breadth of the Australian tropics, from the Kimberley region of Western Australia to Cairns and Townsville in Queensland, and includes areas where toads arrived 60 years ago and places they have yet to reach. "Team Bufo" researchers monitor the exact position of the invasion front by chatting with locals and driving the roads every night, when toads move about. At the front, to detect impacts of toad arrival before local predators have time to adjust, we confirm which species of native snakes, lizards, turtles, mammals, and fish in the area might regularly be frog-eaters, and to what degree they prefer frogs over toads. When the toads arrive we fit the front-runners with miniature radio-transmitters strapped to small waistbands in order to follow their progress. We also closely monitor the likeliest victims, including snakes (especially death adders [*Acanthophis praelongus*], which experience about 50 percent mortality within the first year), and locally common lizards. To examine general ecological impacts, we enclose toads in pens to observe both their effect on insect abundance and their competition with native frogs.

Cane toads (*Bufo marinus*) have been introduced to over 40 countries to control insect populations, but they are toxic to many of the native species that prey upon them.

Source: John White.

The initial results from this work reveal a picture that is more complicated, and interesting, than expected. In the enclosures, toads effectively reduce insect numbers. They compete with native frogs, but, intriguingly, toad presence mostly affects frog feeding rates: some native frogs prefer to forgo feeding rather than forage beside a potentially predatory giant toad. The long-term impacts of cane toads on frogs and insects are likely not severe, and frog numbers before and after toad arrival show little change.[9]

Assessing toad impact on snakes, lizards, and other predators is more complicated. Cane toad toxin is indeed deadly to many, but not all, native snakes and lizards. Some species are highly sensitive; for example, a 6-foot-long (2 m) varanid lizard (*Varanus panoptes*) that seizes a toad can die almost instantly. More than once researchers have found a dead varanid frozen in attack posture with a toad sitting happily a few feet away bearing only a scratch from the lizard's teeth. Death adders that feed on tiny juvenile toads swarming from ponds are killed in large numbers. It is difficult to assess the effects on larger, rarer, and highly sensitive predator species like the king brown snake

> Predators such as varanid lizards, snakes, and quolls (marsupial carnivores) die in huge numbers when the toads first arrive in an area, but . . . these populations gradually recover.

Source: David Fischer.

The varanid lizard (*Varanus panoptes*) or yellow-spotted monitor is highly susceptible to poisoning by cane toad toxins.

(*Pseudechis australis*)—they could be declining without our knowledge.

Fortunately, however, many other species of snakes, frogs, and mammals distinguish between toads and their native prey and simply are not tempted to eat the toxic newcomers. Some mammals, such as small, shrewlike planigales (*Planigale maculata*), try, but tend to immediately spit out the toads and quickly learn to avoid them. In fact, our survey has not detected widespread mortality among native predators in the floodplain; instead, mortality has been species-specific, mostly hitting varanid lizards and death adders. However, previously common snake, lizard, and frog species are still common about two years after toads arrive, and even the varanid lizards and death adders are present in areas colonized long ago by toads, which suggests that their populations recover over time.

How do sensitive predator populations manage to recover in the face of a toxic invasive species? One possibility is natural selection based on individual animal feeding preferences: for example, some death adders refuse to eat toads even though they happily consume native frogs. These fussy eaters survive after toads arrive in the area, whereas their less choosy relatives die. Such choosiness probably rests on a genetic basis (as is known to be true in other snake species), and since the "choosy" gene survives to future generations, we can expect rapid evolution of feeding preferences among death adders, leading to future populations much less likely to eat cane toads.

Comparisons between toad-exposed and toad-naïve populations of black snakes (*Pseudechis porphyriacus*) have shown exactly that shift. About half of the toad-naïve black snakes that we tested were happy to feast on cane toads, but all of the snakes collected from toad-settled areas simply ignored toads as a food source.[10] Laboratory experiments suggest that these snakes are slow learners—even a series of near fatal meals does not convince a hungry black snake to leave the next cane toad alone, nor is it enough to confer resistance to the toxin. So the shift in feeding responses appears to be an example of rapid evolution rather than learning.

By demonstrating the longer-term persistence of predators after toad invasion, these studies illustrate how quickly evolution can work and reaffirm that living beings have a remarkable ability to adapt. As long as external changes are not too massive or too rapid, evolutionary processes should buffer the disruptive effects of human activities and major biological changes—at least over time. When widespread species with greater genetic variation and higher reproductive rates are faced with specific challenges to their viability, the Darwinian demon of natural selection may be a powerful ally.

Rapid evolutionary change is emerging as a significant conservation issue worldwide. For example, heavy exploitation by motorized trawlers in the Barents Sea early in the twentieth century not only drastically reduced the numbers of Arctic cod, but, by removing the larger, older fish, also caused rapid evolution of earlier maturation, making it more likely for a fish to mature and reproduce before it was caught.[11] Sometimes native species evolve rapidly to exploit opportunities rather than to escape the negative effects of human activities. The American checkerspot butterfly (*Euphydryas phaeton*), which once was rare and fed on only one native plant, increased in abundance after it evolved to exploit an invasive weed.[12]

> When widespread species with greater genetic variation and higher reproductive rates are faced with specific challenges to their viability, the Darwinian demon of natural selection may be a powerful ally.

It is still too early for us to confidently evaluate the ecological impact of cane toads in Australia, but it is already clear that the impact is unlikely to be as severe, widespread, or long-lasting as previously thought. Some other challenges facing Australia's reptiles will be harder to address: habitat destruction by urban development and agriculture, feral predators, and invasive plants may eliminate some reptiles from large areas, precluding gradual adjustment to the new conditions. Predation by introduced cats and foxes on adult reptiles and their eggs has been catastrophic for some taxa and is likely to prove far more dangerous than cane toads. Introduced diseases, such as chytrid fungus, have already exterminated several species of native frog,[13] and exotic viruses from imported captive snakes pose a potential threat to Australia's wild reptiles.[14]

Compounding all this is climate change, which may affect reptiles by modifying their established ecological niches. Most of Australia is hot and dry, and climate experts predict that southern Australia will become warmer and drier, challenging mountain ecosystems there and the reptiles specialized to a mon-

> There is value in long-term, in-depth wildlife science: cane toads in Australia provide a cautionary note about the dangers of trying to solve a problem based on too little information.

tane existence. For example, montane snakes and lizards bear live young rather than lay eggs because, in cooler climates, keeping gestating offspring warm by shuttling between patches of sunlight is a useful life-history tactic. However, if mountain regions grow warmer, larger or more fecund egg-laying reptile species from lower elevations can extend their ranges upward and outcompete these montane specialists. Similarly, climate warming might allow lowland predators, such as the kookaburra (*Dacelo* spp.), a large kingfisher, to move up into the high country.

No single conservation approach can solve all of these problems. Perhaps the greatest challenge is to genuinely understand the ecological functioning of the systems we wish to conserve. There is value in long-term, in-depth wildlife science: cane toads provide a cautionary note about the dangers of trying to solve a problem based on too little information. In hindsight, the ecologists in the 1930s should have evaluated the likely impact of toad introduction more carefully. That lesson seems to have been ignored in current schemes to control toads, which have largely involved simple-minded—and, at least so far, expensive but unsuccessful—attempts at mass destruction, with surprisingly little understanding of toad biology or the ecological interactions by which toads influence the Australian biota. The study reviewed in this essay provides a basis for more robust approaches to threat mitigation based on ecological and evolutionary understanding. In predicting the consequences of human actions, we need to explore not only the immediate effect but whether (and if so, how rapidly and how completely) a natural system may be able to adapt to new challenges.

Source: Julie Larsen Maher/WCS.

Kookaburras kill their prey (oftentimes snakes and lizards) by dropping them from a height or battering them with their large bills.

For the present at least, Australia remains a land of lizards. So far, our reptile fauna has coped well. Hopefully, the resilience derived from a long evolutionary history of dealing with harsh conditions and weather fluctuations will help them survive new threats. But we cannot simply rely on their tenacity to meet future challenges. Instead, we need to invest more effort in understanding reptiles and widen our conservation priorities to incorporate the small, cold-blooded beasts that dominate so many Australian ecosystems. 🐦

Settling for Less

Disappearing Diadromous Fishes

JOHN WALDMAN

Few sights are as compelling as thousands of salmon on their spawning runs, powering through rapids and leaping up waterfalls to get to the very upstream reaches where they were born. Salmon are one of many diadromous fishes—species that move between fresh- and saltwaters to spawn and mature. Many have complex life histories and long, cryptic migrations. Diadromous fishes constitute less than 1 percent of the world's fish fauna, but their importance to humanity far exceeds this proportion.[1] Salmon, sturgeons, and eels are among the most commercially valuable fishes, and almost all of these species have declined, some to the point of near-extinction. I believe the management of diadromous fishes would benefit from a focused look back at their halcyon days, when they filled our rivers and coastal seas.

Diadromous fish exhibit several types of life cycles: salmon are anadromous, meaning they spawn in freshwater and mature out at sea. Pacific salmon (*Oncorhynchus* spp.), such as chinook and coho, leave their home river and return to it only once to propagate and die. The other, more common type of anadromy is seen in Atlantic salmon (*Salmo salar*) and sturgeons, in which individuals ascend rivers, spawn, and migrate back to marine waters several times during their lives.

Another major type of life cycle is catadromy, exhibited by American and European eels (*Anguilla rostrata* and *A. anguilla*), in which the young are born at

---

JOHN WALDMAN is professor of biology at Queens College, City University of New York. Prior to this appointment in 2004, he was employed for 20 years by the Hudson River Foundation for Science and Environmental Research. His research focuses on the ecology and evolution of fishes, urban aquatic environments, and historical ecology. He is author of several popular books, including Heartbeats in the Muck: The History, Sea Life, and Environment of New York Harbor.

Celilo Indians catching Pacific salmon at Celilo Falls, Columbia River, 1950. This famous fishery was lost when the Dalles Dam was completed in 1957.

sea, enter freshwaters to mature, and then return to saltwaters to spawn. American and European eels have dramatic life cycles, beginning as eggs spawned deep in the Atlantic's Sargasso Sea. From there, the Gulf Stream deposits their larval stages along the North American and European coastlines, and most eels then ascend rivers where they grow over two decades, some reaching deep within the continental interiors—as far as Lake Superior or the Caspian Sea—before returning to the Sargasso to spawn and die.

Not all diadromous fish are as well traveled as eels. Nonetheless, each year Atlantic sturgeon (*Acipenser oxyrinchus*), some weighing a hundred pounds, glide quietly past Manhattan to reproduce in New York's Hudson River, schools of striped bass (*Morone saxatilis*) invade the many tributaries of Chesapeake Bay, and silvery shoals of Allis shad (*Alosa alosa*) migrate to the interiors of France and Spain. Yet these spawning runs are, for the most part, mere fractions of what they were in preindustrial times. The phenomenon of shifting baselines, in which succeeding generations of natural resource managers settle for successively lesser conservation goals, has allowed us to become inured to the enormous declines of these fishes, hindering our vision for their potential numbers, and the potential for conservation in our rivers and coastal areas.

The legacy of past abundance is preserved in old photos of great harvests, and early eyewitness accounts from the eastern seaboard of North America tell of awe-inspiring numbers of fish struggling upriver in numbers that once reliably replenished major fisheries. Although difficult to fathom today, in the 1600s, colonists in New England used salmon to fertilize their fields.[2] River herring (i.e., alewives [*Alosa pseudoharengus*] and blueback herring [*A. aestivalis*]), among the smallest of anadromous fishes, glutted many rivers and streams—and were free for the taking.[3] An observer in Virginia conveyed sheer wonder at the magnitude of the river herrings' run, writing in 1728 that, "In a word, it is unbelievable, indeed, undescribable, as also incomprehensible, what quantity is found there."

Contrast this with their present status: in 2007, diadromous fish have so greatly declined that, for example, river herring are tightly regulated in Virginia and other coastal states, with all harvest banned in Connecticut, Rhode Island, and Massachusetts. What happened between then and now? In simplified terms, spawning runs were whittled away or eliminated by the combined pressures of overfishing, damming, and contamination.

> In the US, early harvests of Atlantic sturgeon for caviar resembled the clear-cutting of forests; everything caught was taken until it became uneconomical to continue.

Overfishing

The most prized caviar, that from beluga sturgeon (*Huso huso*), can retail for more than $150 *per ounce* where it is still sold (it is banned in the US). Caviar sturgeon have fetched exorbitant prices ever since the international "caviar craze" of the late nineteenth century, which led to intense overfishing around the Caspian

Source: USFWS.

Highly prized as a food source, American shad (*Alosa sapidissima*) populations have been depleted by overfishing. Shad bakes remain a popular custom celebrating the annual shad spawning run.

Sea basin—the main source of beluga—and in the Amur River between China and Russia. In the US, early harvests of Atlantic sturgeon for caviar resembled the clear-cutting of forests; everything caught was taken until it became uneconomical to continue. Even by 1901, the landings at the main US sturgeon fishery in the Delaware River were only 6 percent of their peak just two years earlier.[4] Similarly, American shad (*Alosa sapidissima*, meaning "most delicious of herrings") have long been harvested, and many rivers have seen pronounced declines. Some "shad bakes" that celebrate the spawning run as a symbol of spring cannot obtain enough locally caught fish to continue.

Source: John J. Mosesso/NBII.

The South Bend Fish Ladder, St. Joseph River, Michigan, was erected to allow the passage of trout and salmon around the South Bend Dam.

> The number of dams in the world is staggering—and growing.

Like most anadromous fishes, shad show high homing fidelity and thus form discrete populations. Harvests are therefore best managed when shad populations are separated into their different home rivers, which should allow the catch to be adjusted to each population's size. However, these fishes bear the double burden of being harvested in rivers *and* in marine waters as well, and in the sea, fisheries are based on mixed stocks—aggregations of a species composed of several populations.

Marine fisheries of this sort obscure the true capacity of each shad population to sustain offtake, and in the 1980s, American shad was caught in coastal waters in such a directed "intercept" fishery. Because it was nearly impossible to determine the damage to the many separate shad populations, this fishery declined and was shut down by 2004. Likewise, some Atlantic salmon ocean fisheries with mixed populations from North American, European, and Greenland rivers have closed, thanks to international negotiations and the North Atlantic Salmon Fund.

Bycatch—the accidental capture of diadromous fish in other fisheries—is another, less easily quantified, threat. As diadromous fishes disperse through coastal seas, mortality as bycatch significantly slows their recovery, particularly for long-lived, late-maturing species, such as Atlantic sturgeon, whose populations dwindle if individuals are removed before they have the chance to reproduce. Atlantic sturgeon, for example, might not reproduce until they reach 20 years of age.[5] A ban on directed fishing in US coastal waters enacted in 1998 may extend for 40 years to protect at least two generations.

Short-Circuiting Life Cycles: Dams

Rivers must flow freely to allow anadromous fish passage to their upstream spawning grounds and to allow catadromous fish to migrate between inland waters and the sea, but the number of dams in the world is staggering—and growing. In the US alone there are an estimated 80,000 dams of six feet or greater height, and perhaps as many as 2 million of all sizes,[6] ranging up to behemoths such as the 200-foot-high Bonneville Dam on the Columbia River in Oregon.

Dams do much to block the upstream passage of adult diadromous fishes, and any young born upstream must sometimes swim through spinning hydroelectric turbines to get to the sea. A river's basic ecology is also compromised by these barriers: other river wildlife loses the ability to move seasonally among fragmented river reaches; dams impound water flows, creating still water and essentially replacing river habitat with lakes; and nutrients and sediments are trapped behind dams, starving ecologically important downstream estuaries, deltas, and coastal areas.

There are ways to assist diadromous fishes past dams, but they are only partially beneficial. Fish "ladders" may allow spawners to ascend, but they create bottlenecks to movement, and sturgeons and striped bass do not even use them. Fish lifts—essentially elevators—move some fish over large dams but may gather only a fraction of those individuals heading upriver. Rather pathetically, some fish runs persist only by the fish being trucked past dams.

Many river systems have multiple dams, requiring migratory fish to negotiate a gauntlet. For example, American shad once ran up the Susquehanna River from the Chesapeake Bay to Otsego Lake in central New York, nearly 620 miles (1,000 km) from the sea. This drainage was liberally dammed until all but the first 10 miles of river were cut off, and diadromous fish must now work their way through several passage facilities to reach just a fraction of the river's length. The ecological consequences of damming rivers are beginning to come to the attention of national and international communities. In the US, some dams are being removed, most notably the Edwards Dam on Maine's Kennebec River in 1999,[7] which allowed Atlantic sturgeon, striped bass, Atlantic salmon, and American shad to reach their historical spawning grounds. But there are still many aging dams with little or no economic value throughout North America and much of the world, and in China and Southeast Asia, construction of new dams is under way. Overcoming societal inertia concerning dams is a premier challenge for the conservation community.

> Bycatch—the accidental capture of diadromous fish in other fisheries—is another, less easily quantified, threat. As diadromous fishes disperse through coastal seas, mortality as bycatch significantly slows their recovery.

Contamination

In the US, the Clean Water Act of 1972 initiated enormous gains in water quality, but a century's worth of noxious chemical wastes dumped in rivers still persists in sediments. In the Hudson River, polychlorinated biphenyls released by the General Electric Company have contaminated the river's fishes, including most of its diadromous species, to the extent that commercial fisheries in the river, and in some cases beyond, were closed.

Sewage, too, has been discharged to rivers from cities throughout the world, creating a thick layer of bottom sludge that, as it degraded, consumed oxygen and rendered waters uninhabitable. Such fouling creates "chemical dams" that block upstream migration of anadromous fishes.[8] In some developing countries, untreated sewage still flows into rivers.

Source: Susan M. Cormier.

A 1-year-old Atlantic tomcod (*Microgadus tomcod*) with multiple hepatocellular carcinomas, appearing as dark circles on the liver. River pollution has detrimental effects on the health of many diadromous fishes.

Glancing Backward to Move Forward

In one of his lesser-known works, *A Week on the Concord and Merrimack Rivers*, Henry David Thoreau wrote, "Dim visions we still get of miraculous draughts of fishes, and heaps uncountable by the riverside, from tales of our seniors."[9] Thoreau made his trip in 1839 and was so struck by the contrast between historical accounts of abundance and the apparent hopelessness for these fishes that he wryly postulated, "Perchance after a thousand years, if the fishes will be patient, and pass their summers elsewhere, meanwhile nature will have leveled the Billerica dam, and the Lowell factories, and the Grass-ground [Concord] River run clear again, to be explored by new migrating shoals." Today, a few salmon and much-reduced numbers of other fishes make it part of the way up the Merrimack, stuck in that netherworld in which most of these runs persist—far below their original richness but just enough to remain on the plus side of extirpation.

> "Dim visions we still get of miraculous draughts of fishes, and heaps uncountable by the riverside, from tales of our seniors."
> —Thoreau

A sampling of diadromous fishes with official threatened status or of high concern include Gulf sturgeon (*Acipenser oxyrinchus desotoi*) along the Gulf of Mexico; Atlantic whitefish (*Coregonus huntsmani*) in Nova Scotia; Japanese eel (*Anguilla japonica*) and Masu salmon (*Oncorhynchus masou*) in Japan; freshwater mullet (*Myxus capensis*) in South Africa; beluga sturgeon; the Chinese sturgeon (*Acipenser sinensis*) in the Pearl and Yangtze rivers; and the Australian grayling (*Prototroctes maraena*).

Some anadromous species have already gone extinct, such as the New Zealand grayling (*Prototroctes oxyrhynchus*) in the mid-1900s. As of this publication, others species like the Syr-Darya shovelnose sturgeon (*Pseudoscaphirhynchus fedtschenkoi*), native to the Aral Sea, appear to have died out.[10] Others are hurtling toward extinction, the European sea sturgeon (*Acipenser sturio*) being a leading example. Its original range extended from the Baltic Sea, around the entire European coast, to Black Sea tributaries, but is now reduced to one relict population in France's Gironde River, with no recent evidence of natural reproduction.[11] Two East Asian shads are also close to disappearing. One of these, *Tenualosa thibaudeaui*, was once among the most abundant fish in its only domain, the Mekong, but has declined drastically as the river suffers overfishing and damming.[12]

More commonly, diadromous fish species exist in a pattern of mixed statuses among populations, with some remaining viable while others fail. For instance, in the Canadian Maritimes Atlantic salmon fisheries are still reasonably productive, but salmon runs in some Maine rivers number in the single digits. A 40-year, $200 million restoration effort in the Connecticut River—once a great salmon spawning ground—has failed to generate even a hint of a sustained comeback. Twaite (*Alosa fallax*) and allis shad are moderately abundant in Europe but have been reduced to relict populations in Africa.

Not only must diadromous fishes cope with the ongoing stresses of fishing, damming, and pollution, but they must now also contend with climate change. Just recently and without fanfare, a run of rainbow smelt (*Osmerus mordax*) in the Hudson River went extinct—an annual monitoring survey that had captured tens of thousands of smelt larvae most years yielded only four individuals since 1995.[13] Rainbow smelt is a boreal species whose range

Source: John Waldman.

Shortnose sturgeon (*Acipenser brevirostrum*) are no longer endangered in the Hudson River, thanks to effective species and habitat protection efforts.

reached south to the Delaware River in the cooler 1800s. Thus warming is the obvious suspect, and there is evidence that Atlantic tomcod (*Microgadus tomcod*) may soon follow.

There have been three recent recoveries on the US Atlantic coast: mid-Atlantic migratory striped bass populations have rebounded due to sharply reduced allowable harvests;[14] American shad are now moderately abundant in the Susquehanna River due to improved upriver passage;[15] and shortnose sturgeon (*Acipenser brevirostrum*) have quadrupled to perhaps 65,000 in the Hudson River thanks to rehabilitated spawning and nursery habitat and the sturgeon's endangered species listing.[16] But effective restoration programs are rarely undertaken unless a crisis occurs. The will to ratchet down lucrative striped bass fisheries was not found until they crashed to truly worrisome levels; the shad run of the Susquehanna was not restored until it flirted with extirpation.

What Thoreau knew, and what we too frequently overlook, is that historical population levels matter—vitally. There is a widespread acceptance that greatly reduced diadromous fish populations are the status quo, which prevents us from realizing the potential of these fishes to provide food, sport, and natural spectacle, and to contribute to healthy river ecosystems. And in assessing only the most recent declines known to us, we too often respond with easy "patches," such as hatchery programs that do more harm than good, rather than addressing the root causes for the losses.

In his essay "Apostrophe to the Ocean," James Carlton asked, "What were the coastal oceans like in 1899, in 1799, in 1699?" and noted that as we enter the twenty-first century, we do not have even a rudimentary synthetic picture.[17] He also noted that 99 percent of the available historical record remains essentially unread by conservation biologists. Having such an understanding of historical rivers and seas could be the sine qua non of modern conservation science. Indeed, we could use diadromous fish spawning runs to broadly evaluate river management: Because they are so susceptible to overfishing, damming, and contamination, their present-day state is an integrative and appropriate metric for how we oversee our rivers and estuaries—the persistence of any respectable runs is a sign of admirable stewardship in these rivers.

I believe the historic record of abundance can be marshaled to achieve great benefits for diadromous fishes. Conservation organizations and government agencies are more likely to mobilize if they are inspired by a scientifically accurate picture of what the waterscape looked like and how it functioned in the past. Historical ecology—that is, the unearthing and synthesis of hitherto forgotten or disregarded historical information—could guide management efforts toward restoration with a firmer knowledge of "what could be." Waiting a thousand years for Thoreau's migratory shoals to appear doesn't seem quite good enough.

Conservation of Wild Places

The following essays illustrate wild places, from truly wild, to threatened, to partially restored, and are written by the conservationists who know these places best.

In the first essay, "Mapping the State of the Oceans," little degradations add up—one degree warmer, one more catch of deep-sea fish—and mapping the last of the marine wild becomes a valuable tool.

In the second essay, "Africa's Last Wild Places: Why Conservation Can't Wait," a remote area that is both politically and ecologically wild is influenced by global ivory trade policy.

The third essay, "The Deep Sea: Unknown and Under Threat," covers a vast and little-known area of the planet that is becoming easier to explore and to destroy.

Alpine areas of the tropical Andes offer a first glimpse of how climate change will gradually alter the natural world in the essay, "Climate Change in the Andes."

Finally, hanging in the balance between wild and human-dominated landscapes are the world's grasslands, and their restoration is described in "Grazers and Grasslands: Restoring Biodiversity to the Prairies."

The combined scientific knowledge on these pages will help identify how best to conserve our wild places.

Herd of Buffalo Crossing the Missouri on Ice

If dragonflies can mate atop the surface tension
of water, surely these tons of bison can mince
across the river, their fur peeling in strips like old

wallpaper, their huge eyes adjusting to how far
they can see when there's no big or little bluestem,
no Indian grass nor prairie cord grass to plod through.

Maybe because it's bright in the blown snow
and swirling grit, their vast heads are lowered
to the gray ice: nothing to eat, little to smell.

They have their own currents. You could watch a herd
of running pronghorn swerve like a river rounding
a meander and see better what I mean. But

bison are a deeper, deliberate water, and there will
never be enough water for any West but the one
into which we watch these bison carefully disappear.

WILLIAM MATTHEWS

Mapping the State of the Oceans

ERIC W. SANDERSON

On land we have an intuitive image of a wild place. A wild place is untrammeled by human endeavor and is full of life, and in a wild place, people feel connected to nature. Unfortunately, of these three attributes of wildness, only the first is easy to map. The "Human Footprint," which was featured in *State of the Wild 2006*, mapped the geographic pattern of human infrastructure on land through proxies like global human population density, land use, access, and technology. The antithesis of the human footprint, the "Last of the Wild" is a map highlighting the areas in terrestrial ecosystems of the world where the influence of humans is the least.[1] Together these maps provide a visual way to understand the state of the wild on land, a tool for scientists to study the consequences of the cumulative influence of human societies, and a framework for conservationists to plan how and where to save what nature remains at the beginning of the twenty-first century. The only problem was, we left out 70 percent of Earth's surface: the oceans.

In the oceans, all these same concepts, and thus the maps on which they are based, are a bit more slippery. Wild places in the water are harder for people to imagine because we typically see only the surface of the full, three-dimensional world that lies below. As a result, our appreciation of the oceans as a place full of life is confounded. Even with scuba gear or submarines, we are but brief, alien visitors. Although we might have some idea of the remarkable abundance of coral reefs, few of us know in our hearts

ERIC W. SANDERSON is the associate director of the Landscape Ecology and Geographic Analysis Program at the Wildlife Conservation Society. He was one of the principal architects of the landscape species approach to conservation, rangewide priority setting, and the human footprint. He also is the leader of the Mannahatta Project, an effort to understand the historical ecology of New York City.

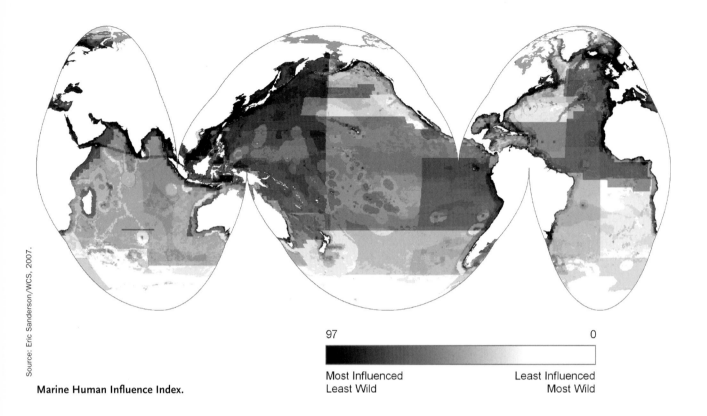

97   0

| Most Influenced | Least Influenced |
| Least Wild | Most Wild |

Marine Human Influence Index.

the monumentality of sea mounts or the teeming fertility of an estuary.

Equally confusing is the vastness of the oceans—in our land-locked way, we take them for granted. On the one hand, we have pulled life from the depths for generations. We have known the ocean as mystical and terrorizing—the manatee mermaid, the narwhal unicorn—and prolific, what once seemed an unending bounty. On the other hand, we have treated the ocean as the ultimate repository of our pollution, which seemed for most of our history to swallow our discards without effect, the consequences washed out on the latest tide. The past century has shown us how naïve we were, especially as our numbers and powers have swelled, enough in fact to diminish the mighty sea and devastate the life it supports.

Mapping the marine human footprint started out with the same logic as that used for the terrestrial sphere. Map the threats, add them up, find the wildest places, and thus motivate and direct conservation action to save the ocean's ecosystems. We use computer software—geographic information systems—and we worry a lot about map projections, data resolution, and the quality of the source material. Some of the maps are based on real-world measurements, some from satellites; others are based on models and on a scientific understanding of the drivers of oceanic threats. These maps would not exist except for the labor of scientists all over the world documenting what is happening in the oceans and placing much of this information into the public domain. None of the maps are perfect, but here is what we are discovering.

Foremost, it is daunting what people have done to the oceans. Fisheries that lasted hundreds of years have disappeared because of too much fishing; some species, like the Atlantic cod (*Gadus morhua*), have yet to return even after moratoriums on fishing for a decade or more.[2] Large predatory fishes, like tunas and sharks, ocean giants at the top of oceanic food chains, have lost nine out of ten of their numbers.[3] Bottom-tending fishing gear annually churns up seafloor habitat at up to 150 times the rate at which forests on land are clear-cut.[4] Raw sewage, fertilizer runoff, chemical wastes, oil pollution, and altered sediment and freshwater inputs[5] continue to add their burdens to the ocean. New biological introductions are reported every year, and now climate change is rewriting basic patterns of temperature, water chemistry, ocean currents, and productivity on which marine life depends.[6]

When we map all these threats together, we confirm the patterns that others have documented for individual threats and show that these threats cumulatively influence all of the ocean—over 90 percent of it. In some cases, eight, nine, ten threats are simultaneously acting, especially in the coastal seas, which are as productive for ocean wildlife as they are for us. Understanding the cumulative impact of threats—not just fishing, but fishing plus pollution, and fishing plus pollution plus habitat destruction—is the next direction for ecosystem-based management of the oceans.

> Large predatory fishes, like tunas and sharks, ocean giants at the top of oceanic food chains, have lost nine out of ten of their numbers.

The Marine Human Footprint allows us to identify the last of the wild in the oceans. These wilder places do exist, and, to the extent that they can be protected, as in the Northwest Hawaiian Islands or over the Great Barrier Reef, they can form the basis for a long-term conservation strategy.

What is the state of the wild in the oceans? Poor, in general, one would have to conclude. But nature, whether on land or in the water, is resilient if given a chance, and, fortunately, human beings have an ability to learn and a capacity to make a difference. Science and sustainable management of ecosystems offer ideas about what we can do to positively influence the oceans. Patience and understanding and love still rest in the human soul. Now people, as individuals, as institutions, as governments, can choose a future for the oceans, which are no longer so vast or so poorly understood that we naïvely abuse them. Our actions, forbearance, and stewardship can help restore the bounty of marine life that is our natural heritage.

Africa's Last Wild Places

Why Conservation Can't Wait

J. MICHAEL FAY

Twenty-five years ago I arrived in Manovo-Gounda-St. Floris National Park in northern Central African Republic as a Peace Corps volunteer to be the botanist for an elephant project. It was a dream job. They gave me a 125 cc dirt bike and said, go out into this vast African wilderness of 5 million acres and collect every plant you can find. The park covered grassy floodplains and wooded savanna. I built a cozy camp down in the park's southern reaches, where there were beautiful, rich gallery forests full of life. I often saw elephants, sometimes in herds hundreds strong. There were a fair number of black rhino roaming the landscape, too. I found hundreds of plant species and learned them all. But, quickly, I was distracted by the most horrific killing a person could ever witness.

I often made long forays off any dirt road deep into the park. More often than not I would be cruising along and the familiar stench of rotting elephant flesh would make that knot form in my throat. Day after day we would find them, piles of dead elephants, sometimes 20 or more in an area the size of a basketball court. There they would be lying, mostly females with a few younger individuals, their faces hacked off and the scant tusks they possessed carried away. As I would circle around the carcasses, yet another terror would reveal itself. There would be horse tracks all around, the haunches of the elephants would have four-inch-wide wounds, and the trunks would be sliced in half, from tip to face.

These were signs that the hunters were Arab horsemen who came from

---

J. MICHAEL FAY is a conservationist with the Wildlife Conservation Society and a Conservation Fellow at the National Geographic Society. His 1997 "megatransect" through 1,200 miles of Congo and Gabon led to the creation of a network of 13 national parks in Gabon and the Congo Basin Forest Partnership. He is currently flying a 60,000-mile voyage over Africa, evaluating human impacts on the environment.

Elephant carcass in Tsavo National Park, Kenya, 1986. The animal's head and tusks were taken by poachers.

Sudan in horse and camel caravans of 100 or so. They traveled across hundreds of kilometers of hot savanna to visit these lands that their ancestors had been raiding for slaves and ivory for centuries. The elephants in the park were their target—they would leave their camps in hunting parties and track the elephants on horseback. These horsemen were the same types of bands—the Janjaweed— who would become infamous decades later for raiding Sudanese villages in Darfur. Their old-fashioned yet lethal method was to get within range of the elephants and gallop forward, their spears with two-foot-long blades at the ready. The elephants would stampede. The horsemen would charge and hamstring any elephant in range, plunging those spears deep into the perfect debilitating spot, and then go for another. Once the remaining elephants escaped, the horsemen would double back and with their sabers slice the trunks of the downed elephants, which would then bleed into enormous pools that we would find blackened in the scorching sun. To see these animals—that we followed daily, observing their gentle nature, their nurturing ways, their intelligence—lifeless and bloated, transformed us.

It transformed us from scientists who came to Africa to study natural history into people who thought only about death—death of elephants, of wildlife, and how to stop those who were doing the killing. We started carrying guns and made feeble attempts to help stem the tide of killing, but it was hopeless. The French Foreign Legion based in the Central African Republic came to join the fight, but with only tacit orders from

> Their old-fashioned yet lethal method was to get within range of the elephants and gallop forward, their spears with two-foot-long blades at the ready. . . . To see these animals—that we followed daily, observing their gentle nature, their nurturing ways, their intelligence— lifeless and bloated, transformed us.

above. They had Puma helicopters, jeeps, and armed men, but this wasn't their war. Killing Sudanese poachers was probably not going to be good for their oil interests across the border. And at the same time the government of the Central African Republic (which was essentially being run by a French military adviser at the time) was exporting hundreds of tons of ivory. In 1982 a minimum of 202 tons, and in 1983, 107 tons of ivory were legally exported from the Central African Republic.[1] Between 1971 and 1984 a minimum of 33,000 elephants' worth of ivory was exported from the Central African Republic.[2] Ivory, laundered between the Central African Republic, Zaire (now Democratic Republic of the Congo [DRC]), and Congo would typically have a false certificate of origin from an adjacent country. This didn't include the thousands of tusks that went into Sudan. Many were making money, but no one was being held accountable for the slaughter.

In 1985, Iain Douglas-Hamilton landed in our camp. It was the wet season and Andrea Turkalo and I were the only two Europeans for well over 100 miles (160 km) in all directions. We had a small team of 12 park guards armed with World War II infantry rifles and I with a Weatherby 300 magnum. A week before, a contingent of French soldiers had visited and we found about 16 dead elephants 24 miles (40 km) from camp but never found the culprits.

Iain had come with Jean Marc Froment to do a sample count of the entire region to quantify wildlife populations and elephant killing. As the days wore on, Iain became furious to the point of deep depression. They were finding dead elephants everywhere. On the fourth day of the survey Iain flew low over the camp, having spotted carcasses just to the south. We arrived on the scene to find 12 dead elephants. They had been killed the evening before. The haunches had those familiar slashes and the blood was still red. The killers had not yet returned to claim the tusks. I was outraged, but at the same time felt helpless. What more could we do with what we had?

Iain had witnessed massive slaughter of elephants in Uganda a few years before but these Central African Republic counts seemed impossible. The final number was estimated at 5,840 dead elephants to 2,701 live ones.[3] The high grasses would have obscured older carcasses, so these killings were a maximum of two years old, and most were relatively recent. At this rate the elephants would be driven to extinction in northern Central African Republic in less than a decade.

Iain was embroiled at the time in the ivory wars continent-wide. His data indicated that elephants were being driven to extinction by poaching not just in the Central African Republic but in Kenya and Tanzania and most everywhere else in Africa (except four countries in southern Africa). The price of ivory had risen to over US$200 a kilo and the poachers would stop at nothing to get it. The dealers took every opportunity to launder and sanitize the killing. Ivory showed up in markets with no link to the lives that had been sacrificed

Part of an illegal consignment of 5,000 pounds (2.5 t) of ivory seized by Taiwanese authorities in July 2006 at Kaohsiung harbor. The ivory was en route from Tanzania to the Philippines. Two days later, a further 6,000 pounds (3 t) were seized at the same port.

for it. Hong Kong and Japan were the largest importers of ivory from Africa.

America was one of the largest consumers of worked ivory. I would write to my mother about the killing. She wrote complaints to Macy's and Saks Fifth Avenue, whose catalogs were full of gorgeous ivory bracelets, necklaces, and earrings. She got a letter back from some public-relations person who said that their ivory was certified to be legally harvested. Seeing the slaughter firsthand and the rampant trade into Sudan, we knew it was not difficult to falsify certification for a piece of ivory.

At the same time, the debate among the suits at the Convention on International Trade in Endangered Species of Wild Fauna and Flora (CITES) and other international policy venues was not about the slaughter but whether all these observations from the field were accurate. Would it really cause extinction of these populations of elephants? The government in Khartoum was one of the biggest offenders in the laundering, but CITES failed to call them on it.

Jean Marc and Iain went to Bangui, the Central African Republic's capital, and showed President Kolingba the pictures of the carnage and the numbers of dead elephants they had found. It wasn't hard to convince the president: Sudanese horsemen had shot at him when he landed his helicopter in an elephant-poaching camp only a few months before. Kolingba immediately issued a decree to outlaw the ivory trade in the Central African Republic and promised to make things happen.

By 1988, Manovo-Gounda-St. Floris National Park became a United Nations Educational, Scientific, and Cultural Organization World Heritage Site. By 1989, the slaughter of elephants became so obvious that a decision was made at the CITES Conference of Parties to ban the international trade of ivory. The protrade lobby warned that the ban would propel ivory prices to astronomical levels, stimulating more trade, and that this would indeed mean the end of elephants. In the face of this new territory—regulating wildlife trade—a few brave souls like Iain and Richard Leakey spoke out and helped convince the rest of

Source: Elizabeth Bennett/WCS.

Poaching for ivory is a threat to Asian and African elephants. This intricately carved ivory sculpture is on display in a museum in Guangzhou, China.

the CITES members to support the ban, despite the efforts of a well-financed lobby from southern African countries to block it.

Soon after the ban was in place, the bottom fell out of the ivory market. Traders who had stockpiles of ivory couldn't sell it. Sabena Airlines would no longer take their shipments. Many poachers stopped hunting elephant because it was hardly worth their while. The full-scale international ban on ivory was working, at least in part.

In the meantime, the European Union financed a large project to help shore up development in the areas surrounding the Manovo-Gounda-St. Floris, to the tune of tens of millions of dollars, with wildlife protection as a

> In the north of the park, in a place where there had been well over 200,000 antelope in the 1960s, there were none. All we saw there were some 10,000 refugees who had fled the Janjaweed raiders from the north.

central focus. The park was abuzz with new Toyota Land Cruisers, a dedicated airplane, well over 100 guards, and a game plan to end the poaching.

But the Sudanese horsemen kept coming to northern Central African Republic. There was still an illegal ivory market. And, as elephant numbers diminished and black rhinos went extinct, they started killing buffalo and antelope on a grand scale. They would smoke the meat and caravan it back to Darfur, which, during the drought of 1984, brought them good money and some sustenance.

Giraffes are hunted for their meat, skin, and hair. Giraffe, with impala in background, drinking in the Great Ruaha River, Pawaga-Idodi Wildlife Management Area, Tanzania.

In 2005, I went back to the Central African Republic. I had a copy of Iain's 1985 report and a plan to fly his exact survey lines to replicate his study. The funding for the European Union project, after almost 10 years, had run its course. The camps were more or less abandoned and only a Toyota or two were still working. The guards were not being paid and were not patrolling. Four park staff had been shot in 1997. The park seemed to have been abandoned.

We counted only 74 elephants in the entire park. The killing was continuing. We found fresh carcasses of elephants, with telltale speared haunches. We found piles of dead elephants with their tusks hacked from their faces. It was obvious where this was going: toward complete extinction of the elephant in the entire north and east of the Central African Republic, southwestern Sudan, and northern DRC. In three decades, this area that may have contained 100,000 elephants had been emptied.

We found the same to be true for most other species of wildlife in Manovo-Gounda-St. Floris. The estimate for giraffe had gone from 1,492 to 223, for buffalo from 8,078 to 1,489. For the nine major species, including hartebeest, topi, and kob, estimated populations had dropped by over 87 percent.[4] In the north of the park, in a place where there had been well over 200,000 antelope in the 1960s, there were none. All we saw there were some 10,000 refugees who had fled the Janjaweed raiders from the north.

This brought back a piercing memory of a paper Richard Ruggiero and I had written 20 years earlier. Richard had firsthand experience with the Sudanese horsemen because he had worked doing antipoaching in Manovo in the mid-1980s. We had written that if the killing continued and the international community did not intervene, these horsemen would not stop at elephants and ante-

African elephant (*Loxodonta africana*) family. The demand for ivory could lead to the extermination of this magnificent species across most of the continent.

lope. We predicted that they would start killing people and destabilize the entire region. Now the United Nations has a major international crisis on its hands. The world community is spending billions just to try and keep people alive. Darfur is now experiencing massive genocide at the hands of the Janjaweed, the same groups who had carried out the mass extermination of elephants, not just in the Central African Republic, but in southwest Sudan and northeast DRC.

The international response to this violence and destabilization has been sporadic. In October 2006, the French military sent Mirage fighter jets to bomb two towns in northern Central African Republic, Ndele and Birao, near Manovo-Gounda-St. Floris National Park. They were bombing so-called rebels who had taken these towns by force. The northern Central African Republic has become a no-man's-land.

By the time this book is published, CITES will have determined, once again, the fate of the elephant by deciding what humans should do about ivory. South Africa wants to kill several thousand elephants and sell ivory because they claim Kruger National Park is overcrowded with them. Although that could be true, Kruger only covers 1.5 percent of the surface of South Africa and less then 0.1

percent of the entire elephant range in 1900. There are alternatives to culling elephants, such as opening up borders to neighboring parks like the Great Limpopo in Mozambique. Should our leaders open up the ivory trade for a special interest that represents such a small part of the equation, unleashing the illegal trade that has characterized men and ivory for the past century? Should they make decisions that are much more far-reaching than just elephants—decisions that can lead to destabilization and hardship for humans in southern Sudan, Central African Republic, and DRC?

> Should they make decisions that are much more far-reaching than just elephants—decisions that can lead to destabilization and hardship for humans in southern Sudan, Central African Republic, and DRC?

There are better solutions. In 1989, leaders in Kenya decided to champion a continent-wide fight to stop the ivory trade because of its obvious impacts: it made parks meaningless, and invited poaching and violence to rural areas and corruption in government. I went back to Kenya in 2005 to Tsavo National Park. It had been the epicenter of poaching wars decades earlier, but elephant populations have been steadily increasing since 1989. At the same time the Somali raiding had declined, security was strengthened in the area, and tourism is booming. People and wildlife are content, for now.

My experiences with all of the elephant slaughter and deforestation and general degradation of the wild in the past 25 years has led me to a few conclusions. If you live on the landscape day after day, year after year, you realize that you do not need the absolute proof of science to act. Often the trends are as real as massive piles of dead elephants at your feet. If you witness these things that will obviously impact the future of wild places, you must ask your politicians to act—because others with less noble motives are doing just that.

Ice sheets melting, forests dying, and fish disappearing are all real, just like the killing of elephants was in the 1980s. Yet our politicians are either leading us to believe that the scientific evidence is not sufficient or they are acting much too late, and with no accountability. It is high time that we pay attention to what we witness so clearly with our own eyes and that we require our leaders to lead us toward a future that can sustain the presence of 6.5 or 9 billion people on this earth.

The killing of elephants should not have been ignored in central Africa two decades ago. Their populations suffered greatly and have not been given the chance to rebound because of another problem we ignored: violent cross-border raids by the Janjaweed. As CITES decides what to do about ivory, and Africa decides what to do about elephant populations in parks that are not large enough, we shouldn't be tempted to think that culling thousands of elephants and selling their tusks is a solution to anything.

The Deep Sea

Unknown and Under Threat

LES WATLING

> I imagined this colossal volume of water, cloaked in permanent darkness, and I pictured the fantastic creatures that swam there, far from our gazes, the surrealist results of an ever inventive Nature.
>
> CLAIRE NOUVIAN, *THE DEEP*,
> UNIVERSITY OF CHICAGO PRESS (2007).

The landscape of a cold, dark world develops into color under the powerful lights of the deep-diving submarine *Alvin*. This is a quiet world; the only noise is the whir of the motors. We are on the side of a mountain that rises more than 11,500 feet (3,500 m) from a broad, muddy plain to its rock- and sand-strewn summit. The bottom consists of large, billowy rocks, with occasional white or purple fan structures about three feet across, festooned with orange serpent stars. There are purple parasols about two feet high, and giant ten-foot white stalks, often twisted Dr. Seuss–like, bearing light pink polyps along their sides. Welcome to Kelvin Seamount, western North Atlantic, depth: 6,730 feet (2,050 m).

This is the first time *Alvin* has landed anywhere on Kelvin Seamount, and we are the first to see this particular landscape. We feel like real explorers, knowing that humans have seen less of the deep sea than we have of our moon and other planets. Only one *Alvin*-class submarine operates in the United States, and only a few submarines and deep-sea-capable remotely operated

---

LES WATLING is a biological oceanographer interested in understanding the adaptations of bottom-dwelling marine species to their environment. His concerns about fishing with trawl gear extend into the deep sea. He has recently dedicated himself to becoming an expert on the taxonomy and ecology of deep-sea octocorals, and has so far described four new species.

Source: Courtesy of Les Wating for the Deep Atlantic Stepping Stones Science Party, IFE, URI-IAO, and NOAA.

The claw of the ROV *Hercules* collects a clump of the octocoral *Acanthogorgia* spp., which has some comatulid crinoids sitting on it. Rehoboth Seamount, on the New England Seamount chain, depth 6,000 feet (1,900 m).

vehicles exist worldwide. Consequently, less than 5 percent of this most extensive habitat on Earth has been viewed by humans, either directly or through samples brought to the surface. There are whole mountain ranges and vast expanses of the abyssal seafloor yet to be seen.

One hundred and fifty years of scientific research has revealed that one of the most intriguing aspects of the deep ocean—the benthos—is that it is a place of constants: constant darkness, constant temperature, constant salinity, constant oxygen levels. Unlike shallow waters, these constants hold true over hundreds or thousands of miles, and for long periods of time. In fact, the water flowing over any one place on the deep ocean floor moves so slowly that it can have nearly the same characteristics for a hundred years and vary little for several thousand. Animals on the deep-sea floor live in a pitch-black world that has changed little in the past 15 to 20 million years.

The deep ocean was once thought to be devoid of life because it is dark and subject to unbelievably high pressures —at 6,500 feet (2,000 m), the pressure is approximately 1.4 tons per square inch. Yet the benthos is rich in bizarre creatures. Species diversity is surprising here, and many species live for a hundred, or even a thousand, years—although one has to wonder whether the term *year* is meaningful in a world with no light or change in temperature. For example, the deep-water black coral (*Leiopathes glaberrima*) is

> Animals on the deep-sea floor live in a pitch-black world that has changed little in the past 15 to 20 million years.

estimated to be more than 2,300 years old, and the gold coral (*Gerardia* spp.) may be 1,470 years old, both collected at 1,480 feet (450 m) off Oahu, Hawaii.[1] To deep-sea benthic inhabitants, time is marked by periods when abundant food particles sink from the sunlit ocean surface water following plankton blooms, and long periods of low or no food. Most of the sea fans (gorgonian octocorals), for example, feed on microplankton that they catch with the tentacles of their

Source: Courtesy of Les Watling for the Mountains in the Sea Science Party, IFE, URI-IAO, and NOAA.

Sea spiders like the one pictured here (of the genus *Collosendeis*) use a long proboscis to feed on the juices of soft-bodied invertebrates, such as sea anemones.

polyps. An individual sea fan may have thousands of polyps, but each one catches food only rarely, and the scarce but sufficient food supports these slow-metabolizing and long-lived species. Most deep-sea species remain to be fully observed or described. Unfortunately, humanity is putting a lot of these creatures in danger of extinction before we have the chance to know them.

Deep-Sea Habitats

The deep sea is considered to be that part of the ocean deeper than 700 to 900 feet (200 to 300 m), meaning that about 65 percent of Earth's surface is deep-sea waters. The average depth of the ocean is over 2.5 miles (about 4 km). Much of that floor is broad, muddy plains 3 miles down (exceeding 5 km). Interestingly, the muddy plains are not truly flat. Small hills rise, creating gradual undulations, and at extremely small scales, burrows, tracks, and fecal mounds made by various animals provide a limited topography. For example, at a depth of about 2.5

miles off northwest Africa, a large single-celled organism called a xenophyophore glues small sediment particles together to make two-inch-wide mounds, and there may be a thousand of these in each 1,000 square feet (93 m^2) of seafloor. From *Alvin*, we sampled xenophyophore mounds on Bear Seamount, off the eastern coast of the United States, and found that each was home to a small shrimplike crustacean called an amphipod. In other areas, as much as 70 percent of the abyssal seafloor contains ferromanganese nodules or metalliferous sediments—sediments that form small stones of high concentrations of iron, manganese, and other metals—and these provide habitat for a wide diversity of worms, crustaceans, and single-celled creatures called forams.[2]

Despite its depth, the muddy seafloor is the best-studied benthic habitat because it can be sampled from research ships. Typically, a box corer lowered from the ship, sometimes to 13,000 feet, is hauled back with a large sample of mud. Its contents reveal a surprising diversity: a sample of 100 animals may contain 80 or 90 separate species, most no more than a millimeter or so in length. (Larger species exist, such as sea cucumbers, but they are relatively rare and usually captured by trawl or on film.)

Thanks to television nature programs, the best-known deep-sea habitats are the hydrothermal vent fields, with their black smoker chimneys, fields of giant clams, translucent, blind shrimp, and mounds of rose-colored tube worms (*Riftia pachyptila*).[3] These communities capture the imagination because they show that life on Earth can exist without any connection to the sunlit surface: their entire food chain is fueled by hot liquids and gases, especially hydrogen sulfide, which is poisonous to virtually all life, but at these vents, bacteria convert it to useable substances.

> These communities . . . show that life on Earth can exist without any connection to the sunlit surface: their entire food chain is fueled by hot liquids and gases, especially hydrogen sulfide, which is poisonous to virtually all life.

Vent communities are not permanent: the chimneys may cease exuding hot water due to geothermal shifts, and when the water cools and the sulfide dissipates, the entire community dies. Because vent fields are widespread, with distances between them potentially thousands of miles, scientists have searched for other deep-sea habitats that support these organisms on their vent-to-vent journey. Most of these species are not mobile as adults, and their larvae precariously depend on the slow flow of the deep ocean waters for transport to the next site.

Interrupting the muddy flat plains in the deep sea are more than 14,000 seamounts (undersea mountains that rise more than 3,300 feet [1,000 m] from the surrounding seafloor) that we have been able to map in great detail with satellite radar surveys and multibeam echo-sounders.[4] Most seamounts originated as volcanoes, and many towered almost a mile above the ocean surface before erosion and the cooling of the crust caused them to sink below. Some seamount groups, such as the Hawaiian-Emperor chain (which extends from Hawaii to northeast of Japan) and the New England Seamount chain (from off Boston to the Mid-Atlantic Ridge), are arrayed in long, nearly straight lines, having being formed as the ocean floor moved over a mantle plume or "hot spot." Others appear in clusters or are volcanoes on spreading ridges, such as the Mid-Atlantic Ridge.

Recent discoveries show that seamounts, no matter where they are, support a diverse community of suspension-feeding corals, sponges, and smaller invertebrates. Many of these species require the hard substratum for attachment, and benefit from water flows around large topography. Seamounts may also be areas where animals like the dumbo octopus (*Grimpoteuthis* spp.) secure their eggs. Seamounts attract congregations of pelagic and bentho-pelagic fishes for protection, and to take advantage of the food-laden currents deflected by the bottom relief.

Despite being remote, these wild places are threatened by deep-sea fishing, mining, and dumping.

Fishing

After coastal nations declared exclusive economic zones over resources within 200 miles offshore, and fisheries on the continental shelves of the North Atlantic were depleted, the fishing industry sought new species further out in the ocean. Industrialized nations developed factory trawlers, ships capable of pulling large nets through the water, and commercial vessels began reaching fish at depths of 6,500 feet (2,000 m). Now, seamounts and deep ridges are targeted because many pelagic and bentho-pelagic species, such as orange roughy (*Hoplostethus atlanticus*) and Patagonian toothfish (marketed as Chilean sea bass) (*Dissostichus* spp.), tend to aggregate there. Their size and market value make them targets.

A dead coral skeleton (*Chrysogorgia* spp.) covered with barnacles (*Glyptelasma hamatum*), Lyman Peak, Yakutat Seamount. Ocean dumping, mining, and bottom trawling have inflicted damage upon many species of the little-known benthos.

Source: Courtesy of Les Watling for the Deep Atlantic Stepping Stones Science Party, IFE, URI.IAO, and NOAA.

Some other deep-water species currently caught commercially include oreos (*Allocyttus niger, Pseudocyttus maculatus*), roundnose grenadier (*Coryphaenoides rupestris*), blue ling (*Molva dypterygia*), Greenland halibut (*Reinhardtius hippoglossoides*), and sable fish (*Anoplopoma fimbria*). The pelagic armorhead (*Pseudopentaceros wheeleri*) is already considered commercially extinct.

These deep-sea species are very slow to reproduce and are long-lived—orange roughy can live longer than most humans, between 50 and 100 years—and only begin to reproduce between 22 and 36 years of age.[5] The Patagonian toothfish only reproduces at nine and ten years. This limits the resilience of their populations, and they can quickly become overfished.

Another major impact of fishing on deep-sea benthic communities is the col-

Bathygadus spp. swimming over Lyman Peak on Yakutat Seamount, depth 5,000 feet (1,600 m). Seamounts are targeted for fishing deep-sea and open-ocean species, as well as for mining.

lateral damage inflicted by metal trawl gear. To reach these depths, the gear must be extremely heavy, with trawl "doors" weighing several tons. Although fishing technology has advanced, the bycatch of corals and sponges brought up during fishing operations suggests that it is not possible to know precisely where the gear is. As a result, bottom communities take a severe beating in areas where trawl use is common.[6] Seamounts in Australian and New Zealand waters fished for orange roughy have been denuded by trawl-gear collisions.

The deep-sea fishing industry is capable of scraping life from seamount after seamount. These habitats are not resilient. They are deep enough that they have no history of strong currents or heavy wave action—factors that might predispose resident organisms to withstand physical impacts. Organisms here grow slowly, so recruitment of new individuals to replace those removed by fishing and collisions is very slow. Deep-sea fishing now occurs in every ocean, so seamounts and ridges that have never been explored and species that have not yet been documented are possibly being fished out. In 2006, the United Nations General Assembly had the opportunity to ban high-seas bottom trawling and protect benthic life, but the effort failed due to the objections of Iceland, Russia, and Spain.[7] A resolution supporting such a ban will almost certainly be introduced again.

Mining

The manganese nodules that occur over wide areas of the abyssal plains contain high-value metals such as copper, zinc, and cobalt.[8] Interest in mining the nodules, and the increasing development of the technology to do so, has resulted in seven international consortia licensed to explore extraction techniques in a combined area of 203,000 square miles (525,000 km²), mostly in the Clarion-Clipperton Fracture Zone area of the eastern Pacific.[9] To be economically feasible, about 6,600 tons (5,987 metric tonnes) of nodules would need to be lifted from a depth of 16,000 feet every day. Because these nodules are the only hard substrate in the muddy deep basins, and because each has taken 10 to 20 million years to grow, such intensive mining would completely alter the microhabitat characteristics of wide areas of the ocean floor, essentially forever. One estimate suggests that fifteen years of mining by two or three companies would severely disturb about 69,500 square miles (180,000 km²) of seafloor.

Another source of metals can be found in seamounts. As volcanoes become seamounts, they are gradually coated with layers of manganese and

> Bottom communities take a severe beating in areas where trawl use is common.

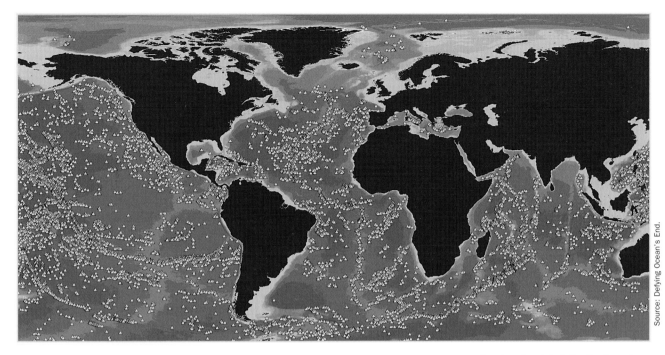

Source: Defying Ocean's End.

Map showing the global distribution of seamounts (represented by triangles) based on ETOPO2 satellite data.

other metals that precipitate out of seawater. These crusts are also becoming more valuable as the worldwide price of metals increases. Recently, high concentrations of cobalt, a metal used in jet engines and computer disks, were found in the manganese crusts of deep-sea mountains.[10] Obtaining cobalt from seamount crusts at 8,200 feet (2,500 m) would be more accessible than reaching seabed nodules, but these areas near the higher flanks of seamounts are favored by hard corals and octocorals. Stripping the surface would eliminate many organisms from the immediate mining area, and the spread of the tailings from the mining process would have wider impacts. There is, at present, no nodule or crust mining. However, with increasing prices of these metals (cobalt prices doubled between 2006 and 2007) comes the likelihood that deep-sea mineral extraction will soon be a concern for conservationists.

Dumping

For 150 years, the ocean was considered a limitless place to dump everything from trash to hazardous waste with little concern that it would be seen again. Increased understanding of ocean chemistry and circulation has made it clear that much of what is dumped in the ocean comes back.

Materials dredged from harbors, notorious for their contaminated sediments, metals, and complex organic molecules from petroleum hydrocarbon, were routinely dumped directly into deep-ocean communities. Between 165 and 440 million tons (150 and 400 million tonnes) of dredged material are still dumped annually in international waters,[11] and metals and complex organic molecules have been found in fish and marine mammals. In regulated countries, most of this activity has slowed, and toxic sediment is usually capped with "clean" sediment.

In addition, the US military disposed of munitions at a deep-water site off the Farallon Islands near San Francisco, and chemical-weapons containers were dumped off Barbers Point, Hawaii. Together, Europe and the US have dumped more than 300,000 drums of low-level radioactive waste into the sea.[12] For a while the deep-sea abyssal plains were considered a useful nuclear disposal site because the mud is thousands of meters thick and wastes would eventually (in several million years) be subducted into Earth's mantle.[13] However, risks associated with the transport and disposal of nuclear waste has halted this practice for now.

> With increasing prices of metals comes the likelihood that deep-sea mineral extraction will soon be a concern for conservationists.

A recent disposal plan involves carbon dioxide sequestration in the deep ocean.[14] Carbon dioxide, pressurized to its liquid form, could be pumped to the seafloor and trapped there for a few centuries. Unfortunately, in the meantime, liquid carbon dioxide would pool in seafloor depressions, smothering most of the organisms there.[15]

As we work our way up the side of Kelvin Seamount, we pass vertical cliffs several hundred feet high. We will reach the summit seven hours later. The conversation in the submarine is about the specimens to be collected, but returns to how lucky we feel to see what few will ever see, and what a shame it would be to lose it all. The deep sea is a place used to hide waste and remove resources. But it is also the least-known habitat on Earth. Part of our mission is to see that people come to know this place, to value the strange beasts that live here for their uniqueness and beauty, and to understand that its protection is essential.

Climate Change in the Andes

CAROLINA MURCIA

To frame discussions of current global climate change, scientists often compare its speed and intensity with that of cyclic glaciations over the past 500,000 years. Each of these periods of warming and cooling lasted thousands of years, allowing plants and animals many generations to migrate and disperse in response to changes in temperature and availability of water and food. Some species went extinct and new ones evolved. The result was a significant change in the composition of communities, ecosystems, and biomes. In the last glacial cycle, moist forests converted to savannas in Africa and South America, and marine areas became terrestrial. These changes were profound, but slow.

In contrast, in just the past 150 years, Earth's average surface temperature has increased by 1.33°F (0.74°C)—with a sharp acceleration in the past three decades.[1] Due to the recent buildup of greenhouse gases, climate warming is occurring about three times faster than in previous warming cycles.[2] Although the temperature increase may not be remarkable to an individual organism that experiences freezing winters and scorching summers, it is enough to cause year-round hotter temperatures in the tropics, more rainfall in some areas, drought in others, and dramatic changes in polar, temperate, and high-elevation ecosystems. Over the next century, these trends will bring yet new challenges to Earth's wild places. Of concern is how climate change will affect highly biodiverse areas such as the tropical Andes.

The Andes are the world's longest mountain range at 4,500 miles (7,200 km), stretching from tropical Colombia and Venezuela to Patagonia and containing

CAROLINA MURCIA is the program director of Fundación EcoAndina, a Colombian NGO. She conducts research on tropical cloud forest ecology and dynamics, restoration, and the impact of global warming. She is the author or coauthor of 25 scientific publications and nine policy documents.

102 mountains taller than 19,700 feet (6,000 m). They provide the source of most major rivers in the continent, including the Amazon and all of its main tributaries in the upper watershed. The Andes cradled the ancient civilizations of South America and today support the core of human settlements in Colombia, Ecuador, Peru, and northern Bolivia.

The tropical Andes, which run from Bolivia to Venezuela, contain almost every type of tropical and temperate ecosystem—from dry to wet tropical forests, from lowland evergreen jungles to highland scrublands and savannas, to permafrost and permanent snow—and are the largest source of biological diversity in the Americas. The wealth of plant diversity spawned by this alpine region is due primarily to three factors: the large altitudinal and latitudinal gradients, over 19,700 feet in elevation and 65 degrees in latitude, and the prevalence of endemic species (native species with small geographic ranges).

Elevation creates the most dramatic changes in fauna and flora. As one ascends the mountains, with every 490 feet (150 m) in elevation the average ambient temperature drops 1.8°F (1°C). This cooling, and the coinciding drop in oxygen concentration, defines the altitudinal distribution of most species. Thus, species that thrive at one elevation may not succeed lower or higher, and groups of plants, trees, insects, and animals form communities within altitudinal belts, creating a succession of ecological zones up and down mountains.

Any cross-section of the Andes yields four to five predictable ecological zones defined by elevation[3]: In the northern portion, Venezuela through northern Peru, the altitudinal belts are piedmont, lower montane (1,300–2,200 m), montane (2,200–3,000 m), upper montane (3,000–3,600 m), and *páramo*, or high-elevation scrubland and grassland (3,600–4,000 m). Areas above 16,400 feet (5,000 m) are covered in snow all year. As one moves south, in the central Andes of Peru and Bolivia, ecological zones are the Yungas between 3,300 and 6,600 feet (between 1,000 and 2,000 m), followed by the cloud forests of Ceja de Montaña until about 3,500 meters, and Puna between 3,500 and 4,800 meters. The forest structure varies with elevation and available moisture, with 115-foot (35 m)-tall forests at lower elevations to mere 3-foot (1 m)-tall woodlands in the *páramo*, and even smaller vegetation in the Puna. The latitudinal extension of the Andes provides a gradual substitution of species as one travels south toward Argentina and Chile.

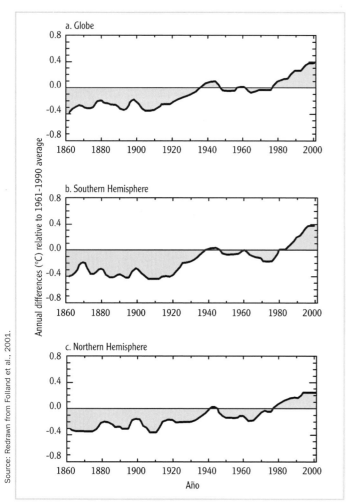

Temperature trends for the last 140 years, showing the difference between the annual average temperature (integrates air and sea surface values—dark wavy line) and the average temperature for the period 1961–1990 (straight horizontal line). The upper panel shows totals for the whole planet, and panels b and c show values for the Southern and Northern hemispheres, respectively.

Such extreme geographical and topographical gradients have led to the evolution and prevalence of endemic plants and animals that are particularly vulnerable to habitat loss. For example, in the northern Andes, 70–80 percent of frog species are endemic. Once their small habitat disappears, so do they. The Cauca guan (*Penelope perspicax*), a bird limited to the Colombian Andes, has a total range spanning only 290 square miles (750 km^2), with much less actual usable habitat, limited to only four forest fragments in two separate mountain ranges. Even more extremely localized is the Quimbaya toad (*Atelopus quimbaya*), also in Colombia, whose estimated geographic range is just 0.4 square miles (1 km^2). Regional protected areas currently cover the toad's range, but this may be insufficient in the face of the shifting conditions caused by climate change.

Climate Change in the Tropical Andes

Meaningful analyses of climate change must incorporate processes acting at both global and local scales. This is challenging in the Andes because mountain topography generates highly localized climatic effects, such as mountain-valley air-circulation patterns and rain shadows. These have not yet been adequately incorporated into the General Circulation Climate Models,[4] so many predictions cannot be readily applied to the particularities of montane regions.

Nevertheless, the current network of meteorological stations in the Andean region provides evidence of warming (although the spatial resolution and history of data are limited). From 1966 to 1990, the longest-running meteorological stations (in Venezuela and Colombia) recorded an increase in temperatures and a reduction in the daily temperature range (which in turn affects water temperatures and wind patterns) relative to the previous half century.[5] Interestingly, mountain stations recorded greater temperature increases than lowland stations. In addition, six stations in the Central Andes of Colombia located between 6,000 and 8,000 feet (1,800 and 2,400 m) recorded a 1.6°F (0.9°C) increase in temperature in the last five decades.[6] This may mean that the tropical Andes is experiencing a faster temperature increase than the world average, which would render Andean wildlife and ecosystems more vulnerable to the effects of climate change.

An outstanding feature of the Andes is its many mountain glaciers, which are receding.[7] In the highlands of Colombia, eight glaciers disappeared during the twentieth century.[8] Today, six glaciers remain, but all receded between 60–80 percent over the past century. Based on this trend, the Colombian Meteorological Institute estimates that two glaciers will disappear as soon as 2015, another three will be gone by 2055, and the last will completely melt over the next century.

The significance is great: glaciers control river water at the regional scale via

> Endemic plants and animals . . . are particularly vulnerable to habitat loss: once their small habitat disappears, so do they.

a balance between their melting and forming. Increased melting creates an initial abundance of runoff. This may benefit agriculture at lower elevations, but is a short-lived bounty that will dry up when the glaciers disappear, compromising future water availability for wildlife, aquatic ecosystems, and humans.

Warming temperatures also affect rainfall, snowline elevation, evaporation, and air humidity. The spatial and temporal distribution of water determines the distribution and reproductive cycles in plants and animals (e.g., rainfall provides cues for breeding in many plants and insects). Predicting how precipitation will change with global warming is complex, particularly in the Andes. Current climate models predict generalized drying of the Andes, but central Colombia has had no change in total precipitation in the past 50 years.[9] The difficulty in generating accurate predictions may again lie in the fact that topography affects local wind patterns and how moisture is distributed in the atmosphere.

To complicate matters further, large-scale deforestation may contribute to regional rainfall variation. When lowland forests surrounding Costa Rica's Monteverde Mountains were cleared for pasture, less moisture from evaporation and transpiration flowed up the nearby slopes to the cloud forests. As a result, less fog reached the cloud forest vegetation, threatening epiphytes—tree-dwelling plants that get moisture from the air.[10] The combined effects of climate change and large-scale forest transformation occurring across the tropical parts of South America make predicting rainfall changes challenging.

Climate-Driven Biological Effects

Climate affects almost all aspects of life—from limiting geographic distributions to modulating cycles of reproduction in plants and animals. Increasingly, ecologists are finding changes in the biology of organisms that are linked to climate change. The most obvious changes are seen in temperate zones such as Europe and North America. There, seasonality ties phenological events—life-cycle events that recur annually or in cycles, such as leaf and fruit emergence, migration, and breeding—to climate, and there have been recent changes in these predictable events. For example, 20 bird species in the United Kingdom advanced their egg-laying by an average of nine days between 1971 and 1995, and adult butterflies now emerge up to a month earlier than they did 20 years ago.[11]

Specific information of this sort does not exist for the tropical Andes because phenological cycles are more complex and not tied to temperature-driven sea-

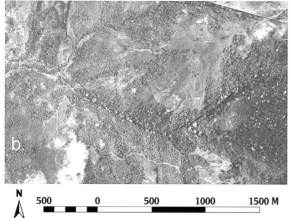

N
500   0   500   1000   1500 M

Change in the altitudinal distribution of the white cecropia (*Cecropia telealba*) due to warming. The upper panel shows an aerial photograph of the forest remnants at El Bolo watershed (Valle del Cauca, Colombia) at 7,380 feet (2,250 m) in elevation in 1982. The lower panel depicts the same site in 1998. The white crowns are adult cecropia trees.

sons. However, changes in rainfall will likely influence the timing of fruit production. Canopy-dwelling frugivorous birds in the Andean forests, such as quetzals (*Pharomacrus* spp.) and oilbirds (*Steatornis caripensis*), track fruit availability by migrating at a regional scale. Changes in fruiting patterns may determine whether these birds and other frugivores reliably find food at a site or elevation in a given month.

As the Andes warm, species will potentially adapt by expanding, contracting, or shifting their distributions or range. Those species whose distributions are defined primarily by elevation will begin to move upward as climates uphill become more benign, or because key resources have moved up.[12] In Colombia, the white yarumo (*Cecropia telealba*), a pioneer tree, has expanded its upper altitudinal limit by 500 feet (150 m) in elevation over the past 40 years, possibly tracking the 1.6°F (0.9°C) warming in this region.[13] As a bird-dispersed species, white yarumo is one of the first trees to colonize forest gaps or abandoned pastures. Consequently, it has expanded its range upward as the climate has changed. The current density of juveniles at the upper edge of the tree's distribution indicates that the species is continuing to move uphill.

In Peru, other species have expanded their ranges upward. Retreating glaciers have exposed more ground, and cushion plants, which live at the edge of glaciers, have colonized new mountain areas. Their current upper limit is 330 feet (100 m) higher than it was in 1931. Retreating glaciers have also left new vernal pools, and toads of three genera have moved up into them, tracking the creation of new habitat.[14]

Despite these examples, moving uphill is not easy and most species—particularly plants—require several generations to adjust their ranges. For some, the rate of dispersal is only a few feet per generation, and each generation may last several decades. Assuming a plant or insect needs to ascend 490 feet (150 m) every 50 years to stay within the climate conditions to which it is adapted, populations would need to move 690 feet (210 m) in actual distance (assuming a slope of 45 degrees). Plants that disperse 50 feet (15 m) per generation (say, every 40 years) may take over 500 years to keep pace with climate change. Many will not be able to track changes in temperature or moisture availability, or will be unable to compete with species ascending from lower elevations. Furthermore, the area available higher up dwindles because mountains taper upward, and elevations above 16,400 feet have no soils—soils form

Source: Negative No. 0-103 Photo: Shippee-Johnson Collection. Department of Library Services, American Museum Natural History (AMNH).

Aerial view of the Cordillera Vilcanota, a section of the tropical Andes range in southern Peru, showing glacial recession: Above, 1931. Below, 2005. Notice the new lake formed near the center of the image.[15]

Source: Anton Seimon/WCS.

over hundreds of years. There is a great chance that some plants will be pushed to the edge of the exposed rock before soils form. Although no extinction has yet been attributed to climate change, the fast-paced changes will very likely become an extinction force.

Changes in individual species and their ranges add up to changes in the composition of ecological communities. Several global models, assuming differing magnitudes of temperature increase and precipitation change, predict shifts in the location and extent of biomes: four models agree that tundra will decline by 40 percent, deserts will decline by 25 percent, and grasslands and dry forests will increase by 40 to 50 percent. However, they are inconclusive on the extent that moist forests will change.[16]

> As the Andes warm, species will potentially adapt by expanding, contracting, or shifting their distributions or range. Those species whose distributions are defined primarily by elevation will begin to move upward as climates uphill become more benign, or because key resources have moved up.

Conserving the Tropical Andes

Information available for the tropical Andes raises many new conservation questions. Will species with slower dispersal rates be able to keep up with warming? If only a few species move, and others stay behind, what will happen to communities or ecosystems whose members have interacted for centuries? How will plants and animals cope with new competitors, predators, or diseases? The interactions between pollinators and plants that regularly bloom based on temperature or precipitation will undoubtedly be affected if some plants no longer flower or flower earlier, or if pollinators move out of that area or increase or decrease in number. Because any one major change can have cascading impacts, it is particularly difficult to predict and track climate change's ecosystem-level effects. Doing so requires thorough knowledge of the behaviors and phenologies of many interacting species and consistent observation over time.

As Earth warms, the Andes may become a Noah's ark for the current biodiversity of nearby lower-elevation ecosystems, particularly two of the most biodiverse lowland ecosystems of South America: the Amazonian piedmont and the Chocó region on the northwestern corner of the continent. But for organisms to move up through the landscape, they need conditions to foster these dispersals: enough forest habitat must be available along an altitudinal gradient to provide green corridors. Current levels of deforestation make this unlikely. In the northern tropical Andes, fragmentation is drastic at mid-elevations of 1,900 to 6,600 feet (580–2,000 m), where the climate is most amenable for crops. At these latitudes, uphill migration is restricted by expanses of cropland and a thick network of roads that, for many species, represent insurmountable barriers. In Colombia, Ecuador, and central Peru, the current location of protected areas along alpine slopes is far from sufficient to ensure necessary green corridors, and efforts to create new protected areas are thwarted by fast-paced infrastructure development projects. Forest conditions in southern Peru and Bolivia are better, although threatened by a transcontinental road network.

Perhaps better than any other region on Earth, the Andes show us that, in

Source: Anton Seimon/WCS.

Green iguana (*Iguana iguana*) in the Bolivian Pantanal. This arboreal species depends on the tropical rainforest canopy for food and shelter. Climate change could affect its geographic distribution and breeding patterns.

the face of climate change, efforts to retain or recuperate connectivity for wildlife require innovative conservation schemes. The Wildlife Conservation Society and others are developing a model for landscape management in the Colombian Andes to allow passage of birds, mammals, and plants through this transformed matrix. Conservation scientists, planners, and managers will have to incorporate the fact that species are shifting ranges or disappearing. It will be a challenge to decide what target areas to conserve or restore. In the face of climate change, conservation involves taking a huge gamble on the planet, and puts to the test our predictions of how individual species will react and our knowledge of how ecosystems work.

Grazers and Grasslands

Restoring Biodiversity to the Prairies

JAMES H. SHAW

In 1942, Aldo Leopold wrote, "While the reestablishment of prairie requires much skill and some expense, its maintenance fortunately requires nothing but an occasional burn."[1]

The founder of wildlife management was, as usual, decades ahead of his time in understanding unique prairie ecosystems. By the time Leopold was born in 1887, much of the original rich grasslands of the United States had already fallen to the plow. At the same time, grassland fires ceased, and some fire-intolerant native plants such as eastern red cedar (*Juniperus virginiana*) invaded and choked the grassland ecosystems, changing their nature over the decades.

Although Leopold was one of the first to recognize grassland fires as a restorative force, he saw wild ungulates such as bison, elk, and pronghorn as residents of the prairie, not integral shapers and maintainers of the grassland ecosystem itself. Today we recognize that the process of grazing by wild ungulates and their domestic livestock counterparts is, like fire, an ecological "driver" without which grasslands cannot be sustained.

Scope of Grasslands Today

In the broadest sense, grasslands cover about 20.5 million square miles (52.5 million km^2) or roughly 32 percent of Earth's land surface.[2] Some of the largest grasslands occur in East and Southern Africa, central North America, Australia,

JAMES H. SHAW has been on the faculty at Oklahoma State University since 1974, where he is a professor in the Department of Natural Resource Ecology and Management. He began studies of bison at the Wichita Mountains Wildlife Refuge in 1981 and later at the Tallgrass Prairie Preserve. He is a longstanding member of the World Conservation Union's Bison Specialist Group.

Grazing by wild ungulates such as bison (*Bison bison*) is key to maintaining the productivity of grassland ecosystems. Bison grazing has influenced how some grasses grow their root systems.

Patagonia, and the Mongolian and Russian steppes. Most are being modified through human activities, including altered fire regimes, continuous grazing, conversion to cropland, and urban/suburban sprawl. These alterations create conditions ripe for invasive plants. Climate change, the twenty-first century's wild card, adds to pressures on grassland ecosystems worldwide by bringing less predictable precipitation and warmer temperatures.

North America's prairies extend from Texas into Manitoba and Saskatchewan and from the Rockies into portions of Ohio, Kentucky, and Missouri. Along the eastern portion are the tallgrass prairies—sometimes called the "true" prairies—in regions of relatively high rainfall (typically 32 inches [80 cm]) and deep, rich soils. Dominant grasses included big bluestem (*Andropogon gerardii*), little bluestem (*Andropogon scoparius*), switchgrass (*Panicum virgatum*), and Indiangrass (*Sorghastrum nutans*).[3] Patches of intact prairie may have a remarkable diversity of grass species, some that are long-lived perennials, many with extensive root systems. Some grasses are as tall as 8 feet (2.5 m), high enough for a horse and rider to disappear from view. Most prairie grasses are fire-adapted, meaning they evolved with and can benefit from fire. Prior to European settlement, fires, which were primarily ignited by Native Americans, occurred on average every one to two years.[4] Tree saplings readily encroach on tallgrass prairies unless frequent fires exclude them.

Large mammals graze on big bluestem (*Andropogon gerardii*), and birds use the plant for nesting as well as cover.

Abundant rainfall and fertile soils made the tallgrass prairies ideally suited for agriculture and, in the nineteenth century, most were converted to family farms. Today only about 4 percent of the tallgrass prairie remains, disproportionately in areas too rocky to plow, such as the Flint Hills of Oklahoma and Kansas.[5]

Further west, in a band from Texas to Manitoba, mixed grass prairies occur where the average annual precipitation is about 12 to 24 inches (30–60 cm) in the northern regions and significantly more in the southern. In mixed grass prairies, large fires occurred about every three to five years,[6] and dominant grasses include little bluestem, wheatgrass (*Agropyron* spp.), and needlegrass (*Stipa* spp.).

To the west, from the Texas panhandle to Alberta and Saskatchewan, are shortgrass prairies, which get less precipitation. Dominant grasses include blue grama (*Bouteloua gracilis*) and buffalograss (*Buchloe dactyloides*), low-growing, nutritious plants resistant to drought and to intensive, short-duration grazing. Shortgrass prairies probably lacked the fuel load to sustain frequent fires on large scales. For example, when fires burned much of Yellowstone National Park during the drought of 1988, only about 1 percent of Montana's shortgrass prairie burned.[7] Even so, infrequent fires may have suppressed the encroachment of woody species such as sagebrush (*Artemisia* spp.), ponderosa pine (*Pinus ponderosa*), and junipers (*Juniperus* spp.) in the north and mesquite (*Prosopis* spp.) in the south.[8]

Prairie Herbivores

Foraging by ungulates also sustains the prairie. In terms of biomass, or weight per unit area, and numbers, bison (*Bison bison*) were historically the dominant mammal of the North American prairies. Estimates of bison numbers in the early nineteenth century range from 4.5 million to 60 million. In 1871, Colonel Richard Dodge encountered one herd along the Arkansas River in southern Kansas that he thought had between 12 million and 18 million bison.[9] The bison's diet consisted almost entirely of grasses and sedges, the nutrients of which were cycled back into the soil in huge quantities by the massive, roaming herds.

Pronghorn (*Antilocapra americana*) were the perfect complement to bison and may even have rivaled bison in numbers. Although bison specialized on grasses and sedges, pronghorn foraged on broad-leafed herbaceous plants (forbs) and leaves, buds, and stems of woody plants (browse). Pronghorn, too, once ranged across the prairies, but they were best adapted to shortgrass prairies, where they reach their highest numbers today.[10]

> Patches of intact prairie may have a remarkable diversity of grass species, some that are long-lived perennials, many with extensive root systems.

Historical accounts show that the American elk (*Cervus elaphus*), a species that is today considered a mountain resident, was once abundant across all three prairie types. A versatile herbivore, elk were capable of foraging on grasses, forbs, and browse.

Black-tailed prairie dogs (*Cynomys ludovicianus*), which were once keystone species common in shortgrass and mixed-grass prairies, created extensive networks of burrows that could cover up to hundreds of square miles. The burrows alter soil properties, microclimate, habitat patchiness, surface topography, and water infiltration.[11] They also provide vital resources for other species, including the burrowing owl (*Athene cunicularia*); the swift fox (*Vulpes velox*); the black-footed ferret (*Mustela nigripes*), a predator that cannot survive outside of the black-tailed prairie dogs' system of burrows; and bison, which are drawn to the variety of fresh, diverse plant growth around prairie dog towns.

Burrowing owls (*Athene cunicularia*) find food and shelter in open, dry grassland habitat. Grassland restoration will benefit this species.

Sustaining Grasslands

Fire is an essential force in creating and sustaining prairies, but so is the interplay, in space and time, between fire and grazing. A burned patch of prairie is flush with nutrients and awash in sunshine. The roots of prairie plants survive fire and grow fresh leaves. Antelopes, elk, and bison find recently burned patches and eat fresh forage. Although the herbivores feast on nutrient-rich green grasses, unburned patches remain largely untouched, a source of fuel for the next fire. Thus a patch burned this year may, thanks to herbivores, be relatively fire-proof the next.

Settlement of the prairies, however, greatly altered the landscape. Elk and free-range bison were extirpated. Plowing destroyed the complex root systems of native prairie plants. Crops replaced the structure and functions of these ecosystems, and the tallgrass prairie, which was largely plowed for corn and other row crops, became a different landscape and a limited habitat for prairie species. Drier shortgrass prairies were plowed to a lesser extent, and the 1930s sodbusting in this region contributed to droughts and the Dust Bowl. The major drivers that had helped create American prairies were halted. After occurring every one to five years for millennia, grassland fires were stopped by settlers, and roads and highways acted as fire breaks. Without periodic fires, woody plants took hold on the native prairie.

> Fire is an essential force in creating and sustaining prairies, but so is the interplay, in space and time, between fire and grazing.

Farther west, settlers replaced bison with cattle, which prompted changes. Both species are grazers of roughly equal body size and have considerable dietary overlap. But more important than dietary choices is the way in which the two herbivores forage. Bison moved in enormous herds over great distances, grazing hard on local prairies for hours or days, and then abandoning them for extended periods. This grazing pattern created successional stages of vegetation and helped determine the structure of the prairie. Cattle, less inherently inclined to move great distances, were often kept from doing so by fences, and they grazed intensively year round on the same portion of land.[12]

Beyond grazing, cattle and bison influence the landscape differently. Bison wallow, creating short-term depressions in otherwise flat prairies that collect rainwater and provide microhabitats for more water-dependent grasses and amphibians. Tree encroachment is often kept in check by bison because they horn and rub saplings. And bison wool has been shown to help disperse more grass seeds as the animals move across the prairie, whereas their shed wool offers nesting material to prairie birds and small mammals.[13]

Bison have a long, constructive history with dry, western ecosystems. They do not trample riparian (streamside) areas, as cattle might, and they wallow, or dust-bathe, which forms depressions in the soil that collect rainwater and enhance vegetation growth.

Source: Julie Larsen Maher/WCS.

Grassland Restoration

As destructive as this history was to native US prairies, restoration is possible, provided that the basic drivers of fire, grazing, and climate can exert the influence that they once did, and that the more pernicious invasive plant species are kept in check. Prescribed fire is essential for prairie restoration and, with proper training and equipment, not especially difficult. But even the best-designed restoration plans may be undermined by climate change. Should the southern plains become hotter and drier, the climatic conditions for tallgrass may no longer occur in important prairie refuges like the Konza Prairie in Kansas and Oklahoma's Tallgrass Prairie Preserve.

A twenty-first-century approach to grassland restoration is patch burning, a management practice that integrates fire and grazing to sustain prairie biodiversity.[14] Patch burning is done by dividing an area into six roughly equal patches. One patch is burned in early spring and the other in late summer, and over three years, each patch is burned once.[15] Grazers, be they bison or cattle, are attracted by the rich forage on recovering burns. Grassland productivity with patch burning is at least equivalent to productivity from more traditional rangeland methods but has the added advantages of suppressing some invasive species and of increasing local diversity of grasshoppers and birds by creating a shifting mosaic of vegetation.[16]

Avian diversity is of special concern because about 77 percent of prairie bird species have declined significantly.[17] The principal reason for bird declines seems to be the trend toward large-scale structural uniformity of vegetation across the landscape. Patch burning reverses this trend by providing a wider range of grass structure to accommodate the nesting and life ecology needs of more prairie bird species.

Source: Terry Bidwell/Oklahoma State University.

Patch burning via prescribed fires is a grassland management practice that creates a mosaic of vegetation types that supports a variety of wildlife species.

Different Visions, Different Futures

North American prairies will likely experience considerable changes as family farms continue to disappear and some forms of ranching and farming become less viable. Economics, demands for new energy sources, and prospects for nature tourism inform the following three proposed plans for North American prairies. With alterations, they may be applicable to grasslands in other parts of the world as well.

Biofuels and Wind Farms

If grassland regions can harness plant growth to produce biofuels, it could restore economies in those regions. Biofuel production may follow either of two pathways. The first, high-input, low-diversity (HILD) biofuels, comes from conventional food-crop plants such as corn, which is already used to produce ethanol, an approach favored by agribusiness. But HILD biofuel production would of itself do nothing to help grassland restoration, nor would it be compatible with fire and wildlife grazing.

The second type of biofuel production is a low-input, high-diversity (LIHD) approach—harvesting a mix of native prairie grasses like prairie hay for biofuel. LIHD holds some promise for restoring a landscape more like that of the original prairies and can, to some extent, be integrated into fire and grazing regimes.

Wind farms, consisting of large rows of turbines placed along prairie ridges, offer an atmosphere-friendly, sustainable alternative to coal-fired power plants, and the Great Plains region seldom lacks for wind. Yet even this has drawbacks: a recent study of wind farm impacts on birds included collisions, displacement due to disturbance, barrier effects (such as possible disruption of migration), and habitat loss.[18] Some prairie birds, including the lesser prairie-chicken (*Tympanuchus pallidicinctus*), are averse to tall structures and will avoid areas within a mile or more. Thus wind farms may be compatible with fire and grazing, but not with endangered prairie birds.

> Avian diversity is of special concern because about 77 percent of prairie bird species have declined significantly.

Buffalo Commons

In the 1980s, Frank Popper, a land-use planner, and his wife Deborah, an economic geographer, analyzed the deteriorating economic and demographic conditions of the western Great Plains. They concluded that traditional farming and ranching practices were unsustainable in this ecosystem and, as an alternative, proposed what they termed the buffalo commons.[19] The plan called for deprivatization of the more economically desolate regions of the Great Plains. Over time, people would migrate away from the region and the federal government would turn over large expanses of the land to bison production. Bison herds would provide a spectacle for tourists and be harvested sustainably, providing some new forms of employment for local residents.

More than anything else, the plan created controversy by seeming unsympathetic to rural communities. Yet long-term economic problems persist in the western Great Plains, and some residents have warmed to the idea of seeking new, more sustainable land uses. Redirecting land use may be a vehicle for prairie restoration. Adjacent land owners can form cooperatives for increasingly larger bison herds to reinstate grazing patterns, and incorporate the use of prescribed fire. Indeed the American Prairie Foundation, which founded a bison population in northwest Montana in 2005, and the Intertribal Bison Cooperative, with member tribes in 19 states, advocate increasing numbers of bison on larger landscapes. The American Bison Society is also exploring the constraints and opportunities of redirecting land use for the larger-scale restoration of bison herds, grasslands, and concomitant species. These ideas could bolster the region's biodiversity and resilience to climate change, and the chance of seeing tens of thousands of bison moving together would deliver an economic boon through nature tourism.

Pleistocene Rewilding

In 2006, a group of conservationists and biologists proposed an ambitious and controversial idea for substantial portions of the Great Plains. Inspired by visions of how rich the continent once was with wildlife, they proposed "rewilding" these open grassland regions. Large mammals like American mastodons (*Mammut americanum* spp.), American cheetahs (*Miracinonyx* spp.), and saber-toothed cats (*Smilodon fatalis*) disappeared from North America about 10,000 years ago at the end of the last Ice Age, but their descendents (or key surrogate species) exist on other continents, including Asian elephants, African lions, African cheetahs, and camels. In "Pleistocene rewilding," some of these species would thrive in the Great Plains, and herbivory would become complex and grand, as elephants and camels would join bison and pronghorn.

Conservationists are keenly aware of the problems of introducing exotic species, and this idea therefore seems radical. But proponents contend that large-scale ecological processes enacted by large wildlife (megafauna) are important, and say that "although the obstacles to Pleistocene re-wilding are substantial . . . we can no longer accept a hands-off approach to wilderness preservation as realistic, defensible, or cost-free. It is time to not only save wild places but re-wild and reinvigorate them."[20]

The prairies of North America will change over the next century, but within the bounds set by climate, prairies will still rely upon the interplay between two drivers: fire and grazing. Recent research has greatly enhanced our understanding of these drivers and our ability to use them. In North America, working *with* the forces of nature to restore at least a portion of the prairie and its wildlife would be a glimpse of this continent's rich ecological history. Yet here and elsewhere in the world, grasslands remain prime areas for crop conversion, and pressures for food and biofuels do not seem to be subsiding.

Whatever the future of grasslands worldwide, we would do well to heed Leopold's description of the healthy interplay of forces that shaped them: "This plant community was adapted, with extraordinary precision, to the vagaries of drouth [sic], fire, grazing mammals, and Indians. The more the Indians burned it, the more legumes it grew, the more nitrogen they pulled out of the air, and the richer it got. So, even among plants, we encounter the 'uses of adversity.'"[21]

Wild Geese

You do not have to be good.
You do not have to walk on your knees
for a hundred miles through the desert, repenting.
You only have to let the soft animal of your body
    love what it loves.
Tell me about despair, yours, and I will tell you mine.
Meanwhile the world goes on.
Meanwhile the sun and the clear pebbles of the rain
are moving across the landscapes,
over the prairies and deep trees,
the mountains and the rivers.
Meanwhile the wild geese, high in the clean blue air,
are heading home again.
Whoever you are, no matter how lonely,
the world offers itself to your imagination,
calls to you like the wild geese, harsh and exciting—
over and over announcing your place
in the family of things.

MARY OLIVER, AMERICAN (1935–)

People, Culture, and Conservation

We have now reached the point where globally, more people live in urban areas than in rural areas, and our relationship to the wild is entering a new era. Urbanized areas are divorced from nature, and each generation might become less aware of the biological connections that string together insects, birds, plants, fungi, mammals, reptiles, and amphibians. Nevertheless, as the following essays on human culture show, there is an intrinsic human connection with the natural world that we must work to maintain.

Despite the urbanizing trend, people in rural areas are still directly dependent on nature's resources. This dependence may put them in conflict with biodiversity conservation, as described in the first essay, "Conservation and Human Displacement."

The second essay, "Conservation Psychology: Who Cares about the Biodiversity Crisis?" grapples with the challenge of reframing the urgent work of protecting wildlife so that more people care about it.

Finally, "Biogenetics and Conservation: Celebrate or Worry?" outlines how our relationship to wildlife and wild places may change as future societies find vastly different technologies at their fingertips.

Our relationship to wildlife and wild places is a dynamic and powerful connection that conservation organizations increasingly recognize.

Conservation and Human Displacement

ARUN AGRAWAL, KENT H. REDFORD,
AND EVA FEARN

The history of displacing rural people is a study of power relations. Through recent colonial periods and times of rapid national development, rural people, particularly in developing countries, were moved to be more easily incorporated into national structures, or because their land was slated for large-scale development projects such as dams, roads, and plantations. Between 100 million and 200 million rural and indigenous people are estimated to have been physically displaced by megadevelopment projects since 1980, with the most significant cases in India, China, and Southeast Asia.[1] This caused social, economic, and health risks for some of those forced to move.[2] In response to severe human rights criticism, lenders like the International Monetary Fund and the World Bank instituted policies to conduct pre-project surveys to assess impacts on people, induce voluntary resettlement, and work with national governments to outline compensation for displacees.

Now, involuntary resettlement is being blamed on another actor—conservation organizations. Indigenous advocates, social scientists, and journalists have criticized conservation organizations, arguing that protected areas, the core

ARUN AGRAWAL *is an associate professor of natural resources and environment at the University of Michigan. Recent interests include the decentralization of environmental policy and the emergence of environment as a subject of human concern.*

KENT H. REDFORD *is director of the Wildlife Conservation Society Institute and vice president for conservation strategy at WCS. He previously worked at The Nature Conservancy and the University of Florida. His areas of interest include biodiversity conservation, sustainable use, the politics of conservation, and the mammals of South America.*

EVA FEARN *is assistant director of the Wildlife Conservation Society Institute. She previously worked at Columbia University and the Council on Foreign Relations.*

strategy of conservation, displaced tens of millions of people who formerly lived in or whose livelihood depended on wild areas that are now protected.[3] These critiques have gained a great deal of attention in high-profile social science and human rights publications and in international forums such as the

Source: Kent H. Redford/WCS.

World Parks Congress, World Conservation Congress, and the Convention on Biological Diversity Conference of the Parties. The sweeping, rhetorical critiques claim that conservation has caused human evictions and suffering comparable to that caused by megadevelopment projects and civil wars.[4] Human welfare and conservation have become increasingly intertwined—politically, philosophically, and practically—and ignoring human displacement undermines the moral basis for conservation. As a matter of both ethics and pragmatism, the conservation community must respond.

Fishing in bay adjacent to Masoala National Park, Madagascar. Economic concerns of local people and sustainable use of natural resources were important factors in the park's design.

Conservation-Induced Displacement

Ever since Yellowstone National Park sparked the modern national park movement in 1872, creating protected areas has been the core strategy for wildlife and biodiversity conservation. Inherently spatial, protected areas involve setting land aside and deciding who has access to an area and the use of its resources—

for homes, farming, hunting, or fishing. This process can result in "physical displacement"—the removal of people from historical or existing home areas, also described as involuntary resettlement—and/or "resource displacement"—the restriction of how, where, and when a group of people can use natural resources in or near a protected area. Loss of access to natural resources occurs more frequently and can be independent from actual physical displacement.

Many protected areas around the world have people living within their boundaries who rely on natural resources for a substantial portion of their livelihood. Protected area regulations generally limit natural resource use, but people often benefit indirectly as abundant wildlife moves outside the park boundaries and can be harvested. However, in some cases when a strict protected area is established, local communities lose access to land, forest resources, and development opportunities, or at an extreme, are forced to relocate. In these cases, conservationists face both moral and practical dilemmas in balancing claims between the public good of protecting species and individual economic and cultural losses.

> Many protected areas around the world have people living within their boundaries who rely on natural resources for a substantial portion of their livelihood.

Much protected areas strategy is based on the need to balance the use of biodiversity with its protection. The World Conservation Union (IUCN) categorizes protected areas according to the nature and extent of human use and habitation permitted. IUCN Category I areas offer the strictest form of biodiversity protection—allowing no use—whereas those in Category VI are managed-resource protected areas that allow sustainable-use activities.

The number of protected areas has grown enormously in the past 50 years, now covering a total of approximately 7.7 million square miles (20 million km^2) of the Earth, including 6 million square miles (15.3 million km^2) of terrestrial protected areas. Although this may seem as if a lot of biodiversity is therefore protected, less than 9 percent of the world's 98,400 terrestrial protected areas fall into the strictest IUCN Categories I and II.[5]

There is growing recognition that it is important to have local people and indigenous communities participate in decision-making regarding protected area management, and that excluding or displacing local people causes resentment that can disable conservation objectives. As a result, conservation strategies seem to be shifting from strict protected areas to "people-centered protected areas."[6]

Even so, the establishment of some stricter protected areas has understandably caused tension between local people and protected areas managers, which include government agencies and nongovernmental organizations (NGOs). In the strictest protected areas where local people are not allowed to live, farm, fish, mine, hunt, or gather nontimber forest products, the reasons for conflict between human welfare and wildlife protection become obvious: displacing people from biodiverse areas or regulating their use of resources for the national or global benefit translates into a loss for local communities—where once villagers could hunt, they may no longer be permitted to do so; where once a village existed, the inhabitants may have been resettled outside the park.

A common assumption in the conservation community is that human presence in protected areas is invariably counter to long-term specific biodiversity conservation goals. Local communities in or near protected areas have been known to grow in number and attract in-migrants. They can also serve as gateways to exploiting wildlife in the protected areas: One or two local people partnering with external traders of timber or wildlife products can upset previously sustainable resource use. For example, a recent study on forest elephants in central Africa found that human encroachment and road-building near protected areas gave access to organized elephant poaching operations, and elephants sought refuge as far away from human habitation as possible.[7] In theory, poaching operations could be targeted, but in actuality, once access roads are created and people move in, with limited governance in the region, depletion of natural resources and wildlife can occur quickly.

> Conservationists face both moral and practical dilemmas in balancing claims between the public good of protecting species and individual economic and cultural losses.

On the other hand, critics of strict protected areas argue that people have historically played a structuring role in the landscapes and that small-scale human activities—such as certain types of cultivation—increase biodiversity.[8] The history of each protected area offers different possible patterns for human use. For instance, in a protected area in Cambodia, resin tapping may be a sustainable way for local people to continue to use a forest. In another instance, sustainable hunting might be well managed by local residents, as in Peru's Pacaya-Samiria National Reserve. There Cocama-Cocamilla Indians comanage the reserve, set hunting quotas, and help control poaching of howler monkeys and white-lipped peccary more effectively than previous strict park management did.[9]

Current Knowledge of Conservation Displacement

At present, there is a serious lack of systematic data about what actually happens in protected areas, in terms of numbers of people asked to leave, the voluntary or involuntary nature of departures, overlap or confusion between physical displacement and resource displacement, and whether or how reducing human resource use impacts specific conservation objectives. In short, data on the magnitude of human displacement resulting from the creation of protected areas is unreliable. Published numbers are often derived from speculation based on disparate case studies. For example, 54,000 people were reportedly displaced from 12 parks in Central Africa,[10] but that number was based on assumptions of preexisting human population densities applied uniformly across diverse regions.[11] Only 50 to 60 studies provide careful information about the impact of protected areas on people living within them.[12] Conservation organizations need to find ways to assess how much human physical displacement is caused by protected areas and how to mitigate its negative impacts on these often already marginalized people. Recent efforts begin to provide a better picture, such as the clearing house established at www.social-impact-of-conservation.net.

Despite the lack of reliable information on numbers and places, when people are displaced, force is often used to influence them to move, and displacement from protected areas causes impoverishment, social disarticulation, and political disempowerment. Few of those evicted have been compensated, and in many cases, displacements are not documented, despite having been executed under the authority of law.[13] There is a growing realization that unless conservation strategies address the rights of local people, little that conservationists argue on behalf of the global benefit of protecting biodiversity will be morally defensible.

Conservation Response

The criticism of historical wrongs committed in the name of conservation—even in the absence of credible quantitative data—grows. And the future of protecting areas for conservation holds the promise of more tension. If conservation organizations are to effectively protect more land and sea, active engagement on this issue is vital.

An important first step is to fill the information gap and empirically answer the generalized criticisms. Case-based data on displacement would help clarify contradictory evidence. One example is the establishment of the Dja Biosphere Reserve in Cameroon, where, despite accusations of human displacement, no evictions actually occurred.[14] Another information gap conservation organizations should help fill is whether and how protected areas benefit local people, and, if there are costs and benefits, how they should be allocated. To gain such information, pre- and post-park-establishment surveys are being conducted in Birougou, Ivindo, Monts de Cristal, and Waka parks in Gabon.[15]

The conservation community must develop and implement transparent policies to minimize human displacement. Such policies might include (1) ensuring that governmental authorities obtain free prior informed consent from all people denied access to land or resources; (2) avoiding involuntary physical displacement or converting involuntary displacement into voluntary agreements to move via incentives; and (3) working with authorities to ensure that local people who lose legitimate access are provided with compensation such as access to equivalent land, resources, or opportunities. It is important to note that financial compensation is rarely sufficient to ensure the welfare of displaced people and must be coupled with social services, infrastructure, capacity-building, social integration, and new livelihoods. If an organization is not convinced that

Agriculture in Rwanda. Communities that depend on the land for their livelihoods may put pressure on available land, which can be a challenge for protected areas and put local people and biodiversity conservation in conflict.

the minimum standards will be met, then it should consider not participating in a given conservation action.

To address compensation of displaced local people, conservation organizations have four potential paths. They can (1) ignore the problem and increasingly promote the strictest nature protection (a negative course of action); (2) change nothing in current protected areas strategies, and disregard potential human displacements (business-as-usual); (3) adopt a policy to avoid involuntary displacements as far as possible, and/or organize for the compensation of local people who may soon be asked to move (a positive course of action); or (4) address not only future but past displacees by retroactively compensating for past evictions from protected areas.

In light of the seriousness of the situation, it seems inconceivable that conservation organizations would follow a negative course (option 1), and continue to aggressively pursue the strictest forms of protected areas, causing even more displacement and exposing the wildlife conservation ethic to critique from a human rights standpoint. Business-as-usual (option 2) may be attractive because it requires no reassessment of current international conservation strategies. However, if the history of development megaprojects serves as a guide, conservation NGOs will ultimately be forced to compensate displaced local people. Therefore, options 3 (compensating future displacees) and 4 (compensating future and past displacees) are the most ethically appropriate courses of action.

> To be sure, the problems generated at the interface of biodiversity protection and human rights agendas cannot be solved by conservation or human rights groups alone—even if they were to work together.

Comparing options 3 and 4 on a cost basis, compensation for future *and* past evictions is likely to be extremely expensive: the lower estimate of 10 million conservation displacees (accuracy unknown) would run upward of $5 billion (assuming an average compensation amount of $500 per displaced person[16]). Although it is ethically superior to compensate past and future displaced people, it might be impossible to determine exactly who was displaced from where, when, and by whom. Rural areas that now contain protected areas often have long histories of social or political movements and natural resource development. It would also be crippling financially.

On balance, option 3 is politically and ethically the most attractive, and although there will be costs to implementing it, they are likely costs that conservation organizations, like development organizations before them, will eventually be forced to bear. To pursue this course of action, conservation organizations will need to more carefully consider how proposed protected areas will affect the people living in them and near them, whether the displacement of those people will substantially improve conservation outcomes, and, if so, how to best work with development agencies to understand and fully address human needs and compensate for displacement. Going forward, conservationists will need to identify the distribution of interests among those likely to be displaced, involve local people in determining a balance between compensation and incentives, and work with national/local governments and development and finance agencies to create appropriate compensation packages. Left unanswered is the daunting and vital question of who is responsible for paying those costs.

When conservation organizations are blamed for disempowering marginalized people, two of the world's least-funded and most-overlooked issues become coupled. To be sure, the problems generated at the interface of biodiversity protection and human rights agendas cannot be solved by conservation or human rights groups alone—even if they were to work together. Unfortunately, what these groups have in common is that the world's most marginalized human populations and biodiversity have little power to affect the actions of the globally powerful. Conservation organizations must work with human rights organizations, local NGOs, and competent sectors of government to minimize the human cost of conservation and design compensation when displacement cannot be avoided. But the world must also question the relative investment made in agriculture, energy development, infrastructure, and military spending. A fraction of this money would help find durable solutions both for local peoples and biodiversity conservation.

Conservation Psychology

Who Cares about the Biodiversity Crisis?

JOHN FRASER AND JESSICA SICKLER

Satellite imagery and other rapidly advancing technologies allow us to measure the entire alarming human footprint on the natural world and to monitor loss of wild places across the planet. Much to the frustration of conservationists, however, publishing and disseminating this data-rich information has not changed global patterns of resource consumption. Clearly, scientific information alone is not enough to promote conservation action at the scale necessary to save wildlife and wildlands. To successfully communicate the importance of conservation we need to decode how people understand their relationship to nature. It is an important puzzle, and perhaps the one most critical for the future of our planet.

Despite a growing awareness that we *could* sustain wildlife and wild places by reworking our business practices and lifestyles, actually making these changes is more complex. It involves human decision making, empathy, motivation, and development of social norms. If humanity is to protect what remains of the world's biodiversity, conservationists need to understand these psychological factors.

We are pleased to count ourselves among a growing group of psycholo-

---

JOHN FRASER is director of the Public Research and Evaluation Program of the Wildlife Conservation Society Institute. A conservation psychologist and architect, John has over 20 years' experience working in the environmental communications field. He is on the planning committee for the Human Dimensions of Wildlife Conference scheduled for September 2008.

JESSICA SICKLER is a research associate with the Public Research and Evaluation Program. Her interests focus on children's development of concern for nature and animals, how they think about environmental issues and science concepts, and the role of parents and teachers in this development.

gists who have joined the conservation movement to build an understanding of how to motivate and change people's behavior. Economists often boil down human behavior to selfishness, factors they define as "rational action." However, psychological research on values and attitudes indicates that most people also have concerns beyond their own self-interest. Most people recognize that their survival is dependent on other people and the services of nature. Yet many do not directly connect their personal experience and actions to the health of the biosphere as a whole. By helping to build this psychological and emotional link, we feel that the social sciences—and conservation psychology in particular—can provide much-needed information to the conservation community. Conservation psychologists can help address why the alarming information about environmental degradation is often ignored and help identify constructive means to ensure that our cultures embrace a more comprehensive environmental ethic.

Conservation and Psychology

For many years social scientists have assessed values associated with the environment, including the study of the biophilia hypothesis (the human bond with other living things), ecopsychology (the value people derive from nature), and the cultural beliefs that influence how we regard nature.[1] This research has primarily considered the psychological benefits nature provides to people. Only recently have social scientists investigated the reciprocal links within the human–nature relationship.[2] This nascent research into conservation attitudes and their relationship to behavioral change may allow us to discover why individuals behave as they do and how to encourage them to engage in environmentally positive activities.

Zoo visitors provide a valuable audience for conservation messages. Here, "Zoo Campers" who researched a group of endangered species share information with interested zoo visitors.

Conservation psychology is an integrative discipline that seeks to build new knowledge on how conservation-minded thinking develops. It was established to provide the conservation community with information in three broad areas: what experiences are necessary to ensure that people develop an emotional concern for nature; how to most effectively present environmental information so people will accept it; and how to encourage people to engage in conservation action.[3]

Conservation Psychology at Work

An early example of conservation psychology involved the conflict between ranchers and environmentalists in Colorado and Wyoming in the late 1990s, when the Preble's meadow jumping mouse (*Zapus hudsonius preblei*) was listed as threatened under the Endangered Species Act. Ranchers were concerned that if mice were found on their property, they would be prohibited from developing, grazing, or irrigating that land. The conflict escalated because both the ranchers and the conservation groups had built up a mutual mistrust of each other's intentions, failing to recognize that they shared similar values about protecting the land.

When conservation psychologists Susan Opotow and Amara Brook looked at this case, they learned that the mistrust had deepened because the two groups had labeled each other as "different," which created an insurmountable division. These entrenched group identities were impeding conservation. The psychologists studied the ranchers' and the environmentalists' emotional value of nature and the limiting and motivating factors both groups held regarding Preble's mouse habitat conservation. They were able to recommend a collaborative strategy to build trust and to generate a plan that was consistent with the values of both the ranchers and the conservation groups. Conservation psychologists demonstrated that an understanding of group identity can be central to implementing a conservation strategy.[4] Unfortunately, in this case, psychology was incorporated too late in the process to be fully effective.

Conservation psychology seeks to understand how we might achieve cultural change by determining how behavior change is fostered in individuals, how those changes ripple through social groups, and, finally, how changes manifest themselves as norms in society. An example that illustrates how an experience helped develop an emotional concern for nature, and how this concern rippled through social groups, comes from a wildlife center in Chendu, China. There, conservation psychologist Sarah Bexell designed an education program in which children repeatedly observed giant panda behaviors. Not surprisingly, the children expressed their innate concern for the animals. However, what was surprising was that the parents were also affected by their children's experience and showed a significant increase in understanding and concern for the species.[5] This broader intensive emotional, educational, and social experience is important for understanding how we can increase concern and care for wildlife across groups of people, which may become important for conservation as human societies become more divorced from wildlife.

Conservation psychology also explores how to best present information about wildlife by understanding how an individual's psychology and prior experiences influence his or her relationship to other species. An example is our recent study on how people reacted to dolphin studies. Over the past 20 years,

The Preble's meadow jumping mouse (*Zapus hudsonius preblei*) was listed as a threatened species throughout its range in 1998. This primarily nocturnal rodent lives in riparian (streamside) areas in southeastern Wyoming and Colorado.

Source: USFWS.

scientists have proven that dolphins recognize themselves in mirrors, recognize symbols, and use those symbols flexibly to communicate with people, signifying a higher level of cognitive ability than previously known.[6] Public reaction to this information, however, has ranged from proof of the supernatural, through disbelief, to distrust that dolphins could have capacities that are humanlike.

To aid dolphin conservation, it was important to understand why people did not accept this information. Our research project at the New York Aquarium interviewed over a thousand people in a series of studies to understand their perspectives on dolphin intelligence. We found that a segment of the public held a worldview that clearly distinguishes between the cognitive abilities of humans and other animals. This underlying special status for humans made it difficult for these people to accept the humanlike abilities of dolphins. We discovered that if educators and exhibit creators reframed discussion about dolphin cognition to focus on *communication* abilities, the information was more easily accepted by more people. In fact, because there is a broad-based acceptance across worldviews that dolphins have unique communication abilities, this served as an entry point for understanding other information about dolphins.[7]

> This broader intensive emotional, educational, and social experience is important for understanding how we can increase concern and care for wildlife.

Conservation Psychology and Zoo Visitors

Our work has primarily focused on the experience of visiting zoos and aquariums, places that provide an unparalleled opportunity for observing people, individually and in groups, as they respond to seeing or interacting with a variety of animals. This work can help expand knowledge about how conservation values

Source: D. DeMello/WCS.

The Bronx Zoo's Congo Gorilla Forest informs zoo visitors about the threats to African rainforests and their inhabitants and about what people can do to help save them. The exhibit also provides the unique and inspiring experience of face-to-face interaction with its resident gorillas, as this youngster discovers.

are developed. Given their broad-based appeal, zoos and aquariums also provide accessible venues where research findings on psychology and communication can be tested and put into action. Once zoos and aquariums begin to use principles of conservation psychology in exhibit design and presentation, they can help visitors build new ways of thinking about nature.

Studies have shown that many zoo visitors have a higher than average motivation and commitment to conservation. Surveys conducted at the Bronx and Brookfield Zoos revealed that visitors believe more strongly than their peers in the utility and existence values of animals and environmental entities (water, trees, plants), and have a greater sense of caring and responsibility for these entities.[8] Studying these already motivated people can offer psychologists a rich opportunity to observe how positive relationships with nature can be strengthened to translate into conservation action. We are cautious, however, because no evidence suggests that all visitors to the zoo are predisposed to conservation. But it is important to work with a gradient of visitors, from disengaged to engaged, to learn how individuals can be influenced to reconsider and change their values, what these changes mean when shared within their social groups, and how that may expand to a community as a whole.

> We often hear that zoos and aquariums cannot compete in content or entertainment value with books, television, or movies.

We often hear that zoos and aquariums cannot compete in content or entertainment value with books, television, or movies. However, when we talk with visitors at the New York zoos or aquarium, they regularly describe these institutions as the source for real, tangible, and personally meaningful experiences that surpass other media for their ability to create awe, wonder, and emotional connection. As one visitor stated, "It presents experiences and information that you don't get in any other venue. You can look up information in a book about a lion, but in front of you, you can see how big he is. You can see how big his claws are. It makes the book-learning real. You can grasp the concept of the animal and have a better understanding of the animal in person."

A 2004 study by three of the founders of conservation psychology, O. E. (Gene) Myers, Carol Saunders, and Andrej Birjulin, confirmed these positive emotional reactions to viewing real animals.[9] Their study showed that visitors reacted to a gorilla, an okapi, and a snake with great feelings of awe and respect, and appreciation of natural "beauty." The surprising discovery was that when animals paid attention to the visitor, or were observed exploring a shared world, visitors felt an emotional connection that increased their desire to help these animals.

Zoo exhibits are also a part of the visitor's experience that both benefits from conservation psychology findings and contributes to our understanding of how audiences respond emotionally and intellectually to conservation information.

Through analyzing zoo and aquarium exhibits, we have consistently found that when information is structured to connect with visitors on a personal level, those visitors are more likely to retain the information and be motivated to act for conservation. For instance, in designing the Tiger Mountain exhibit at the Bronx Zoo, we worked with psychologist Valeria Lovelace to examine visitors' basic knowledge and emotional connection to tigers. To the surprise of our exhibit designers and scientists, we found that visitors arrived at the zoo with fairly robust knowledge of tigers and the threats this species faces in the wild. However, there was a common gap in knowledge about where wild tigers live and where their protection is urgent. Through specific design and content, the final exhibit communicated this necessary information in the context of visitors' prior knowledge. Through postvisit interviews, we found that the exhibit had increased visitors' sense of emotional connection with the tigers at the zoo and empowered them to help save the species in the wild. Had we failed to assess the audience and analyze how knowledge and emotion work together, we would have run the risk of repeating information people already knew, while missing some essential links.

Staff of the Wildlife Conservation Society surveyed zoo visitors' interest levels in water and energy conservation actions through a game called "What do you do at home?" where guests revealed their current conservation interests and actions and the barriers they face to being greener. The activity informed the design of signage outside the zoo's new Eco-Restroom.

We believe that the appeal of zoos could offer the greatest potential access to the conservation hearts and minds of the public. Some visitors feel that scientific content in zoos is more accessible than information from other cultural institutions, such as museums. This accessibility, although it has not yet translated into a commitment to conservation, represents a significant opportunity to promote change. The range of visitors' perceptions helps us to better understand how to motivate the diverse public toward conservation action and how to make conservation values more culturally and socially imperative.

Conservation psychologists are now starting this work in earnest, applying findings beyond the individual, to community and cultural beliefs, values, and behaviors. Conservation psychologists in the US, Germany, Italy, and South Africa are establishing how positive and negative experiences with nature influence social norms. At the Wildlife Conservation Society, we have developed programs in Gabon to foster a local conservation ethic for that country's species-rich forests, coupled with exhibit information at our urban zoos, to connect visitors who are far removed from the wildlands of western Africa.

Although causal links between individual choices, social norms, and wide-scale behavior change have not been fully established, the early results are very promising. As the need for this type of study grows, we see increased interest in the subject from major conservation non-governmental organizations (NGOs). Our colleagues are developing curricula and textbooks for college-level conservation psychology courses.

> The ultimate goal of conservation psychology is to change behavior among individuals and communities, and to motivate conservation action locally and globally.

The ultimate goal of conservation psychology is to change behavior among individuals and communities, and to motivate conservation action locally and globally. An understanding of human psychology can help to refocus current conservation work toward higher-yield activities. Understanding causal relationships between types of experience and effective advocacy can help the conservation community ensure that its efforts will be successful in the long-term. Without this, we will continue to lose biodiversity throughout the world as human communities resist change, despite the excellent work of our conservation and wildlife biologists. Only through an intersection of disciplines will we be able to work collectively toward improving the health of people, communities, wildlife, and the nature on which we all depend.

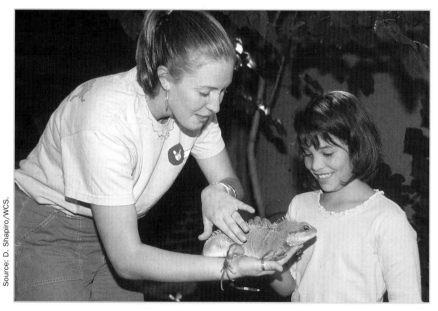

Source: D. Shapiro/WCS.

When people have positive emotional experiences with charismatic animals at a zoo, they are often motivated to be proactive in conservation, on both a local and a global scale.

Biogenetics and Conservation

Celebrate or Worry?

STEPHEN C. ALDRICH

The fantastic achievement of the human genome project at the close of the twentieth century heralded our entrance into a new "bio-era" characterized by rapidly expanding fundamental knowledge and technological reach across the full scope of biology. Recent progress has been breathtaking, particularly the exponential rate of improvement in the speed and unit cost of technologies for reading (sequencing) and writing (synthesizing) the long strings of amino acids that make up DNA. Improvements in these technologies have quietly galloped ahead, at rates comparable to the pace of improvement in the computer chip and Internet industries. The coming era of easy and affordable genetic engineering has potentially positive and negative consequences—including legitimate concern for the impacts on the conservation of existing wild species.

Biotechnology is getting cheaper, diffusing around the globe, and being adopted by younger generations. The result is a rising class of energetic and eager "open source" biologists, pushing the limits of our ability to design and create new forms of life. This is no exaggeration. The 2006 MIT-sponsored International Genetically Engineered Machines competition (iGEM) attracted 37 teams from around the world to showcase their projects for designing and building novel biological systems. Applications to the 2007 competition were almost double. Things are changing fast in the world of biological engineering!

STEPHEN C. ALDRICH is the founder and president of Bio Economic Research Associates (bio-era), an independent research and consulting firm working at the intersection of the economy and our growing knowledge and capabilities in biology. He is the author and coauthor of The Business Significance of Avian Influenza; Thinking Ahead: Using Scenarios to Prepare for an Avian Influenza Pandemic; *and* Genome Synthesis and Design Futures: Implications for the US Economy.

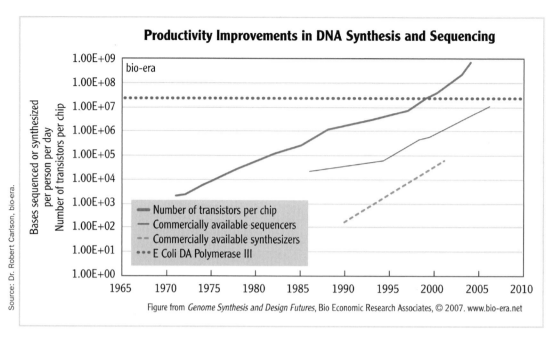

Productivity Improvements in DNA Synthesis and Sequencing

bio-era

Legend:
- Number of transistors per chip
- Commercially available sequencers
- Commercially available synthesizers
- E Coli DA Polymerase III

Figure from *Genome Synthesis and Design Futures*, Bio Economic Research Associates, © 2007. www.bio-era.net

Enabling biotechnologies are advancing rapidly.

> These trends portend a dramatic explosion of human-produced biological innovation in coming years.

These trends portend a dramatic explosion of human-produced biological innovation in coming years, with the potential to deliver benefits—from the drought-tolerant crops we will need to feed 9 billion people, to reducing the net carbon we emit by switching to improved biofuel crops. In the years ahead, wildlife conservationists will have reason to celebrate benefits delivered through our growing capability to engineer life forms to specification. Varieties of genetically engineered crops may require no tillage, less freshwater, and less fertilizer, increasing yields per acre to reduce pressures on land or even taking current agricultural lands out of production. Drought-tolerant crop varieties may reduce diversion of riparian systems—good news for freshwater ecosystems.

Beyond these potential gains, advanced biotechnologies will have an increasingly direct role in conservation work. Hand-held "lab on a chip" genetic sequencing technologies may become a common part of the conservation tool kit for biological surveillance and identification. We see the beginnings of this in Craig Venter's pioneering "ecological genomics" survey of seawater, which dramatically expanded our knowledge of the microbial biosphere, identifying thousands of novel genes and genomes.[1]

The ability to sequence field samples quickly and cheaply will be a big boon to conservation work, as will the ability to rapidly and cheaply synthesize DNA: cloning has already emerged as a tool to help to conserve severely threatened species under captive conditions.[2] Eventually, this may also serve to introduce genetic variation into threatened remnant wildlife populations with diminishing gene pools.

Having confessed optimism for the positive role new biotechnologies can play, let me also admit that these same trends raise profound biosecurity questions that go straight to the heart of conservation ethics and what it means to protect wild or "natural" biological systems. The development and diffusion trajectories for these technologies promise conflict as societies diverge over the extent to which we should encourage and enable biotech innovation. As more genetically engineered forms of life enter the environment, they will inevitably alter the environment, which in turn will put the continued existence of some natural and wild systems at risk.

We must always remember our shared evolutionary history. Everything alive is part of an unbroken living process stretching back to a common origin more than 3.5 billion years ago. We are all parts of this great living process, clearly connected through a bewilderingly complex and poorly understood network of mutually interdependent biological relationships—at all levels. As happened with the advent of industrial chemistry, there is a real potential that our enthusiasm for newfound technologies will run ahead of our understanding of consequences. Because we cannot know in advance how new, self-replicating genetic innovations introduced into the environment will ultimately interact with our existing biological network, caution is warranted. Numerous accidents have already occurred. In the cases of Starlink corn and Liberty Link 601 rice, genetically engineered crops producing proteins not approved for human consumption inadvertently entered the food supply. The cleanup costs were significant. The conservation community can expect analogous problems to emerge as more genetically engineered systems enter vulnerable natural environments. A case in point is creeping bentgrass *Stolonifera L.*, an herbicide-resistant grass engineered for use on golf courses whose seeds dispersed and established small patches in the wild.[3]

> As more genetically engineered forms of life enter the environment, they will inevitably alter the environment.

Such problems may not emerge on a large scale, but it would be wise to expect them—and prepare accordingly. This will mean working together to help ensure that both innovative biotechnologies and conservation are harnessed in the service of enhancing the abundance, diversity, and integrity of life on Earth.

The human race is challenged more than ever before to demonstrate our mastery—not over nature but of ourselves.

RACHEL CARSON
SILENT SPRING

The Art and Practice of Conservation

Because conservation must deal with biological, social, economic, and political systems, it requires innovation, creative solutions, and a deft hand—artistry—as well as a knowledge of landscapes, threats to wildlife, and how to mitigate those threats.

Here, authors from across the conservation community offer insightful analysis of social and political issues that impact wildlife conservation. They highlight some of the more challenging contexts in which conservationists are saving wildlife and wild places.

In the first essay, "Conservation in Conflict: Illegal Drugs Versus Habitat in the Americas," the interplay of lawlessness and coca cultivation in Colombia is beyond the control of conservationists.

The second essay, "Rewilding the Islands," chronicles the innovative techniques and teamwork required to remove invasive mammals, and how this work benefits global biodiversity.

The essay "Addressing AIDS: Conservation in Africa" explains how the disease and increased poverty in sub-Saharan Africa affect conservation.

Finally, foreign policy, or the lack thereof, is the focus of "Conservation as Diplomacy," which highlights why conservationists are still working in war-torn countries.

We have to understand these issues in order to continue to work toward that one unwavering goal—to conserve as much biodiversity as external factors allow.

Conservation in Conflict

Illegal Drugs Versus Habitat in the Americas

LILIANA M. DÁVALOS
AND ADRIANA C. BEJARANO

In 1995, we hiked the Sierra de la Macarena National Park in Colombia, seeking adventure and documenting wildlife. By day, we backpacked across breathtaking rivers and into forests full of surprises—the roar of monkeys, the call of toucans—and sometimes the dark forests would open upon small clearings with tiny huts. The clearings invariably contained rows of lively green shrubs that stood in clear contrast to the shades of the surrounding canopy. At night, small aircraft zoomed above where we slept without a roof over our heads, but Villavicencio, the closest city, was some 82 miles away and had no nighttime flights. It did not take long to discover that the light green fields were coca (*Erythroxylum coca*)—the leaves of which produce cocaine—and that it was being flown out under the cover of darkness.

Today, the Sierra de la Macarena is at the center of a political storm. The clearings carved out of the forest add up to more than 32,000 acres (13,000 ha) of coca planted across the park and its buffer zone.[1] In 2005, the park was the testing ground for a coca eradication policy that involved spraying vast amounts of herbicide. The contradiction became obvious: the government was using

LILIANA M. DÁVALOS's research and writing on the effects of illegal drug trafficking on forests and wildlife was inspired by her visit to the Sierra de la Macarena, Colombia, in 1995. Her work has helped draw the attention of conservationists to this growing threat. Due to the dangerous nature of the work, she used the pseudonym María D. Álvarez until recently.

ADRIANA C. BEJARANO is an environmental toxicologist who has published widely on issues related to pollutants, particularly on pesticide toxicity. She recently joined the Department of Environmental Health Sciences at the University of South Carolina as an adjunct faculty member working on ecological risk-assessment for conservation strategies in the Americas.

toxic chemicals on a park it had promised to protect. Meanwhile, thousands of settlers were encroaching on this land, far from any market or public service, but connected to the rest of the world through clandestine drug-running flights. Trade in illegal drugs damages habitat and threatens species, not just in Sierra de la Macarena but throughout the Western Hemisphere.

Although coca prices have declined over the last 15 years, coca is a valuable commodity in the global market, particularly when compared to legal crops like coffee. In 2005, a farmer could earn about $7,040 annually from a 2.5-acre (1 ha) coca plot,[2] almost four times Colombia's average per capita income, and many times the wealth of a subsistence farmer.

Cultivating coca, opium poppy (*Papaver somniferum*)—the basis for morphine and heroin—and marijuana (*Cannabis sativa*) pays well, given demand for illegal drugs worldwide. But, although marijuana can grow in greenhouses practically anywhere, poppy and coca grow only where adequate habitat is paired with the absence of law enforcement. In the Americas, cultivation of coca occurs in tropical and subtropical regions of Colombia, Peru, Bolivia, and, to a lesser extent, Venezuela and Ecuador. Poppy is grown in the highlands of Mexico, Colombia, and Peru.[3]

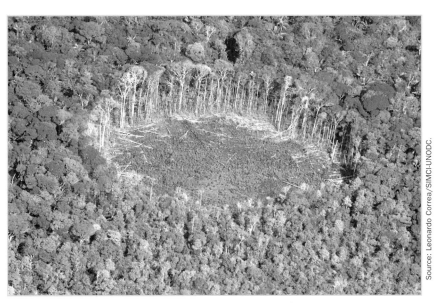

Source: Leonardo Correa/SIMCI-UNODC.

The borders of protected areas do not deter illicit crop growers, as shown in this field cleared in the Amazonian forest of National Natural Park Puinawaii in southeast Colombia.

Until recently, illegal drug cultivation and trafficking in the Americas were not considered drivers of habitat degradation, perhaps because their environmental impact is overshadowed by social and political effects. But the promise of even a fraction of the profits of the international illegal drug trade—estimated between $45 and $280 billion per year[4]—provides powerful incentives to clear Andean and Amazonian forests and wreck coastal habitats and parks throughout Mexico, Central America, and the West Indies. Cultivation, processing, trafficking through remote areas, and eradication by herbicide are threats from Paraguay to northern California. Separated as these four drug-related activities are in time and space, they combine to consistently degrade natural areas, imperil species, and obstruct conservation.

Cultivation

Marijuana is so ubiquitous that national agencies throughout the Americas have practically given up quantifying the total area planted. In California, marijuana-eradication programs operate in nine protected areas, including Sequoia

National Forest.[5] In Chihuahua, Mexico, deforestation and water appropriation for marijuana and poppy cultivation impact the temperate forest and fauna—including the endemic Zacatecan deer mouse (*Peromyscus difficilis*) and several reptile species.[6] The highland ecosystems in Mexico, Peru, and Colombia are prone to erosion, and poppy cultivation there destabilizes fragile water catchments by exhausting the soil's capacity to retain moisture.[7]

Source: Leonardo Correa/SIMCI-UNODC.

Steep slopes and heavy rainfall strip the soil cover from the remnant Andean forests cleared for illicit cultivation, here in northwest Colombia.

Coca is closely monitored by government agencies in the Americas. Cultivated in the Andes since pre-Columbian times and used to stave off hunger and treat everything from altitude sickness to menstrual cramps, the coca leaf contains about 0.15 percent of its weight in cocaine. Traditional uses are still legal in Bolivia and Peru, and in Colombia are restricted to the Kogui community of the Sierra Nevada de Santa Marta.

The rapid expansion of illicit coca crops for the international cocaine market, however, threatens the last repositories of imperiled forest species more efficiently than most other causes of forest fragmentation. Forest-dwelling species have nowhere to go when the forests are burned or cleared for coca plantations, and species such as Todd's parakeet (*Pyrrhura caeruleiceps*) in the Serranía del Perijá, the Baudó guan (*Penelope ortoni*) in the Chocó, or the long-haired spider monkey (*Ateles belzebuth*) in the Macarena park are sometimes hunted for food or the pet trade by encroaching growers and traffickers.[8]

In Peru, coca cultivation is concentrated in the northern Huallaga Valley and the regions of Apurimac, La Convención, and Tambopata. In Bolivia, most of it is produced in the lowlands of Chapare and the highland Yungas. This includes cloud forests and lowland forests. By the 1980s, both countries had hundreds of thousands of coca acres,[9] and international demand had encouraged the clearing of hillsides and steep mountain slopes, causing significant erosion. Subsequent degradation of mountain forests has reduced suitable habitats for threatened bird species such as the southern helmeted curassow (*Pauxi unicornis*) and the cinnamon-breasted tody-tyrant (*Hemitriccus cinnamomeipectus*).[10]

By the end of the 1990s, illegal coca cultivation in Peru and Bolivia declined. But total coca production in the Neotropics did not: instead, Colombia became, and remains today, the world's largest producer. In Colombia, deforestation linked to drug cultivation and transport was likely responsible for more than half the forest loss during the 1990s.[11] Coca cultivation began in small plots at the edge of the Amazonian frontier, far from law enforcement and farther from legal markets. The Colombian conflict, spanning more than four decades, fosters conditions for illegal crops and their trafficking. Guerrillas and paramilitaries struggle against each other and against the state for control of areas of the countryside, and almost every militia controls some production, processing, and even trafficking of coca. In regions effectively beyond the reach of the government, growing coca is not a matter of choice; militias force *campesinos* to grow the crop so the local faction can take a cut of the profit. Even when not coerced, many *campesinos* turn to coca because it is a virtually risk-free investment; processors and traffickers guarantee the purchase and transport of the crop and even provide startup funds and chemicals to clear and fertilize land.

The combination of economic incentive and coercion has allowed coca cultivation to expand swiftly to any part of Colombia with significant forest, including protected areas. In the southern department of Caquetá, the rate of deforestation partly linked to coca peaked during the late 1990s at around 4.1 percent per year, which ranked among the highest in the world and was equivalent to clearing 80,000 football fields annually.[12] Nature reserves are not exempt: in 2005, 12 of the 51 national protected areas had illegal coca production within their borders, and total park area known to be under cultivation increased 14 percent from the year before.[13] Deforestation is only part of the damage caused by coca cultivation: Colombian coca growers use approximately 210 million pounds (95 million kg) of chemical fertilizers and about 3 million pounds (1.4 million kg) of herbicides in their fields annually.[14]

> In Colombia, deforestation linked to drug cultivation and transport was likely responsible for more than half the forest loss during the 1990s.

Quantifying how coca cultivation affects wildlife is difficult. Coca directly threatens with extinction only a handful of endemic birds, because birds generally have large geographic ranges. Nevertheless, intense clearing poses a great risk to less mobile, more narrowly endemic species. For example, a single township in Caquetá encompasses the entire known distribution of the frog

Atelopus petriruizii.[15] This frog is critically endangered precisely because its narrow range is an area where coca has spread quickly over the last 15 years. Habitat loss such as this likely threatens dozens of other narrowly endemic amphibian species.

Yet, although coca production clearly has had a vast environmental impact, an argument can be made that it is the lesser of two evils. Farmers earn more per acre growing coca than they would with any legal crop, which potentially reduces the overall impact of agriculture on forests. But the extent of this reduction is hard to quantify, and in some places lucrative opportunities attract more colonists, converting more forest. For those concerned with wildlife, the overall deforestation rate is also less important than where deforestation occurs: illicit crops in Peru and Bolivia are grown in diverse lowland and upland forest ecosystems that support dozens of endemic and threatened species.[16]

Processing

Aside from sun drying, the processing of coca leaves into cocaine relies heavily on chemicals, including sodium bicarbonate, gasoline or kerosene, sulfuric or hydrochloric acid, potassium permanganate, ammonia, and acetone or ether. The liquid effluents in Colombia alone are estimated around 8.7 million gallons (33 million liters) per year.[17] As befits an unregulated enterprise, these effluents are dumped onto the soil and into watercourses without treatment.

Initial coca leaf processing in Guaviare, Colombia. The white powder is cement.

Coca processing was once limited to large laboratories near airstrips, navigable rivers, or ports. But large laboratories and airstrips were easy to detect, particularly with satellite images, so traffickers adapted and instead help rural growers set up small household labs to prepare the cocaine base. During 2003 and 2004, narcotics police found 14,920 clandestine laboratories in Bolivia, Peru, and Colombia, more than triple the number found a decade before, tripling the number of point sources for the discharge of drug-processing chemicals.[18] Home laboratories throughout the Amazonian forests of Colombia account for most of this growth.

Trafficking

Illegal drug users exist in every country in the world, but it is the purchasing power of users in developed countries that drives most trafficking. There are many more illegal drug users in the United States (and Europe) than in producing countries: less than 1 percent of adults in Colombia reported using cocaine (~280,000 people), compared to almost 3 percent in the US (~6 million people).[19]

Drug trafficking to the US is concentrated along two routes: through the

Drug traffickers target unpopulated parts of the US–Mexico border, often trespassing into protected areas like Organ Pipe Cactus National Monument, shown here, with mortal risks to visitors and park rangers.

islands of the Caribbean and through Central America and Mexico. The latter route is the more used, following post–September 11 restrictions on shipping and air travel. Trafficking requires clearing land for clandestine airstrips, roads, trails, and ports along the route, and sometimes in parks. In the Guatemalan Petén, within the Maya Biosphere Reserve, drug traffickers clear new landing strips about every six months to avoid getting caught. Over the last 15 years, by felling the tall trees bordering rivers, trafficking has eliminated close to half of the nesting sites of the scarlet macaw (*Ara macao*).[20]

Drug trafficking in protected areas poses deadly risks to staff, visitors, and conservationists. Traffickers are ruthless and command vast resources compared to underfinanced park services. In Guatemala powerful cartels have grabbed control of sections of the Maya Biosphere Reserve, undermining the authority of the park service, which has led to more clearing within the park.

> Illicit crops in Peru and Bolivia are grown in diverse lowland and upland forest ecosystems that support dozens of endemic and threatened species.

One of the more insidious effects of trafficking is that the violence it brings precludes wildlife research and monitoring. In Mexico's Baja California, traffickers shipping drugs to the United States have kept conservationists and biologists away from several sea turtle nesting sites, which prevents biologists from knowing how turtle species are being endangered.

Eradication

Although drug cultivation, processing, and trafficking are illegal, enforcing the law by eradicating crops with herbicides likely adds to the environmental damage. The most aggressive eradication program has been in Colombia. There, illicit crop eradication by aerial herbicide spraying began in 1978 when the highly toxic chemical Paraquat—controversially applied to eradicate marijuana in western Mexico—was used in the biodiverse northern areas of Sierra Nevada de Santa Marta.[21] By 1985, glyphosate—commercially sold as Roundup—had been introduced as a relatively benign defoliant. The total area sprayed annually increased from 2,100 acres (870 ha) in 1986 to more than 321,200 acres (130,000 ha) in 2005.

Critics of aerial eradication contend that illicit crops are not eliminated, but merely displaced from one region or country to another, leading to more habitat fragmentation and social upheaval. Data from Colombia support this: the total area under illicit cultivation has risen from approximately 61,700 acres (25,000 ha) in 1985 to around 210,000 acres (85,000 ha) in 2005.[22]

Aerial spraying spares almost no habitat. The effect on amphibians, so susceptible to chemical exposure, is of particular concern. Glyphosate, for example, can reduce larvae survival and may cause DNA damage in tadpoles, leading to population declines.[23] Yet in 2005, the Colombian government permitted defoliants in protected areas over the protest of conservationists worldwide. At the time, more than 1,900 environmentalists, mostly Latin American, addressed the Colombian president in an effort to bar aerial spraying in protected areas, arguing that aerial fumigation was ineffective and threatened amphibian populations, and that alternative development programs would be more successful because they engage the growers and their families. In fact, over the past few decades, Bolivia and Peru succeeded in decreasing the total coca crop by more than half through relatively effective eradication and law enforcement: government officials and coca growers themselves often uprooted coca plants by hand. Nevertheless, the government justified spraying because manual eradication is overtly dangerous in the face of ongoing armed conflict. Again, Colombia's violent conflict magnified the injuries to the country's environment and reduced options for conservation and natural resource management.

The illegal drug trade has far-reaching environmental impacts in the Americas, affecting watersheds, soil cover, protected areas, coastal habitats, and the survival of numerous endemic species. Illicit crops create barren terrains that cannot sustain the many species of the rich landscapes they replace. Though eco-

> Critics of aerial eradication contend that illicit crops are not eliminated, but merely displaced from one region or country to another, leading to more habitat fragmentation.

logical disturbances in such biodiversity hotspots may be low on the priority list of international policy, they should not be ignored, particularly because cultivation and trafficking show no sign of declining.

Conservationists need to establish baseline assessments of critical ecosystems and sensitive species and continuously monitor the damage from the trade. To abate that damage, international collaboration among law enforcement, local governments, and conservationists will be necessary. However, this will be a challenge on many levels.

Source: Leonardo Correa/SIMCI-UNODC.

Eradication by aerial fumigation leaves behind Dantesque landscapes, as in this picture from Guaviare.

Perhaps the best way to minimize the impact of illegal drugs on the environment is to pursue community-based strategies for alternative development and eradication wherever possible. Studies have shown that governance, technical support, and access to legal markets are more important than the price of coca when farmers decide what crops to plant.[24] Since 2001, development programs in Colombia have proved successful at providing support for alternative crops to coca growers, through the combined support of local and international development agencies, NGOs, and the national park system. These projects aim for social and environmental sustainability, and strategies range from incentivizing voluntary eradication to hiring former coca growers as park keepers.[25] Although social goals currently take priority, these projects provide fertile ground for subsequent conservation initiatives. The success of alternative development in Peru, Bolivia, and parts of Colombia shows that the cooperation of coca growers is indispensable to achieving lasting eradication. It also shows that governance, including agrotechnical support for *campesinos* and a reliable justice system, is critical to both antidrug and conservation efforts.

Rewilding the Islands

C. JOSH DONLAN

Islands, the "watered lands" known as *Ieglands* in Old English, serve as microcosms of the interactions between humans and their finite natural environments. Islands comprise approximately 3 percent of total global land area, yet they have harbored a high percentage of biodiversity, including many marvelous endemics such as giant Galápagos tortoises (*Geochelone nigra*), New Caledonia geckos (*Rhacodactylus leachianus*) the size of small dogs, and the pygmy mammoth of Siberia's Wrangel Island (now extinct, *Mammuthus primigenius*). Since the fall of the last pygmy mammoth some 4,000 years ago, the majority of species extinctions have occurred on islands. The islands of Oceania provide a stark example: prior to human settlement, they were home to over 2,000 now-extinct bird species.[1] Humans played a direct role in many of these losses, as in the overhunting of New Zealand's 12-foot-tall flightless moa. But the main culprit was often introduced invasive mammals, such as rats, cats, foxes, and goats. This threat is even more pervasive today; invasive mammals exist on over 80 percent of the world's islands, and consequently nearly half of the threatened mammal and bird species on the World Conservation Union's (IUCN) Red List are island species.

Unique evolutionary histories predispose island plants and wildlife to being

> Invasive mammals exist on over 80 percent of the world's islands.

C. JOSH DONLAN is the founder and director of Advanced Conservation Strategies, which is dedicated to reversing biodiversity loss through the development of innovative, self-sustaining, and cost-effective solutions derived from the integrated analyses of biological, economic, sociopolitical, and technological threats and opportunities. He is a senior fellow at the Robert and Patricia Switzer Foundation and the Environmental Leadership Program.

overly impacted by invasive mammals. Prior to the onslaught of invasive species, islands were generally drama free, with few mammalian predators or large herbivores. Insular species therefore commonly lack behavioral, physical, and life-history defenses: plants are not resilient to mammalian herbivory (overgrazing), and wildlife evolved without knowing predation. Consequently, hardy introduced herbivores, such as feral goats and donkeys, devastate island plant communities by stripping vegetation that may be unable to regrow. As omnivores, feral pigs eat fruits and plants and raid eggs from nests of birds and reptiles. Invasive rats and feral cats have decimated native island rodent, reptile, and bird populations and extirpated numerous seabird colonies by attacking breeding adults or eating eggs and chicks year after year. Invasive rats alone are responsible for at least 50 documented extinctions,[2] including the world's only flightless songbird (*Xenicus lyalli*). Rats drove this wren to extinction on the main islands of New Zealand, and, in 1894, a single cat belonging to the lighthouse keeper of Stephen's Island killed what are believed to have been the last birds of this species.

Source: Bill Henry

Feral cats are a threat to seabird colonies worldwide. Laysan albatross (*Diomedea immutabilis*) colonized Guadalupe Island, Mexico, in 1983, and were growing exponentially until fewer than 20 cats killed 60 individuals, equal to half the breeding subpopulation.

Early Efforts at Eradication

In the 1960s, rats wiped out the last population of yet another wren (*Xenicus longipes*). This time, however, New Zealanders began fighting back. Around the same time, hundreds of white-faced storm petrels (*Pelagodroma marina*) died after rats invaded Maria Island, a speck off the coast of New Zealand about the size of a football field. A group led by biologist Don Merton, a pioneer in the rescue and recovery of birds, spread rodenticide around the island to try to control the rat population. A few years later, much to the group's amazement, the rats were gone. A decade later, in an effort to protect breeding seabirds, biologist Dick Veitch and others conducted a similar rat-control program on the slightly larger 74-acre (30 ha) Titi Island and significantly reduced, but did not eradicate, the rats. Then, in 1976, about 50 New Zealand researchers and conservationists met to discuss how to control invading rats on hundreds of New Zealand's satellite islands. The compounding challenges led them to the dismal conclusion that "[w]e have control methods, and methods for reducing populations, but complete extermination on islands is remote or at least a very, very difficult thing indeed."[3]

Luckily, a handful of conservationists were not deterred. They continued testing new techniques, and developed bait stations armed with rodenticide that could be systematically placed over an entire small island,[4] providing a precise system for dispensing rodenticide while minimizing accidental poisoning of other wildlife. (The most commonly used rodenticide is an anticoagulant; rats

> Twenty years ago, removing rats from an island the size of a football field was a daunting challenge. Today, eradicating rats from a remote sub-Antarctic island larger than Washington, DC, is a reality.

die of anemia.) By 1983, rats had been eradicated from several small New Zealand islands, and silencing the death knell of native birds became a possibility. However, most conservationists remained skeptical about scaling up to larger islands with well-established rat populations.

But the diehards kept at it. In 1988, they placed 743 bait stations throughout the 420 acres (170 ha) of Breaksea Island in New Zealand's spectacular Fiordland. In 21 days, the rats were dead.[5] Breaksea created conservation headlines and became one of the largest invasive-predator-free habitats in the Fiordland. Researchers had "created" new, safe habitat for endangered species like the kakapo (*Strigops habroptilus*), the world's only nocturnal parrot, which was subsequently translocated there. The New Zealanders demonstrated to the world that islands, small and large, could be saved.

Today, the removal of rats and other invasive mammals from islands has become a powerful tool for biodiversity conservation. In New Zealand alone, rats have been eradicated from more than 100 islands. Conservation practitioners elsewhere have successfully adopted these and other techniques, resulting in 332 successful invasive rodent eradications worldwide to date.[6] Those eradications have restored many ecosystems, repatriated hundreds of breeding seabird colonies, and saved dozens of species from extinction. For example, the fewer than a 100 kakapo left in the wild survive only on islands where rats and other invasive predators were removed. In addition, the world's remaining tuataras (*Sphenodon punctatus*), the unique last member of the ancient group of reptiles, persist on only a few New Zealand islands that have been rendered free of invasive predators.

New technology and techniques are also drastically improving our ability to remove invasive mammals. GPS-aided aerial broadcast of rodenticide by helicopter with agricultural bait buckets hanging below can now deliver bait with cutting-edge precision, spreading it onto every square yard of an island. This allows for more cost-effective rat removals on larger and larger islands. In the largest rat eradication to date, in 2001, Norway rats (*Rattas norvegicus*) were removed from the 44-square-mile (113 km^2) Campbell Island, New Zealand.[7] The entire population of Campbell Island teal (*Anas nesiotis*)—a flightless and nocturnal duck—survived only on nearby rat-free Dent Island.[8] In the 1980s, 11 of the remaining teals were brought into captivity for breeding, and, in 2004, the birds were reintroduced to Campbell Island, where broods of new ducklings are now monitored with excitement. Twenty years ago, removing rats from an island the size of a football field was a daunting challenge. Today, eliminating rats from a remote sub-Antarctic island larger than Washington, DC, is a reality.

New wildlife management techniques have also improved our ability to avoid unintentional damage to native island species. In 2002, black rats (*Rattus rattus*) were to be removed from Anacapa Island, off the coast of California,[9] but the island was also home to the endemic Anacapa deer mouse (*Peromyscus maniculatus anacapae*), which is equally susceptible to the poison. To deal with this novel challenge, researchers determined that mice across Anacapa's three islets were genetically similar and functioned as a metapopulation, meaning that individuals occasionally moved among the separated populations. They then ensured that there was at least one free-living population of native deer mice at all times, and staggered the rodenticide broadcast over two years among the three islets. As a safeguard, a captive population of Anacapa mice of requisite genetic diversity was held for future reintroductions. Additionally, raptors and owls that faced potential poisoning from eating dead rats or deer mice were captured and then released after the eradication campaign was completed.

The project was a success. Rats were eliminated, and after a series of translocations between islets and reintroductions from the captive population, native Anacapa deer mouse populations recovered completely. Seabirds also benefited greatly. The endangered Xantus's murrelet (*Synthliboramphus hypoleucus*) and other seabirds that rats had once heavily preyed upon now successfully breed on the island in record numbers. These days shipwrecks, which were the major cause of rat introductions onto islands, are relatively rare. Nonetheless, reintroduction prevention measures are in place on-island to ensure that these benefits are permanent.

Other examples from the Aleutian Islands and the Galápagos illustrate the complexity of invasive mammal removals, but ultimately, their potential for global species conservation.

Foxes in the Aleutian Islands

Alaska's Aleutian Islands are one the world's last truly wild places. The Maritime National Wildlife Refuge encompasses 4.9 million acres (2 million ha) on more than 2,500 islands, providing nesting areas for over 40 million seabirds. Despite their remote location, the Aleutians have not been spared the impacts of invasive mammals. Russians discovered the islands more than 200 years ago and intentionally released Arctic and red foxes (*Alopex lagopus* and *Vulpes vulpes*) on more than 450 islands as food sources and for fur harvesting. Foxes subsequently ravaged waterfowl, shorebird, seabird, and ptarmigan nesting sites, preying on eggs, nestlings, and adult birds.[10] The endemic Aleutian cackling goose (*Branta hutchinsii leucopareia*) was

Source: D. Shapiro/WCS.

An introduced species to hundreds of Aleutian islands, Arctic foxes (*Alopex lagopus*) decimated populations of birds.

Feral goats on Isabela Island, Galápagos, where they were overgrazing and degrading habitat until they were eradicated in 2006.

extirpated from all but three islands. Predation was so severe that it precipitated ecosystem changes: because fewer seabirds transported fertilizing nutrients to land from the ocean via their guano, grasslands converted to tundra.[11]

Refuge staff began removing foxes from the Aleutian archipelago in 1949. Dedicated trappers have spent long, lonely stints year after year on these demanding islands—foxes have now been eradicated from 40 islands, totaling almost 2,000 square miles (5,000 km²).[12] Recovery of waterfowl, shorebird, and ptarmigan populations has been dramatic, and nesting seabird populations have increased four- to fivefold. These successes represent grand strides in protecting the Northern Hemisphere's most important seabird nesting grounds. A translocation program saved the Aleutian cackling goose.[13] Foxes remain on just nine islands, which managers are now targeting, in addition to turning to the challenge of removing rats from the archipelago.

Herbivores in the Galápagos

Both Wallace and Darwin witnessed the destruction of St. Helena Island by goats in the nineteenth century. Introduced in the 1200s, goats are responsible for at least 11 plant extinctions, although the real number is unknown because the first botanical surveyor arrived 300 years after the goats were introduced. Although goats still roam St. Helena, many Galápagos islands are recovering from introduced herbivory.

In 1961, goats were removed from the 29-acre (12 ha) islet of Plaza Sur. By 2000, the Galápagos National Park and Charles Darwin Foundation successfully rid seven other islands of goats via more opportunistic campaigns that involved ground-hunting. In the late 1990s, the Global Environmental Facility (GEF) and others funded Project Isabela—a campaign of unprecedented scale to remove goats from the largest islands of the Galápagos. Their plan was to first eradicate feral pigs and goats from the 224-square-mile (580 km^2) Santiago Island. After refining techniques, the project moved to Isabela Island, an area of 1,771 square miles (4,590 km^2), the largest such action ever attempted.

Removing goats from an area almost the size of Rhode Island required leveraging new technology and new hunting and monitoring techniques. It integrated GPS and GIS technology into all facets of the campaign, large-scale aerial hunting by helicopter, ground-based hunting with specialized dogs, and the use of "Judas goats"—radio-collared individuals that are released to join remaining goats, thereby unwittingly revealing the whereabouts of the stragglers. Altogether, more than 150,000 goats were removed from Santiago and Isabela.[14] Widespread ecosystem recovery has been swift; entire plant communities are rebounding, benefiting giant tortoises and endemic Galápagos rails (*Laterallus spilonotus*). Focus has now shifted toward removing goats from the last four islands in the archipelago. After hundreds of years, the persistent destruction caused by introduced herbivores on the Galápagos is coming to an end.

Densities of the endemic Galápagos rail (*Laterallus spilonotus*) increased on Santiago following the eradication of feral pigs and goats.

The Future of Island Conservation

Similar wildlife conservation gains have been achieved on islands around the globe, targeting other invasive predators and herbivores. To date, there have been close to 800 successful invasive-mammal eradications that have stopped extinctions and restored island ecosystems, safeguarding seabirds and island species on dozens of archipelagos.[15] Importantly, these conservation gains are commonly cost-effective. In western Mexico, a number of organizations have collaborated to remove 42 populations of invasive mammals from 26 islands, resulting in the protection of 88 endemic terrestrial vertebrates and 201 seabird colonies for less than $50,000 per taxon/colony.[16] Tackling even greater challenges, conservationists have now adapted eradication techniques to create habitat "islands" on New Zealand's two main islands. Even though full-scale eradication there remains impossible for now, the expectation is that

> Preventing extinction is at the center of biodiversity conservation, and the removal of invasive mammals from islands is one of society's most powerful tools to do that.

invasive predator populations can be sufficiently suppressed within these habitat "islands," allowing native wildlife populations to stay strong.

Restoration is now taking place on larger islands throughout the world, and conservation practitioners are targeting more biologically complex places—which will bring both vast conservation opportunities and new challenges. We need to continue developing new techniques that increase the cost-effectiveness of eradication campaigns and that mitigate impacts on native nontarget island wildlife. More research is needed on the removal of feral cats and house mice, two of the most difficult invasive mammals to eradicate. Because people live on larger islands, future eradication campaigns will need to integrate education programs to prevent accidental reintroductions of invasive animals and to clarify social and economic gains that come with native ecosystem restoration, such as improved agricultural and

Ecosystem recovery following nonnative herbivore eradication. An exclosure and surrounding area in the highlands of Santiago Island, Galápagos, before (1999) and after pig and goat removal (2005).

human health. Finally, a regional and global analysis to prioritize islands in need of eradication campaigns could maximize native species conservation and particularly benefit seabirds.

From the Indian Ocean to the sub-Antarctic, conservation practitioners are following the lead of those stubborn New Zealanders who were not willing to lose the last of their native wildlife. Preventing extinction is at the center of biodiversity conservation, and the removal of invasive mammals from islands is one of society's most powerful tools to do that. We can no longer afford lengthy eradication campaigns because too many island species are on the brink of extinction. It will be vital that we strive to safely eradicate invasive mammals from islands faster (and cheaper) to maximize the conservation return. With a burning desire to rewild islands, we can.

Addressing AIDS

Conservation in Africa

JUDY OGLETHORPE AND
DAULOS MAUAMBETA

Linda Chibweza of Chiuzira Village, Malawi, had been married for thirteen years and had six children when she fell ill in 1998. Her husband soon married another woman and sent no support home. Linda was bedridden for three years, while her mother and children nursed her and kept her warm by a wood fire; she died in 2001. People said she had died of government disease, *Matenda a boma*, AIDS.

In the three days following Linda's death, mourners converged on her village and slept outside the funeral home at night, around campfires. At the graveyard, wood was burned to heat water for grave diggers to wash. A year later, a tomb was built for Linda—over two tons of firewood was used to bake the bricks, another two and a half tons to brew beer and cook for those who congregated. Over nine tons of firewood were consumed because of Linda's death. Firewood for Chiuzira Village comes from nearby community forests where it has become scarce, in part because of AIDS.

Why should conservationists care about HIV/AIDS? The answers are not

JUDY OGLETHORPE is director of community conservation for World Wildlife Fund–US. Over the last five years she has worked on community conservation approaches, development of broad-scale conservation, and the integration into conservation of socioeconomic issues such as population, health, gender, conflict, and livelihoods. Judy has 14 years' conservation experience in east and southern Africa.

DAULOS MAUAMBETA is the executive director of the Wildlife and Environmental Society of Malawi (WESM). His focus is on natural resource and environmental/biodiversity conservation, organizational development, natural resource based enterprises and livelihood improvement. He is actively involved in increasing the understanding of the linkages of HIV/AIDS and conservation through a program he has developed called the Awareness to Action Campaign.

always straightforward, nor are they as simple as pointing to all the firewood that was used to nurture, mourn, and honor Linda Chibweza. Yet this one story suggests the strong feedback loops between the widespread sickness and death caused by HIV/AIDS and conservation in sub-Saharan Africa. Intertwined are gender issues. It is time for the conservation community to look more closely at these connections, their impacts on conservation, what can be done, and what should concern us as we look forward.

Source: Daulos Mauambeta of Wildlife and Environmental Society of Malawi.

Women cooking food during a typical funeral ceremony in Chiuzira Village, Lilongwe, Malawi. Tons of firewood may be consumed over the duration of a single AIDS victim's funeral alone.

Social Impacts of HIV/AIDS

By 2006, an estimated 39.5 million people lived with HIV globally, 24.7 million of them in sub-Saharan Africa. In that year, about 2.9 million people around the globe died of AIDS-related illnesses (nearly 8,000 deaths daily), and 4.3 million became infected. In sub-Saharan Africa, the disease takes its largest toll on women: approximately three women are now infected for every two men, and in the 15- to 24-year age bracket, three women are infected for every man.[1] In Botswana, in 2002, life expectancy had fallen from 72 years to 34; it is expected to fall to 27 by 2010.[2]

AIDS mainly affects prime-age adults, a group that is rarely selectively hit by serious diseases. This demographic explains the enormous social and economic consequences of AIDS: besides causing untold human suffering, AIDS in sub-

Saharan Africa disrupts families and communities and impacts national economies. Some workforces have been reduced by a fifth or more, and health services are overloaded as the volume of ailing people increases while health professionals themselves become incapacitated by the disease. Teachers, farmers, and parents are drifting out of the social fabric. This is not a one-off effect—losses from AIDS continue over the years, seriously debilitating organizations. In some countries, HIV/AIDS is undermining progress toward the UN's Millennium Development Goals, which steer human development policy and funding.

AIDS and Conservation

Although the direct and indirect impacts of the disease on the conservation sector have not yet been adequately quantified, illness and

> In Botswana, in 2002, life expectancy had fallen from 72 years to 34; it is expected to fall to 27 by 2010.

death at this scale seriously weaken conservation management. The conservation sector in sub-Saharan Africa, hard hit by HIV/AIDS, has lost many experienced and trained people in government, nongovernmental organizations, communities, and private, academic, and donor organizations. For example, the Wildlife and Environmental Society of Malawi has lost 14 percent of its staff to AIDS. When the disease weakens those in physically demanding jobs, such as park guards, some protected areas may be patrolled less: a Rwandan project had to "retire" four national parks service staff from patrols to stationary posts for just this reason.[3]

Losing many staff to AIDS can diminish leadership and endanger institutional memory and continuity of operations. It also whittles away at scarce conservation resources. Staff must take significant time off work to care for family members with AIDS and orphans of relatives, and to attend funerals in their home villages. The epidemic often diverts conservation funds to cover staff medical expenses, sick leave, terminal benefits, and funeral costs. Add the extra expense of training new staff and reconfiguring positions for disabled staff, and a project can spend significant amounts on AIDS rather than on conservation.[4]

At the same time, conservation staff may run a higher-than-average job-related risk of contracting HIV. When staff are stationed far from their families in remote parks or when they are traveling away from home overnight, as are drivers and community conservation workers, they may be more likely to take other sexual partners. As they move through remote conservation areas that lack HIV/AIDS information, or are transferred between posts, they also risk transmitting HIV to remote communities. Boredom, loneliness, and alcohol can exacerbate the risk.

Such was the case in Malawi's Kasungu National Park, which covers about 800 square miles (2,000 km^2) of miombo woodland on the Zambian border. Park management operated from a main camp and five outlying posts, each of which had a team of game scouts living onsite, away from their families, patrolling sections of the park for a month at a time. On payday, scouts congregated in the main camp to be transported to Kasungu Boma for a day off. When scouts showed up for the ride back, many would have been drinking and some would be accompanied by women they had met in bars.

The consequences unfolded a few years later. Between 2000 and 2006, Kasungu National Park lost 17 middle managers and junior scouts to health-related deaths—a staggering 22 percent loss of its workforce. Conservation capacity in Kasungu is now too weak to manage the whole park, and poaching has escalated, leading to the decline of large mammals such as buffalo and elephant. In total, Malawi's Department of National Parks and Wildlife lost 80 park and reserve staff during that period.[5]

Coffins for sale in Malawi. Demand for coffins has greatly increased, and is placing serious pressure on Malawi's forest reserves.

Loss of capacity due to AIDS is also a problem for local communities practicing community-based natural resource management (CBNRM). Through CBNRM arrangements, communities usually play a participatory role in management, control, and monitoring of natural resources for the long-term benefit of the community. Good CBNRM requires governance structures—in Namibia, elected committees manage resources in the communal conservancies' registered land. When champions and leaders die, these management structures erode. When other members must care for the sick and orphans, or refocus livelihood strategies for immediate survival, collective natural resource planning for the future becomes a low priority.

In addition, knowledge of how to harvest natural resources sustainably, and how to farm and practice agroforestry, is being lost. In many families the middle generation—parents—is incapacitated or dead; grandparents are too old to work; children are either burdened with extra duties or orphaned. Traditional knowledge is not being passed from one generation to the next.

AIDS may also intensify natural resource use. Sick fishermen may still fish, for example, but may stay in nearby waters, contributing to localized overfishing.[6] Increased demand for medicinal plants to treat AIDS-related infections such as thrush, shingles, diarrhea, abscesses, and coughs increases harvesting of wild plants, often destroying wild stocks.

Coffins, too, are in greater demand, so much so that forests are being affected. Before the 1980s, ready-made coffins were unusual in Malawi, but today coffin workshops are common. Coffins are sold along roadsides and by Malawi's two main hospitals, which average 20 to 25 deaths a day, many of them AIDS related.[7] Coffins are either made of softwood from pine plantations or hardwood from valuable indigenous trees like mahogany. Hardwood coffins are preferred if families can afford them. But hardwood timber has become scarcer, in part due to the rising demand for coffins, resulting in illegal logging for the timber in forest reserves.

AIDS, Poverty, and Natural Resource Use

Poverty and AIDS are closely related in Africa, in part because the disease affects the economically active age groups, and households with sick family members often lose salaries and agricultural labor. In order to cope, rural households may sell draft animals and land, reducing their future productive capacity.[8] The poor are particularly vulnerable because low nutrition speeds the progress of the virus, shortening the time that people can work.

Female charcoal merchants are at higher risk of contracting HIV because they are often forced to exchange sex for the opportunity to transport their wares.

Natural resources provide a critical safety net for many rural households coping with AIDS and increasing poverty. In Mozambique and Malawi, households that had lost family members tended to collect more forest resources, including firewood, thatch, fruits, mushrooms, and basket-making materials.[9] Some households turned to brewing and food vending as alternative livelihoods, increasing fuel-wood consumption. Elsewhere, hunting and fishing have increased as families struggle to maintain income.[10] Poorer families also fall back on making charcoal, a process of burning wood in kilns. With this intensification of natural resource use, resources can grow scarce and communities near protected areas may be forced to seek resources inside parks and reserves.

Poverty and fewer hands on the farm have also been linked to an increased use of fire to clear land. In the Caprivi region of northeast Namibia—an area with two national parks—fires have increased since 2003 as AIDS orphans and remaining family members use fire as a cheap, labor-saving method to clear agricultural land. Uncontrolled fires destroy forest foods and building materials and threaten to spread into protected areas.[11]

AIDS, Women, and Conservation

Women are disproportionately burdened by the disease and consequent poverty. They care for the sick and orphans, and when a mother dies, her eldest daughter often takes care of the children—in Botswana, it is estimated that families in the poorest quarter of the population will acquire an additional eight dependents as a result of AIDS.[12]

Women are likelier to suffer a downward spiral of poverty resulting from AIDS. Some customs and laws prevent women from inheriting land, putting them at risk of inescapable poverty. Girls in AIDS-affected households drop out of school at a higher rate as they leave to care for sick relatives and younger siblings and to collect firewood and water.[13] Consequently, they will know less about health, have fewer life and employment skills, and become more vulnerable to contracting HIV.[14] As poverty deepens, widows and older daughters may turn to transactional sex to support their families.

A close connection exists between increased natural resource management, AIDS, and women. The natural resources managed by women are in greater demand when caring for AIDS patients (e.g., water, wild food plants, firewood, and medicinal plants). This means women spend more time collecting them. After a death, women may fall back on these resources for survival. One woman from Bushbuckridge, South Africa, commented that after the loss of her household's primary wage earner, her family depends more on wild foods because they cannot afford to

Source: Daulos Mauambeta of Wildlife and Environmental Society of Malawi.

Increased demand for medicinal plants used to treat AIDS-related symptoms has led to the overharvesting of many wild plants.

purchase food: "Locusts are now our beef."[15] Increasing demand strains traditional management systems, and with their additional work loads, women often participate less in enterprise cooperatives. In some places, governance of natural resources has broken down, and forest product collection has become a free-for-all.

Reducing the Threat and Impact of AIDS: Conservation's Role

It is very likely that the effects of AIDS on natural resources will intensify. The epidemic proceeds in four waves: HIV infection, the onset of opportunistic diseases, illness and death, and social and economic disruption at household, community, national, and international levels. Affected countries have not yet fully felt the third wave, or advanced far into the fourth.[16] But they will, and the social and economic impacts, including erosion of human capital in every sector, will last for years. Workforces will be seriously limited: Namibia's agricultural labor force is predicted to drop by over 25 percent by 2020.[17] Many countries are already struggling to keep schools staffed and sustain police forces and armies (whose HIV rate is often higher than the national average).

Against this background, the number of orphans grows, with a predicted 18.4 million by 2010 in sub-Saharan Africa.[18] HIV/AIDS is now widely viewed as a global security threat, in part because unprecedented demographic change is creating a disproportionately large population of young people, and in a few years the "youth bulge" of poorly educated young men could result in political instability.[19] Civil unrest and social upheaval often undermine biodiversity and natural resource management.[20]

The conservation sector cannot tackle the epidemic and its impacts single-handedly, but it can actively reduce the disease's negative effects on conservation. In partnership with the health sector we can develop and implement workplace policies on HIV/AIDS that address awareness, prevention, care, and expected standards of employee behavior toward colleagues, eliminate stigma and discrimination associated with the disease, ensure confidentiality, and promote voluntary counseling and testing. A few conservation organizations have such workplace policies: for example, members of the Namibia Association of CBNRM Support Organizations, KwaZulu Natal Wildlife, and African Wildlife Foundation.

Practical anti-AIDS measures include supplying condoms for staff, particularly in remote field locations and, where feasible, assisting families to accompany staff posted away from home. To help maintain conservation capacity, some organizations have staff wellness programs which may provide antiretroviral drugs (if there is access to good follow-up health care). Sick staff can be assigned to less labor-intensive jobs, while training programs can be adapted to train more people in a broader base of skills so they can take over when colleagues are sick or die.

Conservation programs operating in remote areas, often in partnership with isolated communities that lack good access to social services, are well placed to introduce health projects to these rural communities, either by bringing in health partners or by incorporating HIV/AIDS materials directly into conservation programs. For example, the communal conservancy program in Namibia is main-

Source: Judy Oglethorpe.

Awareness campaigns throughout Africa inform local people and visitors alike about HIV/AIDS prevention.

streaming HIV/AIDS awareness and prevention into its work at the community, conservancy, and support organization levels. It has the potential to reach one-tenth of Namibia's population in remote parts of the country—those with poorest access to health services.

In the course of its work, the conservation sector has opportunities to reduce gender inequality and poverty, those two major drivers of the spread of HIV. The Wildlife and Environmental Society of Malawi, for example, developed non-labor-intensive enterprises to assist AIDS-affected communities, including keeping bees, rearing guinea fowl, planting fruit trees, and producing indigenous fruit juices. The Wilderness Foundation's innovative Umzi Wethu program in South Africa trains orphans from both rural and urban areas to work in ecotourism. Many conservation projects focus on strengthening women's participation in natural resource management and promoting income-generating activities for them. World Wildlife Fund supports schooling for girls from poor families in conservation areas, helping them to develop future careers and empowering them to play a greater role in natural resource governance.

> Much of the conservation sector has been slow to respond because some organizations still see HIV/AIDS as strictly a health problem.

To scale up response to HIV/AIDS, the World Conservation Congress passed a 2004 resolution requesting the World Conservation Union (IUCN) to promote solutions and recommend that its members take action. This has started by raising awareness and developing a workplace policy within IUCN, but much more remains to be done. As one step, the Africa Biodiversity Collaborative Group and World Wildlife Fund have been working with various partners to collect best practices and coping strategies on conservation and HIV/AIDS, and to communicate them in Africa and beyond.

Much of the conservation sector has been slow to respond because some organizations still see HIV/AIDS as strictly a health problem, and stigma around the disease remains high. Even in the face of the disease's very noticeable effects on conservation capacity, little has been done to research and quantify these impacts or to devise larger-scale interventions. Partnerships with the health sector are too rarely forged, and little funding exists for multisectoral approaches to alleviate the pressure of AIDS on conservation.

The AIDS epidemic is inexorably advancing around the world. Conservation organizations in Africa must take action now to mitigate the disease's impacts in coming years, when the full economic, social, and security impacts will be felt. Over the next two years we must scale up efforts to develop and refine approaches, publicize the issues, and ensure much greater mainstreaming of HIV/AIDS best practices in the conservation sector. We must also take action now in the "next-wave countries" in eastern Europe, the Caribbean, and parts of Asia where HIV prevalence is growing but where there is still a window of opportunity for us to be proactive before the disease seriously affects conservation.

Conservation as Diplomacy

STEVEN E. SANDERSON

In the contemporary world of international relations, the Cold War polarities of East–West conflict are long gone and little lamented. In their place is a fractious new world of multiple and changing alliances that may shift in the blink of an eye. Iraq is only the most obvious of these, having gone from American ally (in the war against Iran) to enemy (in the first and second Gulf wars) to ally and then to global millstone, in only one generation. Similarly fluid dynamics of the new post–Cold War world are evident in varying degrees in Indonesia, Myanmar, Congo, Southern Sudan, and countless other places.

Not only are alliances at stake; the entire matter of whether one nation should engage another diplomatically provokes debate. These days, actors on the international stage are prominent for their refusal to negotiate or carry on diplomatic discourse with each other, from the Middle East, Iran, Syria, and Uzbekistan to the durable standoffs in Cuba and North Korea.

What does this have to do with conservation? Simply put, what Clausewitz famously said about war is also true of conservation: it is diplomacy by other means. Yet defining conservation diplomacy is about as easy as engaging in diplomacy itself.

Conservation, both public and private, is suffused with interstate tensions

STEVEN E. SANDERSON is president and chief executive officer of the Wildlife Conservation Society. He has also held fellowships and grants from the Woodrow Wilson International Center for Scholars, the National Aeronautics and Space Administration (NASA), and the Ford, MacArthur, Rockefeller, Tinker, and Heinz foundations. He is a member of the Council on Foreign Relations and a trustee of Fordham University. Among his recent publications are "The Future of Conservation" (Foreign Affairs, September 2002) and "Poverty and Conservation: The New Century's 'Peasant Question'?" (World Development, February 2005).

and the favor or disrepute visited on nation-state actors. Conservationists are often faced with a difficult choice: either align with interstate politics by refusing to engage in certain countries—thereby mortgaging the future of wildlife to the vicissitudes of international conflict—or diplomatically hold conservation apart from interstate politics. If we are to save wildlife and wildlands, we cannot afford the first choice—the politics of enforced abstinence—which these days

Source: Julie Larsen Maher/WCS.

Since 1999, the Wildlife Conservation Society has collaborated with two Cuban agencies—Departamento de Flora y Fauna and Parque Nacional Cienaga de Zapata—to monitor Cuban crocodile (*Crocodylus rhombifer*) populations and develop conservation actions to save the species from human encroachment and other threats.

would leave the Asiatic cheetah abandoned in the mountains of Iran, the tiger marooned in northern Myanmar, and the Cuban crocodile left to its own in the Zapata Swamp.

Thus conservation efforts often choose the second route—attempting to keep conservation separate from interstate politics. In this sense, conservation diplomacy differs from interstate diplomacy in that it behaves in the fashion of relief to the victims of disaster or disease outbreak or famine. Wildlife conservationists are less like proconsuls and more like physicians and administrators of famine relief or rural development in the far outreaches of the globe. These activities are notable for their disinterest in the short-term politics of a given regime or crisis. To work in many high-conflict areas of the world, often in regions where the canons of liberal democracy are notably absent, conservation must studiously avoid—not overlook, but suspend action against—the undemocratic practices of governments and the politics and danger of internal or international conflict. However, to assume that this separation from the directed mandates of interstate politics means that conservation does not play a role in diplomacy is to ignore the inevitable interactions of private actors on the global stage.

Private Actors, Public Mandate

As a first step in exploring the role of conservation in diplomacy, it is necessary to understand a fundamental reality of most conservation efforts. Global conservation is to a significant degree a private matter, undertaken and led by non-profit organizations with private as well as public support. The processes and legitimacy that undergird its efforts vary in their transparency and judgment. In contrast, public diplomacy enjoys public policy processes and diplomatic goals that are sanctioned by political systems, and even the international system through international treaties or conventions of various kinds. Because of its charge to defend national security, every state has diplomatic prerogatives that are explicitly legitimate.

Conservation has no such explicit legitimacy, and this difficulty is compounded because conservation organizations operate on multiple diplomatic footings: as independent agents of civil society in action, as defenders of public agendas through private means, as subcontractors to national governments that lack the capacity to conserve natural resources on their own (or prefer to outsource the capacity), and as technical or implementation agencies for multilateral conventions such as the Convention on International Trade in Endangered Species of Fauna and Flora (CITES). In each of these roles, conservationists are exposed politically, often without sufficient cover from the sponsoring agencies, be they national or multilateral.

The formal interstate system has been designed without private actors in mind, and private actors in general are systematically overlooked as strategic partners, even when playing a leading role on scene. Witness the awkwardness in the councils of the United Nations or in meetings of nations on a subject for which private organizations are the principal knowledge providers—women's reproductive health, conservation, or even education. Brought inside the halls of power for technical advice and then shuffled off when decision making is due, conservationists are like unsuccessful lobbyists, waiting at the doors behind which the future of wild nature is decided.

> Conservationists are often faced with a difficult choice: either align with interstate politics by refusing to engage in certain countries—thereby mortgaging the future of wildlife to the vicissitudes of international conflict—or diplomatically hold conservation apart from interstate politics.

Similarly, little conservation makes its way into the bilateral official development assistance policy dialogue, despite the overwhelming dependence of the world's poorest people on natural resources. For example, there is little biodiversity conservation thinking in the makeup or implementation of the multilateral Millennium Development Goals, a list of priorities for the next two decades that concentrate on poverty alleviation.

Alternately attacked and ignored, independent actors struggle to be relevant. Worse still, the funding sources for their activities are often tightly tied to foreign policy or national objectives of the sponsor, or are missing entirely. Where conservation is linked to official development assistance through bilateral donors, it can be held hostage to official sensibilities or agency capriciousness. At the other extreme, much essential conservation activity comes in the form of an "unfunded mandate," in which the priority is established by intergovernmental bodies or international conventions but the budget is not forthcoming. Thus conservation organizations, like relief agencies, are obliged to fund the unfunded, all the while protecting the threatened.

> Conservation organizations, like relief agencies, are obliged to fund the unfunded, all the while protecting the threatened.

Thus enabling private actors such as conservation organizations in diplomacy is fraught with difficulty because they lack political legitimacy, coercive power, appropriate levels of funding, and the skills and experience of foreign affairs institutions. Yet, often, relief or conservation organizations are the first in and last out of high-conflict or crisis zones, whether or not any government protection is available and despite the risks on the ground. In such circumstances, they often lack the protection of state actors and the legitimacy of government. In contrast to official government delegations, conservationists (and relief organizations) must negotiate their political space with militias, rebels, and local citizens. These private actors are increasingly acting on global public mandates, with or without the necessary support. From Doctors without Borders and CARE to the Wildlife Conservation Society and the World Wildlife Fund network, private actors are struggling to become more significant participants in interstate relations, as well as prime movers in the global commons. The events of the day, from famine and illness to biodiversity loss, demand such involvement, irrespective of international design.

The Role of Conservation in Diplomacy

So how does one define the diplomatic aspect of the precarious and complicated role that conservation takes as a private actor carrying out public mandates—all the while holding itself apart from interstate politics? Scholars and practitioners of international relations have thought of the diplomatic arts of war and peace, national security, and statecraft as high diplomacy, while the rest—economics, interstate relations, and international regime management (and presumably conservation, to the extent it is thought of at all)—are consigned to the lower arts. Likewise, state-directed diplomacy is traditionally considered to be the heartland of international relations, and private relations among international actors a lesser form.

Of course, all of this has been open to new scrutiny in light of trends toward globalization, the rise of the transnational corporation, the proliferation of nongovernmental organizations (NGOs), the institutionalization of the multilateral institutions of the Bretton Woods era, and the negotiation of new international regimes in the "global commons." International relations theory has followed along by generating new and more sophisticated ways of thinking. Appropriately, it is more common these days to hear of public diplomacy by private actors as part of the mix of international relations. Jesse Jackson's long history in the Middle East and independent forays into the Balkans; the Ford Foundation's role in the opposition to Apartheid in South Africa; Donald Kendall's Pepsi diplomacy toward the Soviet Union in the Nixon years, or Armand Hammer's before him. Recently, a task force of the Council on Foreign Relations even called for the creation of an institute of public diplomacy to reflect the changing world and its demands.

In various literatures and guises, some more elegant than others, this form of international relations is known as track two diplomacy, multistakeholder inter-

Okapi (*Okapia johnstoni*) dwell in the rainforests of the Democratic Republic of Congo, where years of civil unrest have threatened many species' survival. Monitoring species in war-torn regions requires diplomatic relations with local governments.

Source: D. DeMello/WCS.

national intervention, or even meddling. The tone of these labels conveys the uneven reputation of unofficial diplomacy among foreign policymakers, despite its growing presence and importance.

This kind of track two activity has a long, venerable reputation in world affairs. During the height of the Cold War, for example, the International Institute for Applied Systems Analysis in Laxenburg, Austria, received multilateral support from the West in order to maintain scientific exchange with Eastern scholars. Similarly, Stanford and Harvard universities played important roles in scholarly exchange with China in the early 1970s, and the Latin American Studies Association has done the same with Cuba since 1959.

Institutionally, it is natural to think of diplomacy as one of the exigencies of a global organization. In certain sectors, such as financial services or retail consumer goods, internationalism and its arts are requirements of the organization. Likewise, in the international nongovernmental world, organizations that focus on poverty alleviation, famine and disaster relief, the delivery of medical services, and the protection of biodiversity all require substantial diplomatic efforts and capacity.

In fact, some argue that certain institutional actors are required to engage in private diplomacy because of their very organizational ecology (i.e., who they are as organizations), their missions, and how they are constituted to deliver their missions. Such is the case with conservation organizations. By our very nature, we are engaged in conservation in the places most appropriate to its need and urgency.

The Realities of Conservation Diplomacy

The Wildlife Conservation Society's global efforts illustrate some of the difficulties in operating as an individual private actor conducting on-the-ground conservation in high-conflict or diplomatically complicated environments. Congo, for example, has suffered 50 years of instability, corruption, and civil conflict. Yet, with or without peace, conservation on the ground is imperative because the Congo Basin is one of the great repositories of biodiversity and where the future of the world's great apes is literally at stake. Congo's Maiko National Park has been surrounded by four different militias and many encampments during the many years of Congo's civil war. In the midst of this, the Wildlife Conservation Society works to clarify land tenure, train park guards, support the government conservation agency Institut Congolais pour la Conservation de la Nature (ICCF), employ forest and wildlife monitors, and conduct ecological surveys of okapi, gorillas, and other important fauna. The task is enriched and complicated by the need to work with local communities of forest people, whose tenure under conditions of war and natural resource exploitation is ever more tenuous.

> Yet, with or without peace, conservation on the ground is imperative because the Congo Basin is one of the great repositories of biodiversity and where the future of the world's great apes is literally at stake.

Afghanistan, as it recovers from a generation of invasion, war, and regime change, still needs to plan for conservation in the Hindu Kush and Pamirs. With 80 percent of the Afghan population dependent on the natural resource base, political stability and wise conservation stewardship go hand in hand. WCS has been working with the fledgling government

A team of scientists travel through the Big Pamir in Afghanistan. Capacity building within Afghanistan's environmental sector is key to sustainable natural resource management in the region.

of Afghanistan to inventory biodiversity, rangelands, and forests; design the first protected area network in the country's history; help write new environmental laws; work with local communities to develop sustainable management systems and increase income opportunities from the natural resource base; and train the next generation of conservation biologists and resource managers. The program is achieving notable successes despite being faced with degrading security conditions and continued fighting in many parts of the country, upward of 10 million landmines across the landscape, and a near-complete lack of physical or technical infrastructure outside of Kabul. Although WCS is an American organization and the program is funded by the US Agency for International Development (USAID), and the American presence receives a very mixed reception in Afghanistan, the role of science and conservation is seen as transcending political boundaries and disagreements by all players in the region. Thus these environmental initiatives have been welcomed by government and local communities alike, and have helped bridge a wide gulf between two countries.

Myanmar, still known as Burma despite the 1989 name change, is a country with extraordinary biodiversity and a near-complete lack of transparency to the outside world. Sitting at the foot of the Tibetan plateau and linked to India and China, Myanmar's northern Hukaung Valley is one of the biggest and most important tiger habitats remaining in the world. But without scientific management, hunting and habitat erosion will mean the end of the region's tiger population. WCS has been working in Myanmar for more than a decade to create what is now the world's largest tiger reserve, the Hukaung Valley Wildlife Reserve, roughly the size of the state of Vermont. Imperiled by separatist rebel activities, gold and precious gem exploitation, wildlife trade to China, and a closed policy process in government, the Hukaung Valley presents great challenges in terms of its protection. Despite these challenges, WCS has outlined a conservation strategy for the reserve that is designed to be viable despite the intensely complicated and intertwined political and conservation contexts, both nationally and internationally.

Other cases abound: WCS has been active in conserving the last Asiatic cheetahs in Iran, crocodiles in Cuba's Zapata Swamp, and forest elephants in the Congo Basin. In this last activity, several NGOs collaborate—using private support—to conserve forest elephants through an internationally sanctioned program of CITES: Monitoring the Illegal Killing of Elephants (MIKE). MIKE was designed to document the often difficult-to-document poaching of elephants. It differs from much conservation in that it has been given official status, yet the monitoring requirements to establish and maintain a politically acceptable and scientifically viable program involve daunting diplomacy indeed. Beyond the difficulty of doing good science under very trying logistical and political circumstances, it is also an "unfunded mandate"—much of the financial support for monitoring must be provided by private organizations, not the CITES budget. The tension in the arrangement includes the prospect that organizations such as WCS or other nonprofit partners may be assigned the task (and the potential liability) of MIKE, but the capacity to deliver will fall short of the regional and continental strategy necessary. The prospect of having all of the responsibility and none of the authority over such important matters as the survival of forest elephants is not attractive.

Conservation organizations stand as important generators of foreign exchange in poor countries (attracting many millions of dollars per year for protected area management and species conservation in the Congo Basin, for example), but they are still foreign interlocutors in the domestic politics of nat-

Building partnerships both in the US and abroad, the Wildlife Conservation Society seeks to provide information and management assistance to the national governments responsible for saving tigers (*Panthera tigris*) in their homelands.

ural resource allocation. Because of this status there are hidden opportunity costs and risks, entirely borne by the NGOs. In 2005–2006, WCS acted as a good faith broker and host for the transfer of an orphaned snow leopard from Pakistan to the Bronx Zoo because no viable housing exists in Pakistan. Given the profile of the bilateral relationship between the US and Pakistan, the difficulties of permitting the transfer of an endangered animal, and the precariousness that attends the global transport of a wild animal, the risk of failure was great. The successful transfer of the animal to New York in September 2006 was accompanied by high-level ceremonies and equally high hopes for increasing the genetic resilience of the species in captivity—and increasing the channels of communication between the two countries. However, the death of the snow leopard while in WCS custody would have produced a different, equally political, result.

Critics who operate from an idealist perspective in international relations have attacked WCS for "enabling" poor governance, such as the dictatorship in Myanmar, by providing foreign exchange (used for conservation) and implied legitimacy. To counter, we offer a kind of conservation realpolitik: conservation must take place wherever an opportunity presents itself. At its most basic, we believe that conservation that waits for good government fails in many places throughout the world. From time to time, these debates are spiced up with crises such as Myanmar's long-term suppression of the political opposition, its alleged complicity in illegal trade in gemstones and wildlife, and, most recently, the apparent continuation of gold mining in the tiger reserve itself, against promises and agreements that accompanied the reserve's establishment. Yet, for those who criticize WCS's presence in countries suffering dictatorships or institutionalized corruption or lacking rule of law, we ask, What is the alternative? The wildlife in crisis around the world did not choose their place or their political system. Irrespective of the governance of wildlife and wildlands, conservation must serve them now and not wait until they are properly governed. To work in hostile countries or those isolated from the international system is to serve as track two diplomats, keeping communication and scientific exchange open and preparing for a better day, all the while conserving what remains. 🦌

The transfer of Leo, an orphaned snow leopard (*Uncia uncia*), from Pakistan to the Bronx Zoo exemplifies how international diplomacy can foster conservation. The Pakistani government invited the Wildlife Conservation Society to raise the cub in the United States until a suitable facility is constructed in Pakistan.

Lost

Stand still. The trees ahead and bushes beside you
Are not lost. Wherever you are is called Here,
And you must treat it as a powerful stranger,
Must ask permission to know it and be known.
The forest breathes. Listen. It answers,
I have made this place around you.
If you leave it, you may come back again, saying Here.
No two trees are the same to Raven.
No two branches are the same to Wren.
If what a tree or a bush does is lost on you,
You are surely lost. Stand still. The forest knows
Where you are. You must let it find you.

DAVID WAGONER
COLLECTED POEMS 1956–1976

Final Thoughts

Profession: Awajun

WALTER H. WUST

Wawain, Mamayaque, and Huampami are the Awajun communities I visited on an expedition through Peruvian forests near the Colombian and Ecuadorian borders. At our last camp on the banks of the Nieva, the familiar call of an *araçari* breaks through the low roar of the river, its large toucan beak rustling the leaves nearby. I have one more day to spend in these drenched and humid lands. One more day of rain; rain that sustains millions of growing plants, some of which produce poisons to protect their ripe fruits. Deep down, the greenery around us is as "alive" as the flock of parrots perched nearby.

In these rich mountains, I got to know the Awajun communities who strive to maintain their traditions while incorporating new knowledge into their culture in order to "join" the national system. For the Awajuns, it is a time of wooden drums and the Internet, cassava beer and Coca-cola. Their ancient wisdom is being severely tested: The elders can give little advice on foreign markets or preparing projects for international foundations. An old *Apu* told me, "Life itself is like the forest and our fate like the channel of a river, ever-changing and unpredictable."

My new friend Abel is solid and good-natured—his profession: Awajun. He has tattoos on his face, marks he "inherited" from his father as a boy, made with ink and copal tree smoke. A line of dots placed above the nose and cheek bones, and two circles on the cheeks are the mark of the Mayants, his countrymen.

WALTER H. WUST is a forester, journalist, editor, photographer, and environmentalist. He is the only Peruvian to have published five articles in National Geographic *magazine, and more than 160 books on nature and local cultures. Among his recent books are* Huascarán, Lord of the Snow; Paracas, between the Sea and the Desert; *and* The Living Desert. *He is currently director of Wust Ediciones and Guías Perú TOP.*

We walk toward the small aluminum motor boat as Abel fixes a net to catch sardines. As we head out on the water, the riverine forest presents its illustrious characters: large *lupuna* trees, the umbrellas of the forest, rise majestically above the others. Clusters of *capirona* trees with svelte trunks, devoid of bark, are tinted an intense ochre. Tree ferns spread their fronds, and impenetrable thickets of bamboo, the well-known *pacales*, defy even the sharpest machetes. *Cecropia* trees abound, home of the shy sloth (or *pelejo*) that, by barely moving and having algae-covered fur, lives a camouflaged existence.

As a motorboat driver, Abel has visited the "land of the five rivers": the Marañon, Chiriaco, Cenepa, Nieva, and Santiago. The jungle rivers are highways, food stores, and a playground for the people here. All that is needed is within a hand's reach. The waters serve to connect villages through areas that an asphalt highway could never reach. If these rivers could talk, they would tell us of the battles, joys, and worries of the ancient Awajun.

Despite his humble appearance, Abel carries worldly memories. He has met the feared Achuar, "who are your friends until you marry one of their women, and then they make you work clearing fields, carrying firewood, and hunting meat." He has lived among missionaries who taught him to speak Spanish, read the Bible, and consider surgery to erase his tattoos. He has also traveled to some US cities, "where they live in houses piled one on top of the other . . . just like termite colonies."

I ask Abel why his people distrust anybody that comes from the outside, anyone who is not a "brother." He says, "This comes from a very long time ago, when the foreigners, *Iwanch*, came to the land where we live. They appeared saying that they wanted to learn, that they wanted to know everything. So the old ones showed them where they got gold and how to braze metals. Afterward, the foreigners killed them. They started with Atahuallpa and just a few escaped, who told us. Later others came with cartridges good for hunting, the type that did not get wet in the rain, and that killed animals even from far away. They spoke English. We called them *inkis*. They took plants, oil, and minerals—even women and children."

As I prepare to leave the forest, I immerse myself in the beauty of the huge *aguaje* palm trees, which soar to the heavens. A few large raindrops drip from their leaves and break the stillness of this jungle asleep in time. From a distance, the sound of the *unku*, made by blowing into a large snail shell, tells friends that a group is about to arrive. Abel says, "I asked myself, 'Where can I find God?' Then, I realized that we find God all over the jungle . . . even in the dens of the animals."

The muddy backpacks are now in my closet, but during those days in the rainforests where the Cenepa and Comainas meander—two rivers born in the craggy peaks of the Condor Mountains—I had uncovered wonders that city-dwelling Peruvians will most likely never see. I had connected with men and women—Peruvians like me—who live every day with the ease of knowing that a rich person is not one who has more, but one who needs less.

From that time I keep a clear message: this jungle asks for, or better said, demands respect from, anyone who floats its rivers. Respect for its extremes—torrential rains followed by 48°C in the shade, its hordes of mosquitoes, and 100 percent humidity. Respect for the *pucacuro* ants, marching through the forest, capable of constructing bridges out of their own bodies to overcome obstacles. And most importantly, respect for its people, who have become distrusting but, despite everything, preserve their welcoming ways.

Awajun: an ethnic group belonging to the Jibaro language family.

Apu: a Quechuan word meaning god, also applied to local chiefs.

Mayants: an Awajun word for an indigenous clan from Northeastern Peru.

Acknowledgments

The WCS Institute would like to thank the many biologists and conservationists mentioned below who took time from their busy schedules to provide valuable information, reviews, photographs, or other support. Their insight, expertise, and advice are greatly appreciated. We also thank the international experts listed on page 47 for writing and reviewing the Global Conservation News Highlights. Auscape International: Sarah Tahourdin; BirdLife International: Gina Pfaff; Conservation International: Gege Poggi; CNRS Photothèque: Christelle Pineau; Defying Oceans End: Tim Noviello; Department for Environment and Heritage (Australia): Kirsty Bevan; Flora and Fauna International: Martin Fisher; Ifremer: Daniele Lemercier and Michel Segonzac; Monterey Bay Aquarium Research Institute: Kim Fulton-Bennett; NASA Goddard Institute for Space Studies: Darnell Cain and Makiko Sato; Nature Picture Library: Tim Aldred and Rachelle Macapagal; The Peregrine Fund: Jack Cafferty and Rick Watson; Seaweb.org/Marine PhotoBank: Reuven Walder; TRAFFIC International: Richard Thomas; Turtle Foundation: Reisa Latorra and Frank Zindel; Turtle Time, Inc.: Eve Haverfield; University of Central Florida: Reed Noss; University of Maryland: Norma Brinkley; University of Washington: Kathryn Kohm; Wildlife Conservation Society: Tim Bean, Kim Berger, Suzanne Bolduc, Stuart Campbell, Nadya Cartagena, Pete Coppolillo, Bryan Curran, Alex Dehgan, Nawang Eden, Dan Erickson, Martin Gilbert, Kevin Gorman, Guillermo Harris, Terese Hart, Matthew Hatchwell, Andrea Heydlauff, Jodi Hilty, Bill Holmstrom, Steve Johnson, Aili Kang, Andrew Mack, Julie Larsen Maher, Roan McNab, Robert Olley, Sarah Pacyna, Lillian Painter, Graeme Patterson, Colin Poole, Jennifer Pramuk, Don Reid, John Robinson, Carlos Rodriguez, Alexandra Rojas, Anton Seimon, Karen Spiak, Patrick Thomas, Susan Tressler, Mariana Varese, Rachael Vinyard, Sarah Werner, Colin Woodward, Gillian Woolmer, and Steve Zack; World Wildlife Fund: Jill Hatzai.

We are especially grateful for the support of Steven E. Sanderson and Ward Woods. Special thanks also go to our editorial board (Debbie Behler, Nancy Clum, Stephen Sautner, Bill Weber, Dan Wharton, Peter Zahler), Catherine

Grippo, Sandra Alcosser, Bronwyn Becker, and Joanna Cagan, and to our patient and supportive team at Island Press, Barbara Dean, Maureen Gately, Erin Johnson, Kat Macdonald, and Barbara Youngblood. This book could not have been produced without all your help.

Notes

By the Numbers: Emerging Diseases and Conservation

1. M. E. J. Woolhouse and S. Gowtage-Sequeria, "Host range and emerging and reemerging pathogens," *Emerging Infectious Diseases* 11(2005): 1842–47.

2. World Health Organization, www.who.int/csr/disease/avian_influenza/country/cases_table_2007_10_25/en/index.html.

3. CIDRAP News, http://cidrap.umn.edu.

4. M. Osterholm, "Unprepared for a pandemic," *Foreign Affairs* 86(2007): 47–57.

5. International Federation for Animal Health, 2006 Annual Report, www.ifahsec.org/annual_report/IFAH%20annual%20report%202006.pdf.

6. S. Shah, "The perfect predator: Malaria makes a comeback." *Orion* (November–December 2006), www.orionmagazine.org/index.php/articles/article/179/.

7. J. Sachs and P. Malaney, "The economic and social burden of malaria," *Nature* 415(2002): 680–85.

8. D. Normille, "Indonesia taps village wisdom to fight bird flu," *Science* 315(2007): 30–33.

9. M. Davis, *Planet of Slums* (New York: Verso, 2006), www.doublestandards.org/davis2.html; Globalis, http://globalis.gvu.unu.edu/indicator_detail.cfm?IndicatorID=136&Country=CN.

10. R. Naylor et al., "Losing the links between livestock and land," *Science* 310(2005): 1621.

11. D. Joly, pers. comm., 2007.

12. Centers for Disease Control and Prevention, www.cdc.gov/ncidod/dvbid/lyme/ld_upclimblymedis.htm; M. Guera, "Predicting the risk of Lyme disease: Habitat suitability for *Ixodes scapularis* in the North Central United States," *Emerging Infectious Diseases* 8(2002): 289–97.

13. D. Turner, "Amphibian Ark planned to save frogs," Associated Press, February 15, 2007; S. Stuart et al., "Status and trends of amphibian declines and extinctions worldwide," *Science* 306(2004): 1783–1786.

14. Panapress, 19 April 2007 [trans. Mod.TY, edited],www.panapress.com/freenewspor.asp?code=por006429&dte=19/04/2007, on promedmail.org.

15. "A deadly scourge," *Economist*, www.economist.com, April 19, 2007; S. S. Twiddy et al., "Inferring the rate and time-scale of dengue virus evolution," *Molecular Biological Evolution* 20(2003): 122–29.

16. Anon. 2003; M. Fenton et al., "Linking bats to emerging diseases," *Science* 311(2006): 1098–99.

17. J. Newcomb, "Thinking ahead: The business significance of an avian influenza pandemic," Bio Economic Research Associates, 2006; Original source, J. Pritchett et al., "Animal disease economic impacts: A survey of literature and typology of research approaches," *International Food and Agribusiness Management Review* 8(2005).

18. Centers for Disease Control and Prevention, www.cdc.gov/ncidod/dvbid/westnile/surv&controlCaseCount07_detailed.htm.

19. Tasmania Department of Primary Industries and Water, www.dpiw.tas.gov.au/inter.nsf/WebPages/LBUN-5QF86G?open; J. Bunce, "Tassie devil tumour break-through," *The Australian*, Oct. 3, 2007.

20. G. Vogel, "Tracking Ebola's deadly march among wild apes," *Science* 314(2006): 1522–23; World Health Organization www.who.int/csr/don/2007_10_03a/en/index.html.

21. Whirling Disease Initiative, http://whirlingdisease.montana.edu.

22. "Trans-boundary diseases hamper livestock development," Botswana Press Agency, June 27, 2005, www.gov.bw/cgi-bin/news.cgi?d=200506278:=Trans-boundary_diseases_hamper_livestock_development.

Introduction: Future States of the Wild by Kent H. Redford

1. J. Marshall, "Future Recall: Your Mind Can Slip through Time," *New Scientist*, March 24, 2007.

Part I: State of the Wild

Tipping Point: Perspective of a Climatologist by James Hansen

1. J. Hansen, "The Threat to the Planet," *New York Review of Books,*, July 13, 2006.

2. J. Hansen et al., "Climate Change and Trace Gases," *Philosophical Transaction of the Royal Society A* 365 (2007): 1925–1954.

3. J. Hansen et al., "Global Temperature Change," *Proceedings of the National Academy of Sciences.* 103 (2006): 14288–93.

4. C. Parmesan, "Ecological and Evolutionary Response to Recent Climate Change," *Annual Review of Ecology and Evolution of Systems* 37 (2006): 637–69.

5. C. Parmesan, "Ecological and Evolutionary Response," 2006.

6. L. Gross, "As the Antarctic Ice Pack Recedes, a Fragile Ecosystem Hangs in the Balance," *PLoS Biol* 3, no. 4 (2005): e127.

7. E. Pennisi, "U.S. Weighs Protection for Polar Bears," *Science* 315 (2007): 25.

8. C. Jordan, "Computers May Help Save Mount Graham Red Squirrel," *Univ. Arizona News*, April 27, 2006; T. Egan, "Heat Invades Cool Heights over Arizona Desert," *New York Times*, March 27, 2007.

9. Fish and Wildlife Service, Loggerhead Sea Turtle, www.fws.gov/northflorida/SeaTurtles%Factsheets/loggerheadsea-turtle.htm.

10. D. Archer, "Methane Hydrates and Anthropogenic Climate Change," *Biogeosciences Discussion* 4 (2007): 521–44.

11. C. Zimmer, "A Radical Step to Preserve a Species: Assisted Migration," *New York Times*, January 23, 2007.

12. J. Hansen et al., "Dangerous Human-Made Interference with Climate: A GISS model Study," *Atmospheric Chemistry and Physics Discussion* 7 (2007): 2287–312.

13. Proven and anticipated reserves are based on Energy Information Administration estimates. Other experts estimate higher or lower reserves, but the uncertainties do not alter our conclusions.

14. J. Hansen, "Dangerous Human-Made Interference with Climate," 2007.

15. J. Hansen et al., "Global Warming in the Twenty-First Century: An Alternative Scenario," *Proceedings of the National Academy of Sciences* 97 (2000): 9875–80.

16. J. Hansen, Political Interference with Government Climate Change Science. Submitted text accompanying oral testimony given March 19, 2007 during hearings on "Political Interference with Science: Global Warming, Part II" of the Committee on Oversight and Government Reform of the U.S. House of Representatives. www.columbia.edu/~jeh1/20070319105800-43018.pdf; http://oversight.house.gov/story.asp?ID=1214

17. K. Z. House et al., "Permanent Carbon Dioxide Storage in Deep-Sea Sediments," *Proceedings of the National Academy of Sciences* 103 (2006): 12291–95.

Discoveries by Margaret Kinnaird

1. B. M. Beehler et al., "A New Species of Smoky Honeyeater (Meliphagidae: *Melipotes*) from Western New Guinea," *Auk* 124 (2007): 1000–9.

2. E. Kranz, "Scientists Believe Bird's Head Seascape Is Richest on Earth," www.conservation.org/xp/frontlines/2006/09180601.xml.

3. A. Singa et al. "*Macaca Munzala*: A New Species from Western Arunachal Pradesh, Northeastern India," *International Journal of Primatology* 26 (2005): 977–89.

4. R. H. Bain et al., "Three New Indochinese Species of Cascade Frogs (Amphibia: Ranidae) Allied to *Rana Archotaphus*," *Copeia* 1 (2006): 43–59.

5. *Bulletin of the British Ornithologists Club*, Vol. 126 (June 2006).

6. K. A. Raskoff and G. I. Matsumoto, "*Stellamedusa ventana*, a New Mesopelagic Scyphomedusa from the Eastern Pacific Representing a New Subfamily, the Stellamedusinae," *Journal of the Marine Biological Association of the UK* 84 (2004): 37–42.

7. E. Macpherson, W. Jones, and M. Segonzac, "A New Squat Lobster Family of Galatheoidea (Crustacea, Decapoda, Anomura) from the Hydrothermal Vents of the Pacific–Antarctic Ridge," *Zoosystema* 24 (2005): 709–23.

8. P. Tyson, "Living at Extremes," Public Broadcasting Service, July 1998, www.pbs.org/wgbh/nova/abyss/.

9. P. M. Kappeler et al., "Morphology, Behviour and Molecular Evolution of Giant Mouse Lemurs (*Mirza* spp.) Gray, 1870, with Description of a New Species," *Primate Report* 71: 3–26.

10. T. Cucchi et al., "A New Endemic Species of the Subgenus *Mus* (Rodentia, Mammalia) on the Island of Cyprus," *Zootaxa* 1241 (2006): 1–36.

11. R. Athreya, "A New Species of Liocichla (Aves: Timaliidae) from Eaglenest Wildlife Sanctuary, Arunachal Pradesh, India," *Indian Birds* 2 (2006): 86–94.

12. T. Jones et al., "The Highland Mangabey *Lophocebus kipunji*: a New Species of African Monkey," *Science* 308 (2005): 1161–64.

13. T. Davenport et al., "A New Genus of African Monkey, *Rungwecebus*: Morphology, Ecology, and Molecular Phylogenetics," *Science* 312 (2006): 1378–81.

The Rarest of the Rare: Some of the World's Most Endangered Animals by Catherine Grippo, Taylor H. Ricketts, and Jonathan Hoekstra

1. "Extinction crisis escalates: Red List shows apes, corals, vultures, dolphins all in danger," www.iucn.org/en/news/archive/2007/09/12_pr_redlist.htm.

2. 2007 IUCN Red List. Summary statistics. Table 1: Numbers of threatened species by major groups of organisms (1996–2007). www.iucnredlist.org/info/2007RL_Stats_Table%201.pdf.

3. S. Stuart et al., "Status and Trends of Amphibian Declines and Extinctions Worldwide," *Science* 306 (2004): 1783–86.

4. "Going up, going down, gone?" www.iucn.org/themes/ssc/redlist2007/going_updown_2007.htm.

5. BirdLife International, "Species factsheet: Abbott's booby," www.birdlife.org/datazone/species/index.html?action=SpcHTMDetails.asp&sid=3651&m=0.

6. Animal Info, "Addax," www.animalinfo.org/species/artiperi/addanaso.htm.

7. G. Morey et al., "*Squatina squatina*," *2006 IUCN Red List of Threatened Species*, www.iucnredlist.org.

8. Wildlife Conservation Society, "Cambodia gives florican room to flourish," www.wcs.org/353624/bengalflorican.

9. Animal Info, "Black-Faced Lion Tamarin," www.animalinfo.org/species/primate/leoncais.htm.

10. S. G. Platt et al., "Noteworthy Records and Exploitation of Chelonians from the Ayeyarwady, Chindwin, and Dokhtawady Rivers, Myanmar," *Chelonian Conservation and Biology* 4 (2005): 942–48.

11. "Disappearing Dragonflies—Sri Lanka's Remarkable Jewels Clearly in Trouble," www.iucn.org/themes/ssc/redlist2006/portraits_in_red.htm#dragonflies.

12. M. Bedjanic, "*Tetrathemis yerburii*," *2006 IUCN Red List of Threatened Species*, www.iucnredlist.org.

13. K. Lips et al., "*Atelopus zeteki*," *2006 IUCN Red List of Threatened Species*, www.iucnredlist.org.

14. Animal Info, "North Atlantic Right Whale," www.animalinfo.org/species/cetacean/eubaglac.htm.

15. J. Ottenwalder, "Ricord's Iguana," www.iucn-isg.org/actionplan/ch2/ricords.php.

16. R. Lewison and W. Oliver, "*Hexaprotodon liberiensis*," *2006 IUCN Red List of Threatened Species*, www.iucnredlist.org.

17. International Rhino Foundation, "Sumatran Rhino," www.rhinos-irf.org/rhinoinformation/sumatranrhino/index.htm.

18. "Fivefold Increase in 'World's Rarest Snake,'" FFI Update No. 5, Summer 2006.

19. Audubon WatchList, "California condor," http://audubon2.org/webapp/watchlist/viewSpecies.jsp?id=56.

20. T. H. Ricketts et al., "Pinpointing and Preventing Imminent Extinctions," *Proceedings of the National Academy of Sciences of the United States of America* 102 (2005): 18497–501.

Continuing to Consume Wildlife: An Update by Elizabeth L. Bennett

1. E. L. Bennett, "Consuming Wildlife in the Tropics," in *State of the Wild 2006: A Global Portrait of Wildlife, Wildlands, and Oceans*, ed. S. Guynup, 106–13 (Washington, DC: Island Press, 2005).

2. J. R. Wingard and P. Zahler, *Silent Steppe: The Illegal Wildlife Trade Crisis in Mongolia* (Washington, DC: World Bank, 2006).

3. M. Lau, Kadoorie Wildlife Farm and Botanical Garden, unpublished data.

4. Education for Nature Vietnam Wildlife Crime Bulletin, Hanoi, Vietnam, January 19, 2007. www.envietnam.org/ENV_Resource_Library

5. E. J. Milner-Gulland et al., "Dramatic Declines in Saiga Antelope Population," *Oryx* 35, no.4 (2001): 340–45.

6. L. Li et al., "Report of a Survey on Saiga Horn in Markets in China." WCS China report to CITES, 2007. www.cites.org/eng/cop/14/inf/index.shtml.

7. J. Watts, "Noah's Ark of 5,000 Rare Animals Found Floating off the Coast of China," *Guardian*, May 26, 2007.

8. TRAFFIC East Asia.

9. Y. Guo et al., "Investigation Report on Sustainable Use of Medicinal Animals," in *Conserving China's Biodiversity*, ed. J. MacKinnon and S. Wang, 190–221 (Beijing: China Environmental Science Press, 1996).

10. H. Shi et al., "Farming Endangered Turtles to Extinction in China," *Conservation Biology* 21 (2007): 5–6.

11. Scott Roberton, pers. comm.

12. Conservation Controversies, in *State of the Wild 2006*, ed. S. Guynup, 147–163 (Washington, DC: Island Press, 2005).

13. J. G. Robinson and E. L. Bennett, "Having Your Wildlife and Eating It Too: An Analysis of Hunting Sustainability across Tropical Ecosystems," *Animal Conservation* 7 (2004): 397–408.

14. "Conservation and Use of Wildlife-Based Resources: The 'Bushmeat Crisis' in Question." Scientific paper to the Convention on Biological Diversity. CIFOR. June, 2007.

15. "EU to Ban Imports of Wild Birds," BBC, January 11, 2007, http://news.bbc.co .uk/2/hi/europe/6253543.stm.

Part II: Focus on the Wild

Little Is Big, Many Is One: Zoonoses in the Twenty-first Century by David Quammen

1. M. E. J. Woolhouse and S. Gowtage-Sequeria, "Host range and emerging and remerging pathogens," *Emerging Infectious Diseases* II (2005): 1842–47.

2. "Puumala virus infections—Belgium," www.promedmail.org (accessed June 1, 2007).

3. "Plague, Feline—USA," www.promedmail.org (accessed May 26, 2007).

4. Ibid.

5. "West Nile Virus Update 2007," www.promedmail.org (accessed May 26, 2007).

6. F. Keesing et al., "Effects of Species Diversity on Disease Risk," *Ecology Letters* 9 (2006): 485.

Land-Use Change as a Driver of Disease by Jonathan A. Patz, Sarah H. Olson, and Jill C. Baumgartner

1. J. A. Patz et al., "Human Health: Ecosystem Regulation of Infectious Diseases," in *Ecosystems and Human Well-Being*, vol. 1, *Current State and Trends* Millennium Ecosystem Assessment Series (Washington, DC: Island Press, 2005): 393–411.

2. N. D. Wolfe et al., "Deforestation, Hunting and the Ecology of Microbial Emergence," *Global Change and Human Health* 1 (2000): 10–25.

3. World Health Organization, *World Health Report, 2004: Changing History* (Geneva: WHO, 2004).

4. S. R. Ostfeld and F. Keesing, "Biodiversity and Disease Risk: The Case of Lyme Disease," *Conservation Biology* 14 (2000): 722–28.

5. K. A. Schmidt and R. S. Ostfeld, "Biodiversity and the Dilution Effect in Disease Ecology," *Ecology* 82 (2001): 609–19.

6. Food and Agriculture Organization of the United Nations, *Global Forest Resources Assessment 2005*, FAO Forestry Paper 147 (Rome: FAO, 2006).

7. M. Coluzzi, "Malaria and the Afrotropical Ecosystems: Impact of Man-Made Environmental Changes," *Parassitologia* 36 (1994): 223–27; W. P. Tadei et al., "Ecologic Observations on Anopheline Vectors of Malaria in the Brazilian Amazon," *American Journal of Tropical Medicine and Hygiene* 59 (1998): 325–35.

8. A. Prüss-Üstün and C. Corvalan, *Preventing Disease through Healthy Environment: Towards an Estimate of the Environmental Burden of Disease* (Geneva: WHO, 2006).

9. J. D. Zulueta, "Malaria and Ecosystems: From Prehistory to Posteradication," *Parassitologia* 36 (1994): 7–15.

10. W. G. Downs and C. S. Pittendrigh, "Bromeliad Malaria in Trinidad, British West Indies," *American Journal of Tropical Medicine and Hygiene* 26 (1946): 47–66.

11. N. Minakawa et al., "Spatial Distribution of Anopheline Larval Habitats in Western Kenyan Highlands: Effects of Land Cover Types and Topography," *American Journal of Tropical Medicine and Hygiene* 73 (2005): 157–65.

12. N. Tuno et al., "Survivorship of *Anopheles gambiae sensu stricto* (Diptera: Culicidae) Larvae in Western Kenya Highland Forest," *Journal of Medical Entomology* 42, no. 3 (2005): 270–77.

13. G. Calderon et al., "Especies de la fauna anofelina, su distribucion y algunas consideraciones sobre su abundancia e infectividad en el Peru," *Revista Peruana de Entomologia* 8 (1995): 5–23.

14. M. M. Povoa et al., "Malaria Vectors, Epidemiology, and the Re-emergence of *Anopheles darlingi* in Belem, Para, Brazil," *Journal of Medical Entomology* 40 (2003): 379–86.

15. A. Y. Vittor et al., "The Effect of Deforestation on the Human-Biting Rate of *Anopheles darlingi*, the Primary Vector of Falciparum Malaria in the Peruvian Amazon," *American Journal of Tropical Medicine and Hygiene* 74 (2006): 3–11.

16. M. C. De Castro et al., "Malaria Risk on the Amazon Frontier," *Proceedings of the National Academy of Sciences of the United States of America* 103 (2006): 2452–57.

17. B. Matthys et al., "Urban Agricultural Land Use and Characterization of Mosquito Larval Habitats in a Medium-Sized Town of Côte d'Ivoire," *Journal of Vector Ecology* 30, no. 2 (2006): 319–33.

18. J. A. Omumbo et al., "Modelling Malaria Risk in East Africa at High-Spatial Resolution," *Tropical Medicine and International Health* 10 (6) 2005: 557–66.; J. A. Patz and J. M. Balbus, "Methods for Assessing Public Health Vulnerability to Global Climate Change," *Climate Research* 6, no. 2 (1996): 113–25.

Transboundary Management of Natural Resources and the Importance of a "One Health" Approach: Perspectives on Southern Africa by Steven A. Osofsky, David H. M. Cumming, and Michael D. Kock

1. SADC consists of Angola, Botswana, the Democratic Republic of Congo, Lesotho, Madagascar, Malawi, Mauritius, Mozambique, Namibia, South Africa, Swaziland, Tanzania, Zambia, and Zimbabwe.

2. E. Koch et al., "SDIs, Tourism-led Growth and the Empowerment of Local Communities in South Africa," *Development Southern Africa* 15 (1998): 809–26.

3. R. Biggs et al., *Nature Supporting People: The Southern African Millennium Ecosystem Assessment, Integrated Report* (Pretoria, South Africa: Council for Scientific and Industrial Research, 2004).

4. S. A. Osofsky et al., "Building Support for Protected Areas Using a 'One Health' Perspective," in *Friends for Life: New Partners in Support of Protected Areas*, ed. J. A. McNeely, 65–79 (Gland, Switzerland and Cambridge, UK: IUCN, 2005).

5. C. W. Schwabe, *Veterinary Medicine and Human Health* (Baltimore, Maryland: Williams & Wilkins, 1969).

6. D. H. M. Cumming and *AHEAD*-GLTFCA Working Group, 2004. "Sustaining Animal Health and Ecosystem Services in Large Landscapes–2nd Draft, Concept for a Programme to Address Wildlife, Livestock and Related Human and Ecosystem Health Issues in the Greater Limpopo Transfrontier Conservation Area," www.wcs-ahead.org /workinggrps_limpopo.html (accessed August 10, 2006).

7. I. R. Phimister, "Meat Monopolies: Beef Cattle in Southern Rhodesia, 1890–1938," *Journal of African History* 19 (1978): 391–414; S. Milton, "The Transvaal Beef Frontier: Environment, Markets and the Ideology of Development, 1902–1942," in *Ecology and Empire: Environmental History of Settler Societies*, ed. T. Griffiths and L. Robin, 199–212 (Edinburgh, UK and University of Natal, Pietermaritzburg, South Africa: Keele University Press, 1997).

8. R. D. Taylor and R. B. Martin, "Effects of Veterinary Fences on Wildlife Conservation in Zimbabwe," *Environmental Management* 11 (1987): 327–34.

9. D. Bourn and R. Blench, eds., *Can Livestock and Wildlife Co-Exist? An Interdisciplinary Approach* (London: Overseas Development Institute and The Environment Research Group Oxford, 1999).

10. T. C. Rodwell et al., "Prevalence of Bovine Tuberculosis in African Buffalo at Kruger National Park," *Journal of Wildlife Diseases* 37 (2001): 258–64.

11. S. A. Osofsky et al., eds., *Conservation and Development Interventions at the Wildlife/Livestock Interface: Implications for Wildlife, Livestock and Human Health* (Gland, Switzerland and Cambridge, UK: IUCN, 2005); S. A. Osofsky et al., "Building Support for Protected Areas Using a 'One Health' Perspective," in *Friends for Life: New Partners in Support of Protected Areas*, ed. J. A. McNeely, 65–79 (Gland, Switzerland and Cambridge, UK: IUCN, 2005).

12. S. A. Osofsky et al., "Conservation Medicine: A Veterinary Perspective," *Conservation Biology* 14 (2000): 336–37.

13. D. T. Williamson and B. Mbano, "Wildebeest Mortality during 1983 at Lake Xau, Botswana," *African Journal of Ecology* 26 (1988): 341–44.

14. D. H. M. Cumming and T. J. P. Lynam, *Landuse Changes, Wildlife Conservation and Utilisation, and the Sustainability of Agro-Ecosystems in the Zambezi Valley*, Final Technical Report to the European Union, Contract B7-5040/93/06 (Harare, Zimbabwe: WWF Southern Africa Regional Programme Office, 1997).

An Ounce of Prevention: Lessons from the First Avian Influenza Scare by William B. Karesh and Kristine Smith

1. Gavin MacGregor-Skinner, pers. comm., 2007.

2. "Bird Watching 101: Expert Offers Basics on What Some Call Nation's No. 1 Spectator Sport," *CBS News*, 2007, www.cbsnews.com/stories/2007/06/01/earlyshow /main2874584.shtml.

3. R. G. Webster et al., "H5N1 Outbreaks and Enzootic Influenza," *Emerging Infectious Diseases* 12, no. 1 (2006): 3–8.

Why Wildlife Health Matters in North America by John R. Fischer

1. US Fish and Wildlife Service and US Bureau of the Census, *2006 National Survey of Fishing, Hunting, and Wildlife-Associated Recreation*, May 2007, http://library.fws.gov/nat_survey.2006.pdf.

2. US Fish and Wildlife Service, "Wildlife Restoration Apportionment History," 2007, http://federalasst.fws.gov/apport/WRAhistory.pdf.

3. USFWS, *2006 National Survey of Fishing, Hunting, and Wildlife-Associated Recreation*.

4. H. K. Cordell et al., "Outdoor Recreation Participation Trends," and J. M. Bowker et al., "Projections of Outdoor Recreation Participation to 2050," in *Outdoor Recreation in American Life: A National Assessment of Demand and Supply* (Champaign, IL: Sagamore Publishing, 1999): 219–351.

5. R. C. Bishop, "The Economic Impacts of Chronic Wasting Disease on Wisconsin," *Human Dimensions of Wildlife* 9 (2004): 181–92.

6. S. M. Schmitt et al., "Bovine Tuberculosis in Free-Ranging White-Tailed Deer from Michigan," *Journal of Wildlife Diseases* 33 (1997): 749–58.

7. M. V. Palmer and D. L. Whipple, "Survival of *Mycobacterium bovis* on Feedstuffs Commonly Used as Supplemental Feed for White-Tailed Deer (*Odocoileus virginianus*)," *Journal of Wildlfie Diseases* 42 (2006): 853–58.

8. M. V Palmer et al., "Investigation of Transmission of *Mycobacterium bovis* from Deer to Cattle through Indirect Contact," *American Journal of Veterinary Research* 65 (2004): 1483–89.

9. M. Powell, "Report of the Committee on Wildlife Diseases," pp. 709–10 in *Proceedings of the One Hundred and Tenth Annual Meeting of the United Status Animal Health Association*, Minneapolis, Minnesota 2006. United Status Animal Health Association.

10. E. T. Thorne, "Brucellosis" in *Infectious Diseases in Wild Mammals*, ed. E. S. Williams and I. K. Barker (Ames, IA, Iowa State University: 2001): 372–95.

11. Ibid.

12. S. M. Schmitt, "Report of the Committee on Wildlife Diseases," pp. 707–9 in *Proceedings of the One Hundred and Tenth Annual Meeting of the United Status Animal Health Association*, Minneapolis, Minnesota 2006 United Status Animal Health Association.

13. Centers for Disease Control and Prevention, "First Human Death Associated with Raccoon Rabies—August 2003," *Morbidity and Mortality Weekly Report* 52 (2003): 1102–3.

14. Centers for Disease Control and Prevention, "Multi-State Outbreak of Monkeypox—Illinois, Indiana, and Wisconsin, 2003," *Morbidity and Mortality Weekly Report* 52: 537–40.

15. J. R. Fischer and W. R. Davidson, "Reducing Risk Factors for Disease Problems Involving Wildlife," in *Transactions of the 70th North American Wildlife and Natural Resources Conference*, ed. Jennifer Rahm (Washington, DC, Wildlife Management Institute: 2005): 289–309

16. J. Baughman and J. R. Fischer, "Programs for Monitoring and Managing Diseases in Free-Ranging Wildlife in the 21st Century," in *Transactions of the 70th North American Wildlife and Natural Resources Conference*, ed. Jennifer Rahm (Washington, DC, Wildlife Management Institute: 2005): 346–58.

17. V. F. Nettles and W. R. Davidson, "Cooperative State Action to Address Research Needs—the Experience of the Southeastern Cooperative Wildlife Disease Study," in *Proceedings of the 61st North American Wildlife and Natural Resources Conference*, ed. Richard McCabe (Washington, DC, Wildlife Management Institute: 1996): 545–52.

Warming Oceans, Increasing Disease: Mapping the Health Effects of Climate Change by Rita R. Colwell

1. R. R. Colwell, "Global Climate and Health—Predicting Infectious Disease Outbreaks," *Innovations* 1 (Summer 2006): 19–23.

2. W. M. Washington, "Computer Modeling the Twentieth- and Twenty-First-Century Climate," *American Philosophical Society* 150 (2006): 414–27.

3. R. R. Colwell and A. Huq, "Vibrios in the Environment: Viable but Nonculturable *Vibrio cholerae*," in Vibrio cholerae *and Cholera: Molecular to Global Perspectives,* ed. I. K. Wachsmuth et al., 117–33 (Washington, DC: American Society for Microbiology, 1994).

4. R. R. Colwell, "Global Climate and Infectious Disease: The Cholera Paradigm," *Science* 274 (1996): 2025–31.

5. B. Lobitz et al., "Climate and Infectious Disease: Use of Remote Sensing for Detection of *Vibrio cholerae* by Indirect Measurement," *Proceedings of the National Academy of Sciences United States of America* 97 (2000): 1438–43.

6. Ibid.

7. E. K. Lipp et al., "Direct Detection of Vibrio cholerae and ctxA in Peruvian Coastal Water and Plankton by PCR," *Applied and Environmental Microbiology* 69 (2003): 3676–80.

8. Common communicable diseases, their distribution, epidemic potential and sensitivity to climate, www.who.int/globalchange/publications/oeh0401/en/index5.html.

9. G. C. de Magny et al., "Regional-Scale Climate-Variability Synchrony of Cholera Epidemics in West Africa," *BMC Infectious Diseases* 7 (2007): 20.

Part III: Emerging Issues in the Wild

The Last of the Great Overland Migrations by Joel Berger

1. J. Berger, "The Longest Mile: How to Sustain Long Distance Migration in Mammals," *Conservation Biology* (2004) 18: 320–32.

2. M. Owens and D. Owens, *Cry of the Kalahari* (Boston: Houghton Mifflin, 1983); G. Child and J. D. Le Riche, "Recent Springbok Treks (Mass Movements) in Southwestern Botswana," *Mammalia* 33 (1967): 499–504.

3. J. Berger, "The Longest Mile"; J. Berger et al., "Connecting the Dots: An Invariant Migration Corridor Links the Holocene to the Present," *Biology Letters* 2 (2006): 528–31.

4. J. Berger, "The Longest Mile."

5. K. M. Berger and J. Berger, pers. comm., 2006.

6. K. M. Berger et al., *Wildlife and Energy Development: Pronghorn of the Upper Green River Basin—Year 2 Summary* (2007 report of the Wildlife Conservation Society, New York) www.wcs.org/yellowstone.

7. J. Berger et al., "Connecting the Dots."

8. Office of Governor Dave Freudenthal (press release, Cheyenne, WY, February 27, 2007).

9. F. V. Osborn and G. E. Parker, "Linking Two Elephant Refuges with a Corridor in the Communal Lands of Zimbabwe," *African Journal of Ecology* 41 (2003): 68–74.

10. Andres Novaro, Wildlife Conservation Society, pers. comm., May 21, 2007.

Downward Spiral: Catastrophic Decline of South Asia's Vultures by Todd E. Katzner

1. V. Prakash et al., "Catastrophic Collapse of Indian White-Backed *Gyps bengalensis* and Long-Billed *Gyps indicus* Vulture Populations," *Biological Conservation* 109 (2002): 381–90.

2. J. L. Oaks et al., "Diclofenac Residues as the Cause of Vulture Population Decline in Pakistan," *Nature* 427 (2004): 630–33.

3. M. Gilbert et al., "Breeding and Mortality of Oriental White-Backed Vulture *Gyps bengalensis* in Punjab Province, Pakistan," *Bird Conservation International* 12 (2002): 311–26; S. Shultz et al., "Diclofenac Poisoning Is Widespread in Declining Vulture Populations across the Indian Subcontinent," *Biology Letters* 271 (2004): 458–60.

4. R. E. Green et al., "Diclofenac Poisoning as a Cause of Vulture Population Declines across the Indian Subcontinent," *Journal of Applied Ecology* 41 (2004): 793–800.

5. G. E. Swan et al., "Toxicity of Diclofenac to *Gyps* Vultures," *Biology Letters* 2 (2006): 279–82.

6. R. Cuthbert et al., "Rapid Population Declines of Egyptian Vulture (*Neophron percnopterus*) and Red-Headed Vulture (*Sarcogyps calvus*) in India," *Animal Conservation* 9 (2006): 349–54.

7. T. Katzner et al., "Population and Conservation Status of Griffon Vultures in the Former Soviet Union," in *Proceedings of the WWGBP, 6th World Conference on Birds of Prey and Owls*, ed. R. D. Chancellor and B.-U. Meyberg, 235–40 (Budapest: WWGBP, 2004).

8. G. Rondeau, "What about West African Vultures?" *Vulture News* 51 (2004): 3–6.

Conserving Cold-Blooded Australians by Richard Shine

1. E. R. Pianka, *Ecology and Natural History of Desert Lizards* (Princeton: Princeton University Press, 1986).

2. F. H. Pough, "The Advantages of Ectothermy for Tetrapods," *American Naturalist* 115 (1980): 92–112.

3. G. Armstrong and J. Reid, "The Rediscovery of the Adelaide Pygmy Bluetongue *Tiliqua adelaidensis* (Peters, 1863)," *Herpetofauna* 22 (1992): 3–6.

4. H. G. Cogger, "Conserving Australia's Reptiles: Are We Serious?" *Community Biodiversity Network*, May 28, 2001, www.cbn.org.au/member/cbn/projects/.

5. X. Bonnet et al., "Taxonomic Chauvinism," *Trends in Ecology and Evolution* 17 (2002): 1–3.

6. B. L. Phillips et al., "Rapid Expansion of the Cane Toad (*Bufo marinus*) Invasion Front in Tropical Australia," *Austral Ecology*, in press.

7. W. J. Freeland, "Populations of Cane Toads, *Bufo marinus*, in Relation to Time since Colonization," *Australian Wildlife Research* 13 (1986): 321–29.

8. C. Lever, *The Cane Toad: The History and Ecology of a Successful Colonist* (Otley, West Yorkshire: Westbury Publishing, 2001).

9. M. J. Greenlees et al., "Effects of an Invasive Anuran (the Cane Toad, *Bufo marinus*) on the Invertebrate Fauna of a Tropical Australian Floodplain," *Animal Conservation* 9 (2006): 431–38.

10. B. L. Phillips and R. Shine, "An Invasive Species Induces Rapid Adaptive Change in a Native Predator: Cane Toads and Black Snakes in Australia," *Proceedings of the Royal Society of London, Series B* 273 (2006): 1545–50.

11. T. Jorgensen, "Long-Term Changes in Age at Sexual Maturity of Northeast

Arctic Cod (*Gadus morhua* L.)," *Journal du Conseil International pour l'Exploration de la Mer* 46 (1990): 235–48.

12. M. C. Singer et al. "Rapid Human-Induced Evolution of Insect Diet," *Nature* 366 (1993): 681–83.

13. D. K. Nichols, "Tracking Down the Killer Chytrid of Amphibians," *Herpetological Review* 34 (2003): 101–4.

14. R. N. Reed, "An Ecological Risk Assessment of Nonnative Boas and Pythons as Potential Invasive Species in the United States," *Risk Analysis* 25 (2005): 753–66.

Settling for Less: Disappearing Diadromous Fishes by John Waldman

1. R. M. McDowall, "Occurrence and Distribution of Diadromy Among Fishes," *American Fisheries Society Symposium* 1 (1987): 1–13.

2. D. R. Montgomery, *King of Fish: The Thousand Year Run of Salmon* (Boulder: Westview Press, 2003).

3. W. J. Bolster, "Opportunities in Marine Environmental History," *Environmental History* 11, no. 3 (2006): 567–97.

4. D. H. Secor and J. R. Waldman, "Historical Abundance of Delaware Bay Atlantic Sturgeon and Potential Rate of Recovery," *American Fisheries Society Symposium* 23 (1999): 203–16.

5. J. Boreman, "Sensitivity of North American Sturgeons and Paddlefish to Fishing Mortality," in *Sturgeon Biodiversity and Conservation*, ed. V. J. Birtsein et al. (Dordrecht: Kluwer, 1997): 399–405.

6. W. L. Graf, "Summary and Perspective," in *Dam Removal Research: Status and Prospects*, ed. W. L. Graf (Washington, DC: Heinz Center, 2003): 1–21.

7. J. McPhee, *The Founding Fish* (New York: Farrar, Strauss, and Giroux, 2002).

8. C. Hardy, "Fish or Foul: A History of the Delaware River Basin through the Perspective of the American Shad, 1682 to the Present," *Pennsylvania History* 66 (1999): 506–34.

9. H. D. Thoreau, *A Week on the Concord and Merrimack Rivers* (Boston and Cambridge: James Munroe, 1849).

10. E. K. Pikitch, "The Gathering Wave of Ocean Extinctions," in *State of the Wild 2006: A Global Portrait of Wildlife, Wildlands, and Oceans*, ed. S. Guynup (Washington DC: Island Press, 2005): 195–201.

11. P. Williot et al., "Status of Caught Wild Spawners and Propagation of the Endangered Sturgeon *Acipenser sturio* in France: A Synthesis," *International Review of Hydrobiology* 87 (2002): 515–24.

12. S. J. M. Blaber et al., "Biology, Fisheries, and Status of Tropical Shads *Tenualosa* spp. in South and Southeast Asia," in *Biodiversity, Status, and Conservation of the World's Shads*, ed. K. E. Limburg and J. R. Waldman (Bethesda: American Fisheries Society, 2003): 223–40.

13. J. Waldman, "The Diadromous Fish Fauna of the Hudson River: Life Histories, Conservation Concerns, and Research Avenues," in *The Hudson River Estuary*, ed. J. S. Levinton and J. R. Waldman (New York: Cambridge University Press, 2006): 171–88.

14. R. A. Richards and P. J. Rago, "A Case History of Effective Fishery Management: Chesapeake Bay Striped Bass," *North American Journal of Fisheries Management* 19 (1999): 356–75.

15. R. St. Pierre, "A Case History: American Shad Restoration on the Susquehanna

River," in *Biodiversity, Status, and Conservation of the World's Shads*, ed. K. E. Limburg and J. R. Waldman (Bethesda: American Fisheries Society, 2003): 315–21.

16. M. B. Bain et al., "Recovery of a U.S. endangered fish," *PLoS One* 1 (2007): e168.

17. J. T. Carlton, "Apostrophe to the Ocean," *Conservation Biology* 12 (1998): 1165–67.

Mapping the State of the Oceans by Eric W. Sanderson

1. E. W. Sanderson et al., "The Human Footprint and the Last of the Wild." *BioScience* 52 (2002): 891–904.

2. J. A. Hutchings, "Collapse and Recovery of Ocean Fishes," *Nature* 406 (2000): 882–85.

3. R. Myers and B. Worm, "Rapid Worldwide Depletion of Predatory Fish Communities," *Nature* 423 (2003): 280–83.

4. L. Watling and E. A. Norse, "Disturbance of the Seabed by Mobile Fishing Gear: A Comparison to Forest Clearcutting," *Conservation Biology* 12, no. 6 (1998): 1180–97.

5. J. P. M. Syvitski et al., "Impact of Humans on the Flux of Terrestrial Sediment to the Global Coastal Ocean," *Science* 308 (2005): 376–80.

6. T. P. Barnett et al., "Penetration of Human-Induced Warming into the World's Oceans," *Science* 309 (2005): 284–87; J. C. Orr et al., "Anthropogenic Ocean Acidification over the Twenty-First Century and Its Impact on Calcifying Organisms," *Nature* (2005) 205: 681–86.

Africa's Last Wild Places: Why Conservation Can't Wait by J. Michael Fay

1. J. M. Froment, *Exploitation des elephants en Republique Centrafricaine*, Document de terrain N. 1 FAO, Report number CAF/78/006 (Rome: FAO, 1985).

2. Ibid.

3. I. Douglas-Hamilton et al., *Amenagement Faune Republique Centrafricaine. Recensemat aerien de la faune dans la zone nord del Republique Centrafricaine*, Document de Travail N. 5 FAO, Report number CAF/78/006 (Rome: FAO: 1985).

4. J. M. Fay et al., "Aerial Census of Manovo-Gounda-St. Floris and Bamingui-Bangoran National Parks and Peripheral Zones in Northern Central African Republic," 2005.

The Deep Sea: Unknown and Under Threat by Les Watling

1. E. B. Roark et al., "Radiocarbon-Based Ages and Growth Rates of Hawaiian Deep-Sea Corals," *Marine Ecology Progress Series* 327 (2006): 1–14.

2. L. S. Mullineaux, "Organisms Living on Manganese Nodules and Crusts: Distribution and Abundance at Three North Pacific Sites," *Deep-Sea Research* 34 (1987): 165–84.

3. C. L. Van Dover, *The Ecology of Deep-Sea Hydrothermal Vents* (Princeton: Princeton University Press, 2000).

4. A. Kitchingman and S. Lai, "Inferences on Potential Seamount Locations from Mid-Resolution Bathymetric Data," in *Seamounts: Biodiversity and Fisheries*, ed. T. Morato and D. Pauly, 7–12, University of British Columbia, Fisheries Centre Report 12 (Vancouver: UBC, 2004).

5. M. Clark, "Are Deepwater Fisheries Sustainable?—the Example of the Orange Roughy (*Hoplostethus atlanticus*) in New Zealand," *Fisheries Research* 51 (2001): 123–35.

6. J. A. Koslow et al., "Seamount Benthic Macrofauna Off Southern Tasmania: Community Structure and Impacts of Trawling," *Marine Ecology Progress Series* 213 (2001): 111–25.

7. See www.savethehighseas.org/index.cfm for updates on UN actions.

8. A. K. Ghosh and R. Mukhopadhyay, *Mineral Wealth of the Ocean* (Rotterdam, Netherlands: A. A. Balkema, 2000).

9. International Seabed Authority, "Polymetallic Nodule Areas," www.isa.org.jm/en /scientific/workshops.

10. P. Halbach and F. T Manheim, "Potential of Cobalt and Other Metals in Ferromanganese Crusts on Seamounts of the Central Pacific Basin," *Marine Mining* 4 (1984): 319–35.

11. www.oceansatlas.com/unatlas/uses/oceandumpingwastes/dumping/ dumping_at_sea.htm#Dumping.

12. A. G. Glover and C. R. Smith, "The deep-Sea Floor Ecosystem: Current Status and Prospects of Anthropogenic Change by the Year 2025," *Environmental Conservation* 30 (2003): 219–41.

13. C. D. Hollister and S. Nadis, "Burial of Radioactive Waste under the Seabed," *Scientific American* January 1998, 40–45.

14. P. G. Brewer et al., "Direct Experiments on the Ocean Disposal of Fossil Fuel CO_2," *Science* 284 (1999): 943–45.

15. M. N. Tamburri et al., "A Field Study of the Effects of CO_2 Ocean Disposal on Mobile Deep-Sea Animals," *Marine Chemistry* 72 (2000): 95–101.

Climate Change in the Andes by Carolina Murcia

1. IPCC, *Climate Change 2007: The Physical Science Basis—Summary for Policymakers* (Geneva: IPCC, 2007), www.ipcc.ch.

2. During the recovery phase from the last Ice Age, Earth warmed at a rate of 0.2°C per century. C. K. Folland et al., "Observed Climate Variability and Change," in *Climate Change 2001: The Scientific Basis. Contribution of Working Group I to the Third Assessment Report of the Intergovernmental Panel on Climate Change* (2001).

3. There is no unified classification system for altitudinal belts for the Andes, but a certain degree of coincidence exists among authors in the approximate altitudinal limits.

4. Topography generates complex local climatic patterns because it interferes with the general circulation of the atmosphere at different scales and creates local air currents resulting from differential warming and cooling of different elements.

5. R. A. Quintana-Gomez, "Trends of Maximum and Minimum Temperatures in Northern South America," *Journal of Climate* 12 (1999): 2104–12.

6. M. Vuille et al., "20th Century Climate Change in the Tropical Andes: Observations and Model Results," *Climatic Change* 59 (2003): 75–99; N. L. Lasso, "Cambio en la distribución altitudinal del Yarumo blanco (*Cecropia telealba* Cuatrecasas, Cecropiaceae) asociado al cambio climático" (master's thesis, Universidad del Valle, Cali, Colombia, 2005).

7. R. G. Barry and A. Seimon, "Research for Mountain Area Development: Climatic Fluctuations in the Mountains of the Americas and Their Significance," *Ambio* 29 (2000): 364–70.

8. Instituto de Hidrología, Metereorologia y Estudios Ambientales, *Los glaciares colombianos: expresión del cambio climático global*, technical report, www.ideam.gov.co /publica/glaciares/glaciares.pdf.

9. H. H. Shugart, *Terrestrial Ecosystems in Changing Environments* (Cambridge: Cambridge University Press, 1998); Vuille et al., "20th Century Climate Change."

10. R. O. Lawton et al., "Climatic Impact of Tropical Lowland Deforestation on Nearby Montane Cloud Forests," *Science* 294, no. 5542 (2001): 584–87.

11. H. Q. P. Crick et al., "U. K. Birds Are Laying Eggs Earlier," *Nature* 388 (1997): 526; D. B. Roy and T. H. Sparks, "Phenology of British Butterflies and Climate Change," *Global Change Biology* 6 (2000): 407–16.

12. C. Parmesan, "Ecological and Evolutionary Responses to Recent Climate Change," *Annual Review of Ecology and Systematics* 37 (2006): 637–69.

13. Lasso, "Cambio en la distribución altitudinal del Yarumo blanco (*Cecropia telealba* Cuatrecasas, Cecropiaceae) asociado al cambio climático"

14. T. A. Seimon et al., "Upward Range Extension of Andean Anurans and Chytridiomycosis to Extreme Elevations in Response to Tropical Deglaciation," *Global Change Biology* 13 (2007): 288–99.

15. T. A. Seimon et al., "Upward range extension of Andean anurans and chytridiomycosis to extreme elevations in repsonse to tropical deglaciation," *Global Change Biology* 13 (2007): 288–99.

16. Shugart, *Terrestrial Ecosystems in Changing Environments*, 346.

Grazers and Grasslands: Restoring Biodiversity to the Prairies
by James H. Shaw

1. A. Leopold, "Prairie: The Forgotten Flora," in *Recovering the Prairie*, ed. R. F. Sayre, 162 (Madison: University of Wisconsin Press, 1999).

2. J. M. Suttie et al., eds., *Grasslands of the World*, Plant Production and Protection Series 34 (Rome: FAO, 2005).

3. S. R. Jones and R. C. Cushman, *A Field Guide to the North American Prairie* (New York: Houghton Mifflin, 2004).

4. F. B. Samson and F. L. Knopf, eds., *Prairie Conservation* (Washington, DC: Island Press, 1996).

5. Samson and Knopf, eds., *Prairie Conservation*.

6. Ibid.

7. Ibid.

8. F. B. Samson, F. L. Knopf, and W. R. Ostlie, "Great Plains Ecosystems: Past, Present, and Future," *Wildlife Society Bulletin* 32 (2004): 6–15.

9. J. H. Shaw, "How Many Bison Originally Populated Western Rangelands?" *Rangelands* 17 (1995): 148–50.

10. J. H. Shaw and M. Lee. "Relative Abundance of Bison, Elk, and Pronghorn on the Southern Plains, 1806–1851," *Plains Anthropologist* 42 (1997):163–72.

11. G. Ceballos et al., "Influence of Prairie Dog (*Cynomys ludovicianus*) on Habitat Heterogeneity and Mammalian Diversity in Mexico," *Journal of Arid Environments* 41 (1999): 161–72.

12. D. Hartnett et al., "Comparative Ecology of Native and Introduced Ungulates," in *Ecology and Conservation of Great Plains Vertebrates*, ed. F. L. Knopf and F. B. Samson, 72–101 (New York: Springer-Verlag, 1997).

13. B. Coppedge, unpublished data.

14. S. Fuhlendorf and D. Engle, "Restoring Heterogeneity on Rangelands: Ecosystem Management Based on Evolutionary Grazing Patterns," *BioScience* 51 (2001): 625–32.

15. S. Fuhlendorf and D. Engle, "Application of the Fire-Grazing Interaction to Restore a Shifting Mosaic on Tallgrass Prairie," *Journal of Applied Ecology* 41 (2004): 604–14.

16. S. Fuhlendorf et al., "Should Heterogeneity Be the Basis for Conservation? Grassland Bird Response to Fire and Grazing," *Ecological Applications* 16 (2006): 1706–16.

17. J. R. Herkert. "An Analysis of Midwestern Breeding Bird Population Trends: 1966–93," *American Midland Naturalist* 134 (1995): 41–50.

18. A. Drewitt and R. Langston, "Assessing the Impacts of Wind Farms on Birds," *Ibis* 148 (2006): 29–42.

19. D. Popper and F. Popper, "The Great Plains from Dust to Dust," *Planning* 53 (1987): 12–18.

20. J. Donlan et al., "Pleistocene Re-wilding: An Optimistic Agenda for Twenty-first Century Conservation," *American Naturalist* 168 (2006): 660–81.

21. Leopold, "Prairie: The Forgotten Flora," 162.

Conservation and Human Displacement by Arun Agrawal, Kent H. Redford, and Eva Fearn

1. M. M. Cernea, "Risks, Safeguards, and Reconstruction: A Model for Population Displacement and Resettlement," in *Risks and Reconstruction: Experiences of Resettlers and Refugees*, ed. M. M. Cernea and C. McDowell (Washington, DC: The World Bank, 2000): 11–55.

2. The impoverishments risks are landlessness, joblessness, homelessness, marginalization, food insecurity, morbidity and mortality, loss of access to common property, and social disarticulation.

3. D. Chatty and M. Colchester, eds., *Conservation and Mobile Indigenous Peoples: Displacement, Forced Settlement, and Sustainable Development* (Oxford: Berghahn Books, 2002); K. Schmidt-Soltau, "Conservation-Related Resettlement in Central Africa: Environmental and Social Risks," *Development and Change* 34 (2003): 525–51.

4. D. Brockington et al., "Conservation, Human Rights, and Poverty Reduction," *Conservation Biology* 20 (2006): 250–52; P. West and D. Brockington, "An Anthropological Perspective on Some Unexpected Consequences of Protected Areas," *Conservation Biology* 20 (2006): 609–16.

5. L. Naughton-Treves et al., "The Role of Protected Areas in Conserving Biodiversity and Local Livelihoods," *Annual Review of Environment and Resources* 30 (2005): 219–52.

6. Ibid.

7. S. Blake et al., "Forest Elephant Crisis in the Congo Basin," *PLoS Biology* 5 (2007): e111.

8. J. Gajaseni et al., "Ecological Rationalities of the Traditional Homegarden System in the Chao Phraya Basin, Thailand," *Agroforestry Systems* 46 (1999): 3–23.

9. R. Bodmer, "Impacts of Displacement in the Pacaya-Samiria National Reserve, Peru," in *Protected Areas and Human Displacement: A Conservation Perspective*, 20–29, Wildlife Conservation Society Working Paper, No. 29 (2007), ed. K. H. Redford and E. Fearn, Wildlife Conservation Society, NY.

10. M. Cernea and K. Schmidt-Soltau, "Poverty Risks and National Parks: Policy Issues in Conservation and Resettlement," *World Development* 34, no. 10 (2006): 1808–30.

11. F. Maisels et al., "Central Africa's Protected Areas and the Purported Displacement of People: A First Critical Review of Existing Data" in *Protected Areas and Human Displacement: A Conservation Perspective*, 75–89, Wildlife Conservation Society Working Paper, No. 29 (2007), ed. K. H. Redford and E. Fearn, Wildlife Conservation Society, NY.

12. See *Conservation and Society* 4, no. 3 (2006), dedicated to this issue.

13. K. Schmidt-Soltau, "Conservation-Related Resettlement." Much of the case

work on this aspect of conservation-induced displacements is in the gray literature. See the reports by the International Human Rights Advocacy Center and by the Legal and Human Rights Center.

14. F. Maisels et al., "Protected Areas and Human Displacement."

15. D. Wilkie, "Parks and People in Gabon," in *Protected Areas and Human Displacement: A Conservation Perspective*, 70–74, Wildlife Conservation Society Working Paper, No. 29 (2007), ed. K. H. Redford and E. Fearn, Wildlife Conservation Society, NY.

16. Government of India, *The Report of the Tiger Task Force: Joining the Dots* (New Delhi: Project Tiger, Union Ministry of Environment and Forests, 2005).

Conservation Psychology: Who Cares about the Biodiversity Crisis? by John Fraser and Jessica Sickler

1. E. O. Wilson, *Biophilia: The Human Bond with Other Species* (Cambridge, MA: Harvard University Press, 1984); T. Roszak et al., eds., *Ecopsychology* (San Francisco: Sierra Club Books, 1995); K. Milton, *Environmentalism and Cultural Theory: Exploring the Role of Anthropology in Environmental Discourse* (London: Routledge, 1996).

2. C. Vlek, "Essential Psychology for Environmental Policy Making," *International Journal of Psychology* 35 (2000): 153–67.

3. C. D. Saunders and O. G. Myers, Jr., "Exploring the Potential of Conservation Psychology," *Human Ecology Review* 10, no. 2 (2003): iii–v.

4. S. Opotow and A. Brook, "Identity and Exclusion in Rangeland Conflict: Identity and the Natural Environment," in *The Psychological Significance of Nature*, S. Clayton and S. Opotow, eds. (Cambridge: MIT Press, 2003), 249–72.

5. S. M. Bexell, "Effect of a Wildlife Conservation Camp Experience in China on Student Knowledge of Animals, Care, Propensity for Environmental Stewardship, and Compassionate Behavior toward Animals" (Ph.D. diss., Georgia State University, 2006).

6. D. Reiss and L. Marino, "Mirror Self-Recognition in the Bottlenose Dolphin: A Case of Cognitive Convergence," *Proceedings of the National Academy of Sciences* 98 (2001): 5937–42; L. M. Herman, "Cognitive Characteristics of Dolphins," in *Cetacean Behavior: Mechanisms and Functions*, L. M. Herman, ed. (New York: Wiley Interscience, 1983), 363–429.

7. J. Sickler et al., "Thinking about Dolphins Thinking," Wildlife Conservation Society Working Paper, No. 27, New York, 2006.

8. C. D. Saunders et al., "The Environmental Ethics of Zoo Visitors," (presentation at the Society for Human Ecology Annual Conference, Salt Lake City, Utah, 2005).

9. O. E. Myers et al., "Emotional Dimensions of Watching Zoo Animals: An Experience Sampling Study Building on Insights from Psychology," *Curator, the Museum Journal* 47 (2004): 299–321.

Biogenetics and Conservation: Celebrate or Worry? by Stephen C. Aldrich

1. D. B. Rusch et al., "The *Sorcerer II* Global Ocean Sampling Expedition: Northwest Atlantic through Eastern Tropical Pacific," *PLoS Biology* 5, no. 3 (2007).

2. B. P. Trivedi, "Scientists Clone First Endangered Species: a Wild Sheep," *National Geographic Today*, October 29, 2001, http://news.nationalgeographic.com/news/2001/10/1025_TVsheepclone.html.

3. J. R. Reichman et al., "Establishment of Transgenic Herbicide-Resistant Creeping Bentgrass (*Agrostis stolonifera L.*) in Nonagronomic Habitats," *Molecular Ecology* 15, 13 (2006): 4243–55.

Conservation in Conflict: Illegal Drugs Versus Habitat in the Americas by Liliana M. Dávalos and Adriana C. Bejarano

1. L. Correa, Sistema Integrado de Monitoreo de Cultivos Ilícitos, unpublished field data, 2006.

2. Ibid.

3. UN Office on Drugs and Crime, *World Drug Report*, vol. 1, *Analysis* (2006); Correa, unpublished field data.

4. F. E. Thoumi, "The Numbers Game: Let's All Guess the Size of the Illegal Drug Industry," *Journal of Drug Issues* 35 (2005): 185–200.

5. National Drug Intelligence Center, *National Drug Threat Assessment 2006: Marijuana*, www.usdoj.gov/ndic/pubs11/18862/marijuan.htm.

6. R. Gingrich, "Long Journey to Save the Sierra Madre," *Earth First!* 19 (1999): 8; G. Galster, "Mexican Deforestation in the Sierra Madre," Trade and Environment Database (TED) Case Studies 5, case 287 (1996); J. Walker and J. Leib, "Revisiting the Topia Road: Walking in the Footsteps of West and Parsons," *Geographical Review* 92 (2002): 555–81.

7. Gingrich, "Long Journey"; M. D. Álvarez, "Environmental Damages from Illicit Drug Crops in Colombia," in *Extreme Conflict and Tropical Forests*, ed. W. de Jong et al. (Dordrecht: Springer, 2007): 133–47.

8. M. D. Álvarez, "Illicit Crops and Bird Conservation Priorities in Colombia," *Conservation Biology* 16 (2002): 1086–96.

9. K. R. Young, "Threats to Biological Diversity Caused by Coca/Cocaine Deforestation," *Environmental Conservation* 23 (1996), 7–15.

10. J. Fjeldså et al., "Illicit Crops and Armed Conflict as Constraints on Biodiversity Conservation in the Andes Region," *Ambio* 34 (2005): 205–11.

11. Correa, unpublished field data; M. D. Álvarez, "Illicit Crops and Bird Conservation Priorities in Colombia," *Conservation Biology* 16 (2002): 1086–96.

12. A. Etter et al., "Unplanned Land Clearing of Colombian Rainforests: Spreading Like Disease?" *Landscape and Urban Planning* 77 (2006): 240–54.

13. UN Office on Drugs and Crime, *Coca Cultivation in the Andean Region: A Survey of Bolivia, Colombia and Peru* (2006), 1–228.

14. UN Office on Drugs and Crime, *World Drug Report*, vol. 2, *Statistics*.

15. M. C. Ardila-Robayo, *Atelopus petriruizii* in *Ranas Arlequines*, ed. J. V. Rueda-Almonacid et al., *100* (Bogotá, Colombia: Conservación Internacional, 2005).

16. Fjeldså, Álvarez, Lazcano, and León, "Illicit Crops and Armed Conflict."

17. This may be an overestimate because the reagents are routinely reused; see M. D. Álvarez, "Environmental Damages from Illicit Drug Crops in Colombia," in *Extreme Conflict and Tropical Forests*, ed. W. de Jong, et al. (Dordrecht: Springer, 2007): 133–47.

18. UN Office on Drugs and Crime, *World Drug Report*, vol. 2, *Statistics*, 259.

19. Ibid.

20. WCS Guatemala program, pers. comm., 2007.

21. R. Vargas Meza, *Cultivos ilícitos y proceso de paz en Colombia* (2000), 1–55 (Bogotá: TNI/Acción Andina, 2000); R. Jeffrey Smith, "Spraying of Herbicides on Mexican Marijuana Backfires on US," *Science* 199 (1978): 861–64.

22. UN Office on Drugs and Crime, *World Drug Report*, vol. 2, *Statistics*; L. Sherret, "Futility in Action: Coca Fumigation in Colombia," *Journal of Drug Issues* 35 (2005): 151–68; M. D. Álvarez, "Environmental Damages from Illicit Drug Crops in Colombia," in *Extreme Conflict and Tropical Forests*, ed. W. de Jong, et al., 133–47 (Dordrecht: Springer, 2007).

23. R. A. Relyea, "The Lethal Impact of Roundup on Aquatic and Terrestrial Amphibians," *Ecological Applications* 15 (2005): 1118–24.

24. E. Dávalos, "Modelo de toma de decisiones de los sembradores de cultivos ilícitos" (undergraduate thesis, Universidad del Valle, Cali, 2004), 1–29; L. Correa, unpublished field data, 2006.

25. Asociación Interamericana para la Defensa del Ambiente, Estrategias de desarrollo alternativo en Colombia: la necesidad de acciones más allá de las fumigaciones a cultivos ilícitos (Oakland, California: Asociación Interamericana para la Defensa del Ambiente, AIDA, 2006): 1–23.

Rewilding the Islands by C. Josh Donlan

1. D. W. Steadman, "Prehistoric Extinctions of Pacific Island Birds: Biodiversity Meets Zooarchaeology," *Science* 267 (1995): 1123–31; T. H. Worthy and R. N. Holdaway, *The Lost World of the Moa: Prehistoric Life of New Zealand* (Bloomington: Indiana University Press, 2002): 718.

2. D. R. Towns et al., "Have the Harmful Effects of Introduced Rats on Islands Been Exaggerated?" *Biological Invasions* 8 (2006): 863–91.

3. B. W. Thomas and R. H. Taylor, "A History of Ground-Based Rodent Eradication Techniques Developed in New Zealand, 1959–1993," in *Turning the Tide: The Eradication of Invasive Species*, ed. C. R. Veitch and M. N. Clout (Gland, Switzerland: IUCN SSC Invasive Species Specialist Group, 2002): 301–10.

4. I. MacFadden, P. Moors, R. Taylor, and B. Thomas were among the New Zealand conservationists who developed the initial bait stations.

5. R. H. Taylor and B.W. Thomas, "Rats Eradicated from Rugged Breaksea Island (170 Ha), Fiordland, New Zealand," *Biological Conservation* 65 (1993): 191–98.

6. G. Howald et al., "Invasive Rodent Eradications on Islands," *Conservation Biology*, 21 (2007): 1258–68.

7. P. McClelland and P. Tyree, "Eradication: The Clearance of Campbell Island," *New Zealand Geographic* 58 (2002): 86–94.

8. P. J. Seddon and R. F. Maloney, *Campbell Island Teal Re-Introduction Plan*, DOC Science Internal Series 154 (Wellington: New Zealand Department of Conservation, 2003): 1–30.

9. G. R. Howald et al., "Eradication of Black Rat from Anacapa Island: Biological and Social Considerations," in *Proceedings of the Sixth California Islands Symposium*, ed. D. K. Garcelon and C. A. Schwemm (Arcata, CA: Institute for Wildlife Studies, 2005): 299–312.The Anacapa project was conducted by the US National Park Service and Island Conservation.

10. E. P. Bailey, "Introduction of Foxes to Alaskan Islands: History, Effects on Avifauna, and Eradication," US Fish and Wildlife Service Resource Publication 193 (Washington, DC: United States Department of Interior, 1993): 1–52.

11. J. L. Maron et al., "An Introduced Predator Transforms Aleutian Island Plant Communities by Disrupting Spatial Subsidies," *Ecological Monographs* 76 (2006): 3–24.

12. S. E. Ebbert and G. V. Byrd, "Eradications of Invasive Species to Restore Natural Biological Diversity on Alaska Maritime National Wildlife Refuge," in *Turning the Tide: The Eradication of Invasive Species*, ed. C. R. Veitch and M. N. Clout, 102–9 (Gland, Switzerland: IUCN SSC Invasive Species Specialist Group, 2002). The team since 1983 has been led by Ed Bailey, Vernon Byrd, Steve Ebbert, and Art Sowls.

13. G. V. Byrd et al., "Removal of Introduced Foxes: A Case Study in Restoration of

Native Bird," *Transactions of the North American Wildlife and Natural Resources Conference* 59 (1994): 317–21.

14. K. Campbell et al., "Eradication of Feral Goats (*Capra hircus*) from Pinta Island, Galápagos, Ecuador," *Oryx* 38 (2004): 328–33; F. Cruz et al., "Conservation Action in the Galápagos: Feral Pig (*Sus scrofa*) Eradication from Santiago Island," *Biological Conservation* 121 (2005): 473–78; V. Carrion et al., "Feral Donkey (*Equus asinus*) Eradication in the Galápagos," *Biodiversity and Conservation* 16 (2007): 437–45. Project Isabela was led by Felipe Cruz, Victor Carrion, and Karl Campbell.

15. M. Nogales et al., "A Review of Feral Domestic Cat Eradication on Islands," *Conservation Biology* 18 (2004): 310–19; K. Campbell and C. J. Donlan, "Feral Goat Eradications on Islands," *Conservation Biology* 19 (2005): 1362–74; Howald et al., "Invasive Rodent Eradications."

16. This work was led by Island Conservation, Grupo de Ecología y Conservación de Islas, A.C., and Universidad Nacional Autónoma de México, and in particular Jesús Ramirez, Jose Angel Sanchez, Bernie Tershy, and Bill Wood.

Addressing AIDS: Conservation in Africa by Judy Oglethorpe and Daulos Mauambeta

1. UNAIDS, *AIDS Epidemic Update: December 2006* (Geneva: UNAIDS, 2006).

2. U.S. Census Bureau, "The AIDS Pandemic in the 21st Century," *International Population Reports WP/02.2* (Washington, DC: US Government Printing Office, 2004).

3. M. Masozera, Wildlife Conservation Society, pers. comm., February 2007.

4. N. Bell Gelman et al., "The Impact of HIV/AIDS: How Can It Be Anticipated and Managed?" *Parks* 15, no. 1 (2005): 13–24.

5. B. Kumchedwa, Department of National Parks and Wildlife, Malawi (official unpublished data, 2007).

6. E. Torell et al., "Examining the Linkages between AIDS and Biodiversity Conservation in Coastal Tanzania," *Ocean and Coastal Management* 49, no. 11 (2006): 792–811.

7. S. Sakala, Hospital Statistician, Health Management Information System (HMIS) Unit, Queen Elizabeth Central Hospital, Malawi, pers. comm., 2007.

8. T. Barnett and A. Whiteside, *AIDS in the Twenty-first Century: Disease and Globalization* (Basingstoke and New York: Palgrave Macmillan, 2006).

9. M. Barany et al., "Firewood, Food and Medicine: Interactions between Forests, Vulnerability and Rural Responses to HIV/AIDS," in proceedings from the IFPRI Conference: HIV/AIDS and Food and Nutrition Security, Durban, South Africa, April 14–16, 2005.

10. Africa Biodiversity Collaborative Group, "HIV/AIDS and Natural Resource Management Linkages," in proceedings, Nairobi, Kenya, September 2002.

11. M. Jurvelius, FAO, pers. comm., 2005.

12. R. Greener, "The Impact of HIV/AIDS on Poverty and Inequality," pp. 167–81 in M. Haacker, ed., *The Macroeconomics of HIV/AIDS* (Washington, DC: International Monetary Fund, 2004).

13. S. Drimie, *The Impact of HIV/AIDS on Rural Households and Land Issues in Southern and Eastern Africa* (Pretoria, South Africa: Human Sciences Research Council, 2002), www.fao.org/wairdocs/ad696e/ad696e00.HTM (accessed December 17, 2006).

14. UNAIDS, UNFPA, and UNIFEM, *Women and HIV/AIDS: Confronting the Crisis* (Geneva: UNAIDS, 2004).

15. L. M. Hunter et al., "'Locusts Are Now Our Beef': Adult Mortality and Household Dietary Use of the Local Environment in Rural South Africa," Working Paper, Institute of Behavioral Science, Program on Environment and Society (University of Colorado at Boulder, 2006).

16. UNAIDS, *2006 Report on the Global AIDS Epidemic* (Geneva: UNAIDS, 2006).

17. International Labor Organization, HIV/AIDS and work: global estimates, impact and response (Geneva: International Labour Organization, 2004).

18. P. R. Lamptey et al., "The Global Challenge of HIV and AIDS," *Population Bulletin* 61 Washington, DC: Population Reference Bureau,2006): 1–24. (note that the reference itself is on p. 6)

19. R. Cincotta et al., *The Security Demographic: Population and Civil Conflict after the Cold War* (Washington, DC: Population Action International, 2003).

20. J. Shambaugh et al., *The Trampled Grass: Reducing the Impacts of Armed Conflict on the Environment* (Washington, DC: Biodiversity Support Program, 2001).

Index

Forever!

The birds chirp waking the morning sun,
As it lifts over the golden horizon.
The frogs croak engaging the evening moon,
As it rises to the peak of the earth.
The trees dance loving the gentle breeze,
As it sweeps by playing a chasing game.
While the flowers cling to their petals,
Determined to hold tight to their beauty.
The leaves glide enjoying the paddleboat ride,
While the dandelions set off for an adventure,
Determined to find a fresh new life.
At last you'll see,
What magic means
Through Mother Nature's eyes.

AGLAIA HO
AGE 11